GENDER ON TRIAL

Sexual Stereotypes and Work/Life Balance in the Legal Workplace

Holly English

2003

ALM Publishing
New York, New York

Cover Design: Michael Ng
Interior Page Design & Production: Amanda Koch

Library of Congress Cataloging-in-Publication Data

English, Holly, 1956-
   Gender on trial: sexual stereotype and work/life balance in the legal workforce/by Holly English.
      p. cm.
   ISBN 1-58852-109-5
      1. Women lawyers--United States. 2. Stereotypes (Psychology)--United States. 3. Sex discrimination in employment--United States. I. Title.

KF299.W6E54 2003
349.73'082--dc21   2003048152

Dedicated to

Alan Taylour English
Jerry Fitzgerald English
Fred Smagorinsky
Tess Curtis Smagorinsky
Karla Catherine Smagorinsky

Preface

I have heard about the law, and about women lawyers, ever since I can remember.

When I was seven years old, I sat in the audience watching the Class of 1963 graduate from Boston College Law School. Also present were my father, Alan English, my six-year-old brother Christopher, and my three-month-old brother Anderson, who slept soundly in my dad's arms. We watched as my mother, Jerry Fitzgerald English, collected her diploma.

Twenty years later my parents sat in the audience while I received my law degree from the same institution. My mother and I were the first mother/daughter pair to graduate from Boston College Law School.

And although we went to the same law school, our careers have been different, although each has been emblematic of our respective generations.

My mother was a "typical" pioneer. She went to law school well before it was fashionable for women, one of four women in a sea of eighty-three men. Only two of the women graduated that year. She has enjoyed a nonstop, distinguished career, starting as a marital lawyer in a suburban New Jersey firm, serving as counsel to the governor of New Jersey, and thereafter as the New Jersey Commissioner of Environmental Protection. She returned to build a successful environmental law practice at her former firm, where she practices to this day, showing few signs of slowing down. She and my father balanced life and work for years before anyone thought it could be knocked askew. (And they produced another child as well: my youngest brother Eric.)

I have been typical of my generation as well. Forty percent of the people in my class were female, a huge increase; 102 women and 153 men graduated in 1983. I have worked as a legal journalist, clerked for the New Jersey Supreme Court, practiced as a litigator, and am a writer and consultant. I have worked in offices and at home, part time, full time, and not at all for various periods, spending time raising my two daughters. Although many of my female classmates are successful practitioners, many have left the practice of law, or taken time off, as have I. We enjoy more options than did the pioneer women in the profession, because we are less unusual and therefore not quite so conspicuous. (Indeed, the Boston College Law School Class of 2003 is 57% female.)

This lifelong perspective informed my approach to writing from a new viewpoint about gender relations in the practice of law.

It is vital to understand that this book is not just about women and how they have fared. The book is just as much about male practitioners and how profoundly their worlds have been altered by the presence of women in large numbers. Men have heretofore been edited out of the "gender issues" picture: they have been onlookers, commentators, assumed to be the lucky beneficiaries in workplaces tailored to "typical" male traits. This book attempts to bring their issues more sharply into focus as they grapple with problems that are both similar to those that women face or that are individual to men.

To this end, this book seeks to broaden the "gender issues" debate so that it becomes an open forum for men and women alike, seeking solutions for working lawyers who are engaged in solving the dilemmas that men and women face working side by side, every day of the year. I hope these discussions about gender roles eventually broaden into more fundamental debates such as, "What makes a good lawyer? What do clients want? Who makes a good parent?" Rather than dividing the sexes, as do so many issues, resolving these questions can unite them.

Holly English
Montclair, New Jersey
March, 2003

Acknowledgments

This project first took shape at a restaurant in New York City, during a lunch that Robert Steinbaum, publisher of the *New Jersey Law Journal,* had arranged so I could meet with Sara Diamond of Law Journal Press. *Gender on Trial* is the result. My thanks to Rob for having spearheaded this project; he is a person who always follows through.

Along with Sara's help, I appreciate the guidance of others at Law Journal Press, including Caroline Sorokoff and Pat Rainsford. My particular appreciation goes to Dory Green for her conscientious editing, thoughtful comments, and championing of my ideas throughout the course of the book's production.

Many people read chapters of this book and commented on them. Thanks to Ann Rasmussen, Deborah Ellis, and Ellen Blaney for giving helpful remarks and insights on the excerpts they reviewed. In particular, I am grateful to my dear friend Suzanne Roth, who, in addition to providing editing assistance, listened with unflagging interest for two years as each chapter took shape.

Dr. Fraeda Klein discussed sexual harassment issues with me, Dr. Ellen Ostrow and Dr. Ron Kimball provided me with the psychologists' perspective, Dr. Ostrow also reviewed a chapter, and Phyllis Weiss Haserot and Ida Abbott provided the viewpoint of law firm consultants. My great appreciation to all of them for giving their time. In addition, I wish to thank Ann Carmer at the library of Montclair State University, who helped me with research.

Attracta Lagan, an esteemed consultant, colleague, and friend in Australia, guided and mentored me as I learned about working with organizations, and my gratitude to her is enormous.

I am grateful to my father Alan English for having carefully proofread the final galleys. More broadly, I thank my father and my mother Jerry Fitzgerald English for setting a lifelong example of the best way to handle gender roles—by ignoring them. They provided limitless moral support throughout the writing of this book.

My husband Fred Smagorinsky was my stalwart at-home editor throughout the research and writing of *Gender on Trial.* His careful weighing of every word in this book was honest, yet tactful; he told me what I needed to know while supporting me each step of the way. Without his help this book could not have been written.

My greatest thanks are to the many people I interviewed whose names I cannot include. They were candid, open, articulate, thoughtful, and fair. They went out of their way, often in second and third interviews, to answer my many questions. I am very grateful to each and every one of them for having spent the time with me to make this book a reality. My favorite quality of this book is the authenticity and immediacy that their quotations lend to the text. May their words, if not their identities, flourish.

Contents

CHAPTER 1

Confronting the Expectations Gap

———————————— ————————————

———————————— ————————————

This project began as a book on women's issues in legal workplaces. When I began researching, however, the women I interviewed kept referring to their male colleagues, saying that they too had gender issues. As a result, I broadened the perspective of the book to include both men and women, asking people from all around the country, in a variety of different legal settings, what gender issues they observe and experience.

What I learned should be set against a dramatic backdrop of demographic change. Men and women in the United States have engaged in a radical experiment over the past forty years: integrating large numbers of women into the workforce. This era is the first time in American history that men and women have worked side by side as peers in professional settings on a major scale.

Part of this phenomenon includes seismic change within the legal profession. In 1872, the United States Supreme Court refused to admit Myra Bradwell to the Illinois bar, reminding her loftily that "[t]he paramount destiny and mission of woman are to fulfill the noble and benign offices of wife and mother."[1] Today, sheer numbers reflect the fact that women now occupy other "offices." Nearly 300,000 women are admitted to the bar in the United States of America, comprising almost 30% of practitioners. Fifty percent of law school students are women. One-fifth of the nation's federal court judges are female. One-quarter of state supreme court justices are women. Two women sit on the United States Supreme Court, and two women have been president of the American Bar Association. The numbers go on and on, but the bottom line is stark: the law is no longer all men, all the time.

Other data—snapshots rather than statistics—also reveal the sweep of change. A male litigator stops work for a few years to care for his children and re-enters the workforce thereafter, openly discussing the choices he's made. A female judge presides over a courtroom featuring a female prosecutor and female public defender. Two men warn a female lawyer, a fellow member of the family law bar, that a male judge is sexist and that she should prepare herself accordingly. A male partner insists that a woman partner's pay and draw remain intact, despite her extended pregnancy leave due to complications.

---

[1] Bradwell v. Illinois, 83 U.S. (16 Wall.) 130, 141 (1872), Bradley, J., concurring. Eventually, Illinois revised its rules for admitting women to the bar. As a result, in 1890 Bradwell was finally admitted to the Illinois bar, and in 1892 she received a license to practice before the U.S. Supreme Court.

A female judge brings her infant daughter on the bench with her when the baby is sick. A male general counsel asks that a recruiter make every effort to find a female as his successor. An African-American woman mentors an Asian trial lawyer, talking her through her fears to bolster her confidence, and the novice improves dramatically in the courtroom. When a client turns to a female partner and asks her to get everyone coffee, a male partner stands up and says, "I'll get the coffee." A woman on a compensation committee points out that a man is being paid more than a woman who performs equally well, and insists they be paid the same. These and countless other stories are miniatures of the massive changes within the profession that have occurred during the past generation.

Indeed, the phase we are in now is a post-sex-discrimination era. I heard virtually nothing about blatant sex discrimination in my interviews, meaning hostility or rejection based strictly on women's gender. The fundamental battle for acceptance has been won, at least in public. Men who accuse women of "taking up a space" in law school, judges who call female litigators "sweetie," clients who refuse to have a woman represent them—these stories make people laugh rather than litigate.

But people continue to feel uneasy about inequities. For instance, the progressive numbers cited above have a flip side. Men constitute 70% of practitioners, still the great majority. They are even more overwhelmingly the leaders. Eighty-five percent of firm partners, 95% of managing partners, and 88% of general counsel in Fortune 500 companies are male. Three-quarters of federal judges and 80% of state supreme court justices are men. The relentless focus on the relative increase of women in the law obscures the continuing reality of a male-dominated profession. Other numbers tracking women's progress also are troubling. Women flee law firms in much larger numbers than do men. As a definitive survey found, the attrition rate for women each year was three to seven percentage points higher than for their male counterparts, and was most evident in the sixth through eighth years following law school.[2] Salary gaps continue: the median gross income of a

---

[2] The study was of 10,300 associates in 154 law firms hired from 1988 to 1996. "Keeping the Keepers" (National Association for Law Placement, 1997).

woman lawyer is 73% of what a male lawyer earns, or $1,054 per week, compared to a man's $1,448 per week.[3]

And along with the upbeat stories chronicled above, other anecdotes strike a more sinister chord. A female managing partner informs visitors pointedly that she's the one in charge, to break their laser-beam focus on the men in the room. A woman who has successfully represented a corporate client for years suddenly is yanked off a "bet the company" case because the client loses his nerve. A shy and retiring man finds it hard to make partner because he doesn't act like a "typical" guy. An ambitious woman, who labors ceaselessly and brings in big revenues, is marginalized and disliked by her colleagues. A woman who prides herself on managing support staff in a "nice" and non-threatening manner finds they do her work only after they do the demanding male partner's work (and not very well at that).

A man freezes up about mentoring women, worried after his wife teases, "What's going on with you and that associate?" A woman complains about a client hounding her for a date; a partner responds, "Would it really kill you to go out for a drink with the guy?" A woman says flatly, "Going part time takes you out of the race." A man longs to cut his hours to spend more time with his three-year-old, but fears he'll ruin his career. Women partners with children are called bad mothers behind their backs—by their female colleagues. A woman avoids talking about her kids and leaves her baby pictures at home, calling it an "experiment" that she hopes will make people take her more seriously. People say they don't want to hire women lawyers because "they'll just get pregnant and leave." These vignettes reveal a darker side of present-day practice.

Defining the Problem

When I asked people to name the most important gender issues of the day, the most frequent response was work/life balance, usually expressed as a problem of retaining women in the workplace. They also frequently cited a disparity in advancement for women, harassment, and negative perceptions and stereotypes, caused by lack of access to social networks, lack of

---

[3] United States Department of Labor, Bureau of Labor Statistics, 2000.

opportunities, lingering gender bias, and rigid workplace structures and business models.

But people also were frustrated trying to articulate the issues and their causes. They said that today's issues were "subtle," "covert," "hard to pin down," and "hard to isolate." As a female partner in a New England law firm points out, "We don't have any blatantly awful guys left. We've done a good job of telling our male colleagues the kind of jokes that aren't acceptable, the kind of comments that aren't acceptable. The obvious things that were offensive in the past, they don't do those things anymore." She's apprehensive about the future, and her words were echoed by many others. "Men don't seem to think there's a problem any more," she reflects. "They're all enlightened. Everything is more subtle now. The harder job is ahead of us." Although the principal battle for acceptance is over, many lawyers are concerned that progress may be slowed or frustrated because of lurking, underground demons that don't surface.

After more than four decades of change, the overriding gender issue in legal workplaces is persistent stereotypes. The contradiction is that even though women have achieved basic acceptance in the workplace, seeming to break out of the confines of rigid roles, many traditional stereotypes are as strong as ever. One woman calls them "the traditional gender roles that I can't seem to avoid thinking about."

For instance, people still assume that women aren't as competent as men. Speculation abounds that successful women "sleep their way to the top" rather than advancing due to merit, whereas men have to protect themselves from assumptions that they are potential sexual predators who will harass the women they supervise. Both males and females who don't look typically confident can be rejected out of hand, before being given a chance to gain more self-assurance. Women who are too passive are dismissed; women who are too aggressive are disliked. "Real lawyers" who work around the clock don't respect people who reduce their hours. Women, once they become mothers, are judged by how well they nurture their children. Men, as they become fathers, must meet a "responsible breadwinner" standard.

Why has this seeming contradiction occurred? For one thing, the stampede of women into the profession and the shattering of many ceilings have resulted in the "no-problem problem," as Stanford Professor Deborah Rhode calls it. As she wrote in an American Bar Association report on gender equity, "A widespread assumption is that barriers have been coming down, women have been moving up, and it is only a matter of time before full equality becomes an accomplished fact."[4]

So if any problems remain, the collective agreement has become that we don't need to address them, because they'll soon be gone. Those who remain troubled by gender issues experience what I call the "expectations gap." At present, expectations have outstripped reality. Many people assumed that by this time, with strength in numbers, gender issues for lawyers would be a thing of the past. "These issues will ameliorate over time," predicts one of the few female managing partners of large law firms, Mary B. Cranston, CEO and chair of Pillsbury Winthrop in San Francisco. "At present it's going slowly, more so than people would have expected given the number of women in the field."

The "no-problem problem" is compounded by the fact that we're also in a post-malice era. Most people believe that they are acting in a bias-free manner. They've had many years of education and reflection about gender bias, and assume they have absorbed the necessary lessons. One man said to me, "This is the hardest thing you're looking at. I think most men don't realize what they're doing. I suspect if you asked any of these people, even the worst offenders, they would say they don't do it and they don't see it. I don't think it's malicious." A very prominent woman in the profession said, "There are covert examples of bias every day, and many times the people who are involved in the activity, when challenged, would absolutely flatly deny it, and would get angry with you for accusing them."

As a result, it's hard to even start a conversation about possible inequities, let alone solve them. There is a disconnect between what people are thinking versus what they say publicly. One reason is that people are genuinely unsure about whether gender bias is the culprit in ambiguous situations. A remark I heard over and over, in describing an anecdote, was, "I can't tell if it's gender or personality." Also, both men and women point out that many of the supposed extra pressures on women often apply to everyone, in a rough-and-tumble, harsh, and unforgiving work environment. Because gender can be one of many factors affecting an individual situation, it can be hard to make a

---

[4] Deborah L. Rhode, "The Unfinished Agenda: Women and the Legal Profession," at 13-14 (American Bar Association Commission on Women in the Profession, 2001).

clear-cut case that gender is relevant, much less the overriding culprit or deserving of special attention.

Therefore, women keep quiet about their suspicions because they don't want to be labeled whiners and complainers, or throw-back "feminists" in the least flattering incarnation of that discredited label. They don't want to anger well-meaning male colleagues who consider themselves bias-free. Men, too, say things they don't believe wholeheartedly, or simply say nothing, too afraid of the consequences of speaking their minds, of being labeled throw-back "sexists" themselves if they air any misgivings about women or advocate traditional views.

As a result, everyone now is a well-rehearsed rhetorician on gender issues. But the yawning space between what people say and what they really believe is the breeding ground for misunderstanding, confusion, and resentment. It also allows private re-confirmation (unchallenged) that the old stereotypes actually make a lot of sense.

Making Sense of the World

What is a stereotype, anyway?

Stereotypes are a set of beliefs and expectations about the roles people fill and how they will behave. Categorizing by stereotypes is a quick and efficient way to cut through the mass of information we use to make decisions and judgments about what we observe. When we see behavior that fits our assumptions, our stereotype is strengthened, and when we see actions that don't conform, we set them aside as aberrations. For instance, we might expect that most nurses will be female. When we see yet another woman nurse, it confirms and strengthens our expectation. A male nurse, then, is an "exception" to our expectation. Stereotypes are a way of making sense of the world.

There are stereotypes about all kinds of things—race, gender, sex, age, nationality, occupation, people from New Jersey (like me)—and countless ones about lawyers. Some are very hardy. Stereotypes about gender, in particular, have stood the test of time well. Psychologist Virginia Valian reports that "[a] quantitative review of studies of personality characteristics conducted between 1940 and 1992 shows several enduring and sizable sex differences." Men throughout that time period were more likely to think of themselves as assertive and action-oriented; women described themselves as communal, trusting, and nurturing. Valian concludes that stereotypes about gender are "alive and well, and have moderated only slightly over the years."[5]

This is confirmed in a February 2001 Gallup poll, in which respondents matched certain traits with one sex or the other. For instance, 72% of respondents associated the quality of "patience" with women, as compared with 19% who associated it with men. Eighty-six percent of respondents thought being "affectionate" typified women, as opposed to 5% who associated this with men; 68% of respondents linked the word "aggressive" with men, whereas 20% called it a womanly trait; 50% associated the quality "courageous" with men, 27% with women. These lopsided results show that we as a society continue to hold strongly traditional views about what men are like and what women are like.

Although stereotypes are hard to budge once they have a foothold, they can ease or change over time. In 1872 society couldn't conceive of Myra Bradwell or any other woman abandoning hearth and home to practice the profession of law; now people are accustomed to women in the workplace. More recently, the original challenge for women as they entered the law was whether they could perform at all, whether they had the ability to make the grade. They passed that test quickly. Few people today suggest that women don't have the basic brainpower to be successful advocates.

The aim of this book is to explore the fact that persistent gender stereotypes present a continuing obstacle that obstructs the availability of broad options and choices for men and women lawyers. There are two prevailing approaches to dealing with stereotypes. Some people feel that gender roles are so engrained and inevitable that it's easiest to conform as gracefully as possible, fine-tuning one's behavior and style to get the job done while not offending social norms. My interviews suggest that, on a day-to-day basis, that's the conclusion most people reach. Indeed, although many studies conclude that stereotypes contribute to gender bias, the assumption seems to be that there's little you can do about it.

Others counsel that we should stifle and ignore all discussion of stereotypes, predicting that over time, with the weight of evidence to the contrary, they will evaporate (in line with the thesis of the "no-problem problem"). To

---

[5] Virginia Valian, *Why So Slow? The Advancement of Women*, at p. 110 (MIT Press, 1998).

this end they urge that women not "perpetuate" stereotypes that confirm typically feminine behavior: crying or getting emotional under stress, invoking child care concerns, expressing uncertainty, being flirtatious. Popular books about women in business echo this dichotomy. Some advise that women take advantage of their womanly traits; others say abandon them altogether and play the guys' game.

Neither is a good approach. Simply caving in to entrenched stereotypes narrows options for both men and women, and doesn't leave room for individuals to reach their fullest potential. And expecting that stereotypes will magically disappear also is unrealistic. Even though some dictates have eased, others, such as those concerning motherhood and fatherhood, are as sturdy as ever. Cautioning women not to "play into" stereotypes actually helps keep the stereotypes alive. Deliberately avoiding traditional behaviors only preserves the bright line between actions expected of one sex and not the other.

To be sure, ignoring root causes of a problem such as the stereotypes animating certain workplace dilemmas often is the right thing to do. Skating over the surface and treating "behavioral" symptoms rather than root causes can be preferable to a prolonged, complicated analysis of deeply engrained motivations. But we've gone as far as we can go with the "no problem" approach. Right now we're at a plateau for lawyers regarding gender issues. We need to restart the debate by going back to first principles.

The better approach is to deconstruct stereotypes, to take them apart and get to know them all over again. Dismantling a stereotype allows us to examine all its assumptions and prejudices—some of which may have escaped our attention—and challenge and debate their validity. Awareness of the genesis of gender roles can lead to questioning and revision of attitudes. In turn, dissolving or softening stereotypes increases options for behavior for both men and women.

Listening to Many Voices

In order to study the tenacious stereotypes described above, I utilized interviews as my major source of information. During 2001 and 2002 I interviewed 180 people (fifty men and 130 women) in all regions of the country (thirty-three states plus Washington, D.C.), who were knowledgeable about a wide variety of practice areas. A majority of the people I interviewed are engaged in the private practice of law, and I interviewed people in firms of all sizes. I also talked with people in corporate departments, government offices (including judges), and public interest organizations. In addition, I talked with people outside the profession, such as psychologists, recruiters, and various consultants (who specialize in marketing, jury work, career counseling, mentoring, and self-image), as well as some attorneys who had left the practice of law entirely. I identified some interview subjects through personal contacts, whereas others were chosen at random from Martindale-Hubbell. Still others were referred by earlier interviewees. I interviewed each person—sometimes face-to-face, more often by telephone—for one to three hours.

The vast majority of interviewees chose to remain anonymous to promote candor and protect themselves and others. Within the text I refer to the people I quote in general terms, such as "a woman partner in Texas" or "a male in a government office." Sometimes I include a fictitious first name if I must refer back to someone. Those individuals who are quoted for attribution have allowed me to include their first and last names and their affiliation. Occasionally I changed details in anecdotes to shield individual identities.

I also reviewed relevant scholarly tracts, surveys, books, and newspaper articles, which are cited in textual footnotes as well as in the bibliography at the end of this book.

I had no preconceived notions when I began writing this book. Rather, I listened carefully to people and organized their thoughts in a structured format, buttressed by other research. As a result, this book resembles an oral history, where my sources do much of the talking.

Of the ten chapters in the book, eight are substantive chapters that discuss a stereotype or a collection of related stereotypes. I use quotations, survey results, and other research materials to establish that the stereotype persists, and then define it by identifying discrete behaviors and attitudes. I then include observations from people who describe what they do in response to these norms—conforming, gently challenging the norm, or flouting convention altogether. Although I give broad conclusions at the end of each chapter, my recommendations for specific change are contained in Chapter 10.

Chapter 2, "Changing Clothes: Erosion of a Stereotype," explores a simple, outdated stereotype—that an attractive woman can't be competent—and shows how it has diminished in force over time. This process provides clues as to how other stereotypes, still entrenched, might erode in the future.

Chapter 3, "Sex and the Bar: Two Steps Forward, One Step Back," examines how some sexual stereotypes have shifted. For instance, sexualized conduct by women, formerly absolutely *verboten*, is now permissible within limits, whereas some male perspectives, such as the automatic assumption that women welcome sexual advances, have been altered. The chapter discusses the persistence of low-level "underground harassment" and speculative "story making" that can plague workplaces even though sexual harassment law has diminished overt sexual harassment. Lawyers explain how they finesse harassing clients, react to low-level harassment, and squelch rumors.

Women faced an original challenge, as noted above, to establish basic competence. Chapter 4, "Question Marks and Quizzical Looks: Closing the Competence Gap," discusses the fact that a generation's worth of data about women's performance, along with suspicions about their commitment (linked to competency) due to work/life concerns, has kept the "competence gap" open.

Leadership styles are discussed in Chapter 5, "Being the Boss: Making Room for the Authoritative Woman," which focuses on the oft-heard dictum that women can't be too passive or too aggressive. The chapter asks why it is that ambitious, striving women are often summarily rejected and their male equivalents are celebrated. It details how "nice" supervisors walk a fine line between being supportive and being authoritative, and also explores the difficulties that men face when they manage women.

Chapter 6, "Getting Ahead: Are 'Confident Insiders' Born or Made?" discusses the formula for success, especially perceived confidence. The chapter describes how men and women who appear to lack traditional, masculine-style self-assurance are left behind, and suggests ways they can achieve greater workplace acceptance and success.

Most people believe that work/life balance is above all a gender issue, chiefly one for women. Chapter 7, "Real Lawyers Don't Work Part Time," isolates non-gender aspects of the debate by analyzing the broader expectations of commitment that apply to all lawyers. The chapter asks why full-timers and part-timers find so little common ground, and discusses the "turf war" between them.

Chapter 8, "The Kid Thing: Redefining Success at Home and at Work," documents the continuing grip of stereotypes about motherhood and fatherhood. It explores the reasons why a woman, once she becomes a mother, is transformed into a person who is judged in relation to how she raises her children, whereas a man, once he becomes a father, is viewed largely as a breadwinner and faulted if he veers from that role.

Although most of the stereotypes discussed within the book are those that cast a negative light on women, some are positive: that women bring a caring orientation to the profession, that they are more honest and humble, and that they are more likely to seek meaning in their work. Chapter 9, "We Care: Debating a 'Good' Stereotype," explores this collection of "good" behaviors and the pitfalls that ensue when people apply these qualities only to women.

Finally, in Chapter 10, "Conclusion: Snapshots, Present and Future," I present some ideas for change based on the views aired in this book. These thoughts reflect ways that an individual can evaluate and alter inner attitudes and convictions, emphasizing the power of one person to make changes large and small. The chapter also includes more expansive ideas about effecting change on an organization-wide basis, when there's a commitment by top management to such initiatives.

Themes and Caveats

Several overall themes define this book. One I have called the "genderation gap." Many people explain present-day gender issues as a rift between generations. They state confidently that any lingering gender issues are a result of the older generation's narrow views. Once the grey hairs turn out the lights and retire, proponents conclude, these issues will be a thing of the past.

There's some truth to this, but I don't think current lawyers should have to wait until some distant day to do something about these issues. (Lawyers are notorious for delaying retirement.) Also, even though one can generalize that there's more overlap between attitudes of young men and women, some younger lawyers retain traditional ideas. Moreover, when the pressures of family intrude, many people who previously experienced their work lives as free of gender bias struggle to reconcile assumptions of equity with the realities of conflicting demands. (Many women said to me that they had no use for "that feminist stuff," and believed they had no gender issues—until they had kids.) As a result, throughout the book I identify "genderation gaps" where they are relevant.

Another frequent theme is how rhetoric, along with metaphors and images, provides insights into how we frame and define a debate (such as "accommodation" and "supportiveness" in relation to flexible work arrangements). I also refer to work/life issues throughout the book, not just in Chapters 7 and 8 where they are the focus, because they affect many topics. Finally, in different contexts I discuss various reasons why men tend to gravitate toward men, and women toward women, especially in informal settings, reflecting the multi-faceted awkwardness that men and women experience working with one another.

I include at the end of most chapters a diagnostic for measuring change. It is a three-part "test" that broadly calculates what change has occurred relating to a particular stereotype over the past generation. I ask, first, whether the options for men and women for new behaviors and actions have increased, meaning whether the unofficial "rules" governing what men and women can do have been modified. Second, I ask whether any applicable "double bind" or contradiction that entraps a person no matter what action he or she undertakes has started to unravel. The classic example of a double bind is a woman who acts submissively and is called ineffective, but is then marginalized and dubbed "unfeminine" if she acts more ambitious and domineering. Third, in some cases I ask whether a particular male or female image dominates a debate. These aren't precise measures, but they help identify where we've come from and where we're headed. I also at times attempt to predict the future path of an issue by using factors enumerated at the end of Chapter 2, which traces the erosion of a stereotype.

Some caveats. First, I did not include law schools among the legal work-places studied. I reasoned that an analysis of gender issues in those settings had more to do with academia than the traditional practice of law.

Second, although I interviewed significant numbers of minority group members, my discussions in this book concerning minority group members are limited. I wanted to avoid sliding into a superficial discussion of race, mistaking controversies that are actually about race for gender issues, or muddling or overlooking differences that exist among and within races and ethnic groups. If problems involving gender are complex, adding race and ethnicity to the mix makes them even more so. Therefore, although there are quotations from various interviewees from minority and ethnic groups, and some relevant data are included, they are intended merely to add some illustrative examples of issues; this book does not pretend to fully analyze the added difficulties imposed by race in addition to gender.[6] Along the same

---

[6] What promises to be a superb, comprehensive new book on one minority group, written by Professor David B. Wilkins, is entitled *The Black Bar: The Legacy of Brown v. Board of*

lines, although I interviewed lesbians and gay men, I also did not include a significant discussion of sexual orientation, again because these issues can be more appropriately treated in a work devoted exclusively to that subject.

Clearing the Underbrush

The primary audience for this book includes people who are thinking about the law as a career, lawyers who are currently in practice, and management groups within legal workplaces. However, people outside the law can draw insight from the book as well. The issues are not unique to the legal profession. In some respects, of course, the law differs from other careers. It is tradition-bound and slow to change, governed by leaders who are older than those in other industries and businesses. The law also may include an "outside the rules" orientation: lawyers make the rules and enforce them, leading sometimes to an above-it-all assumption that fairer rules don't apply within the profession. However, there are parallels that people in other businesses, professions, and organizations might draw from *Gender on Trial*.

This book has three main purposes in addition to its overall mission to demystify stereotypes. First, it provides a new starting point for debate. The modern discussion about gender issues for lawyers has foundered; in part there's too much reliance on well-worn rhetoric and not enough on what people "really think." I hope this book will provide an agreed-upon starting point based upon airing a full spectrum of provocative views about how male and female lawyers work together.

Second, the book is intended to prod both men and women to think more about men's gender issues. The less that "gender issues" are all about women, and more about all people, the more productive the debate will be. At present, the focus on women tends to isolate them further and perpetuate some of their problems.

Finally, this book is meant to help realize a vision for the future in which men and women work together effectively, delivering superb work products

---

Education and the Future of Race and the American Legal Profession (Oxford University Press, forthcoming). Professor Wilkins, Kirkland and Ellis Professor of Law and Director of the Program on the Legal Profession at Harvard Law School, graciously shared some of his findings with me in an interview, portions of which I have included within this book.

that build upon healthy relationships with one another. This vision will require that people have adapted to and overcome the awkwardness and confusion that inhibits conduct in the workplace right now. We continue to be stymied by stereotypes, which arbitrarily limit what men and women can and cannot do. Less reliance on traditional gender roles will clear away the underbrush, so that the walk towards equity is brisk and sure-footed. A "cult of personality" can then emerge—evaluating people on individual characteristics, skills, and traits, on their accomplishments rather than their alleged potential—and push aside the cult of gender. In this fashion reality can catch up with our ambitions and the expectations gap can disappear.

CHAPTER 2

Changing Clothes: Erosion of a Stereotype

Women as Immigrants
Going Feminine
Going Casual
"Pit Bulls in Lip Gloss"
How Change Happens

A female judge, now in her fifties, worked as a trial attorney early in her career. She recalls that she was advised to wear her hair in a bun while she was in the courtroom.

She dutifully did so until the last day of a trial, when she wore her hair down instead. After the verdict, a male juror mentioned to her in passing that he liked her hair better that way. "So do I," she thought to herself, and never wore it up again. She says:

> I didn't feel comfortable with my self-image when pulling my hair back. It was an austere look, and I'm not an austere person. Looking too schoolmarmish wasn't really to my liking.

This woman resolved for herself the contradiction inherent in a long-held stereotype: that an attractive woman is presumed to be frivolous or incompetent. She had been a trial lawyer for many years, with much success, and decided that she could risk looking more like her "real self."

I hadn't intended to write a chapter about dress and appearance. But people I interviewed kept bringing it up. Women described the designers, fabrics, and colors they prefer. Men wondered when they could wear khakis, and when they had to wear a suit. Randi McGinn, a seasoned trial lawyer from Albuquerque, says she frequently gives presentations to bar groups about trial tactics, passing on war stories and tips culled from twenty years of stormy courtroom battles. But the women in her audience have their minds on something else. "The number one question I get from women lawyers is about dress," she reports, a little miffed. "You talk about trial tactics and they want to know, 'What should I wear in the courtroom?'"

So dress is a high-interest topic. And it isn't that much of a gender issue any more, although it certainly used to be in the 1960s through 1980s, when men wore identical suits and women tried to look like them. Over time women decided they didn't like the required masculine look, whereupon they "rebelled" and "demanded" a return to a more traditionally feminine look. One woman changed her look after admiring another woman's fashionable outfit and bright red nail polish. Another heard a jury mock her appearance on videotape and dressed in sleeker fashions to increase her credibility. A dowdy associate got a makeover and then looked and acted confident enough to make partner.

In a generation's time, the arc of the dress issue for women has soared and declined. Indeed, when I asked people whether they thought dress was a gender concern, most were dismissive: "Oh, no-one thinks about that. It's a non-issue." Although some concerns remain—women still get more scrutiny than men, and many people object to overtly sexual clothing on females— "what to wear" is not as charged as it once was. Men and women now have similar concerns about their professional look. They dress down when meeting with the high-tech client, and wear pinstripes for the corporate types; they dress modestly in small towns, saving the Ferragamo suits for the big city. Both sexes have more options than they used to, and tailor their wardrobes based on setting, client, and location.

This chapter will trace how this gender issue and stereotype eroded, and also identify where vestiges of the stereotype persist. The conclusion will explore the effects, especially the benefits, of a gender stereotype that diminishes, and discuss why change occurred for this issue when it's been slower to evolve for other concerns. This prompts the question whether it is possible to predict how change can occur for other issues.

Women as Immigrants

When women first entered the profession in big numbers, in the 1960s and 1970s, the common ground for men and women was that they were expected to look professional. Work required a dressy formality.

But what, exactly, were women supposed to wear? Traditionally, they looked attractive, frilly, and distinctly feminine. In the workplace, however, women were like immigrants in their own land, meeting hostility and rejection as they "invaded" new territory. They dressed in order to blend in, reduce resentment, and be "taken seriously," assimilating in their new "country." And because the definition of "professional" at the time was to dress like a man, women repressed their femininity—donning sober charcoal and navy blue suits, low-heeled pumps, and short hairstyles with minimal makeup and jewelry—to look like some passable version of a male lawyer.

"When we graduated, we were grilled on the 'power look,' and I wore my ugly blue suit like everyone else," gripes a partner in a large West Coast firm. Another recalls, "The clear message that women got was they had to be as *incognito* as possible and melt into the woodwork. They had to be as unnoticed as possible, and wear the most subtle and manlike attire."

However, women's fashion choices didn't escape criticism, whether they tried to blend in or not. A feminine appearance and professional competence couldn't coexist, resulting in a "double bind."[1] As Mona Harrington wrote about women lawyers: "If [women] departed from the code and revealed the shape of their bodies, they were suspect as non-serious. If they did not, if they successfully hid their breasts and hips and legs, if they subdued their hair and fingernails, they were also suspect as nonfeminine, not themselves."[2]

One woman remembers how dismayed partners were about her long, curly brown hair when she was younger. They would say, "Can't you do something about your hair? It just shouldn't be that way." A senior partner barked, "Make it go away!" Although she actually looked too "womanly," another woman offended by not looking feminine enough. A colleague says: "She looked like she hadn't brushed her hair in the morning. She wore ties with her suits. She was coming up for her first trial, and a male partner asked me to tell her how to dress."

Indeed, people noticed what women wore, no matter what option they chose. As sociolinguist Deborah Tannen observed, women in the workplace are "marked" in their appearance and men are "unmarked." We don't notice men's more predictable and unrevealing clothing, she writes, whereas there is no style of clothing, hair, jewelry, and general appearance that women can adopt that doesn't convey some message and is "standard." As she sums it up: "There is no unmarked woman."[3]

Going Feminine

By the late 1980s and early 1990s women started to reject the faux-male power suit in favor of vibrant colors, silk dresses, softer hairstyles, and distinctive jewelry and accessories. How did this come about?

First, women felt uncomfortable with a masculine-type appearance. Dress, hair, jewelry, and overall attractiveness were touchstones for self-worth and

---

[1] This "double bind" is developed and explained in Kathleen Hall Jamieson, *Beyond the Double Bind: Women and Leadership,* at p. 120 (Oxford University Press, 1995).

[2] Mona Harrington, *Women Lawyers: Rewriting the Rules,* at pp. 100-101 (Penguin Books, 1993).

[3] Deborah Tannen, *Talking from 9 to 5: Women and Men in the Workplace: Language, Sex and Power,* at pp. 108, 112 (Morrow/Avon Books, 1994).

identity. Women in their forties and older repeatedly said that a "frumpy" wardrobe "wasn't me" and that "I didn't feel like myself." A partner in a west coast firm commented, "I just liked to look nice. Kind of silly, but don't we all?" A litigator in the southwest remembers:

> When I started guys were the role models, and the women wore severe suits and pseudo-ties, rosette things. We put our hair in a severe bun. Someone saw me on TV and said, "You look just like your mom." That was enough for me to say, "That's bad, that's not who I am, I'm 26."

Another woman recalls leafing through women's magazines in the late 1980s, seeing features on colorful new fashions for professional women, and realizing with a start that there were ways to dress other than the "uniform." Women felt they had been robbed of their true identities. They hadn't made the decision to break the gender mold—it had been thrust upon them. They wanted to reassert control with a traditional appearance, which looked fresh and defiant and "new," in contrast to dressing like men.

As more women entered the profession and formed a critical mass, there was safety in numbers. The "immigrants" were better able to assert a separate identity when there were more of them to support one another. And their expertise and confidence were building as well. If women doubted their legal abilities at the outset, after a few years in the workforce they knew they could perform effectively. And if they were competent when they dressed like men, they were equally so dressed like women. Louisa, a female partner in a large law firm, comments: "I was getting to be more senior, so I didn't feel I had to prove anything by dressing according to a certain code, and I saw more women practicing law, so I didn't feel I had to dress like a guy to fit in."

Restive women who were unhappy in their shapeless blue suits noticed that other women were bucking the system. Louisa, quoted above, says:

> I remember meeting one woman, a big-time tax lawyer, in the early 90s at a seminar on networking. She had long red nails, bright red lipstick, and was wearing a beautiful, attractive outfit. She pointed out that it was great to be noticed—and boy, you noticed her when she walked into a room!—and that you should wear what looks good on you.

The role models urged others to revamp their wardrobes. A law firm partner, Maureen, described a younger woman she worked with, a superb practitioner who looked "too much like a hausfrau" and more "like a little brown mouse." Her looks were getting in the way of a coveted partnership. Maureen, advising that an attorney needs to be "*au courant* and crisp" and not a "nebbish," helped the younger woman revamp her wardrobe so that she appeared more confident and attractive.

The makeover isn't an easy message to deliver to someone who has faithfully dressed in a colorless way. "There was a time when you were told that in order to be successful you had to be kind of drab," says Kathleen Kauffmann, formerly a jury consultant and now with Sommer Barnard Ackerson in Washington, D.C. "If you incorporated that at age twenty-five, and now you're forty-five or fifty, being told that you can be 'not drab and still successful' is a hard message. Also, you're told that you've dressed badly for twenty-five years."

Women were rewarded for "going feminine" with greater power and control, rather than being dismissed. Maureen, who oversaw the makeover described above, recalls:

> In the office, she [her protégé] began to come out, because everyone said, "You look wonderful!" All of a sudden she started being visible and people started listening to her. It became a synergy. She just projected herself more. Maybe it was because we started noticing her and listening more. She wasn't just looking more feminine, she looked packaged, in control. It's the presentation.

A woman who served as executive director of a not-for-profit public interest group felt that the all-male board viewed her as a "daughter figure" and didn't consider her authoritative. Her solution:

> I was careful when I had board meetings to dress up. To give myself the added authority that I lacked because I was a woman and because I was young. I always wore lipstick to make sure I looked older. Not to look more feminine, but to look a little more official, a little bit more professional. Lipstick is a polishing thing. Makeup and clothes can be your armor.

For some women, wearing what they liked was a form of rebellion and risk-taking. Suzanne, now a general counsel in New York City who formerly worked in a large firm there, tells about a turning point that occurred during her sixth year as an associate:

> I woke up on a freezing cold day in 1989. I went to dress in my usual skirt suit, and then said, "Screw this, I'm going to wear a pantsuit." I thought, "It's frigging cold outside, the guys are wearing pants and they're nice and warm, why should I freeze my butt off?" There was a sense of rebellion. I was nervous about it, because there was an informal rule against wearing pantsuits. And the stares I got! Including from my male peers. But no-one said anything to me, no partner came to me and said, "You can't wear pants." I'm not suggesting I set a trend, but I noticed that gradually more women were doing it all over. I thought, "What are they going to do, fire me?" I was senior enough, well-respected. I was more secure. You know that they're not going to fire you for what you're wearing.

Women increasingly didn't care if dressing as they pleased ruffled some feathers, and insisted on wearing what they wanted to within reason. Says a law firm partner, "I'm stubborn and not willing to give up looking female." Roberta, a partner in her fifties, says her distinctive appearance—short leather skirts and patterned silk dresses—also sends a useful message in practice:

> It says to an opposing attorney, for instance, "I have more aspects to me than you may think. Watch out, there may be things about me you don't know. I may be unpredictable. I'm not like that guy in the blue suit where you know what he's going to say. So you'd better be on your toes." It also says, "I like myself, and I feel secure enough in what I do that it doesn't matter to me if you judge me about this. Because the other aspects of me are so strong, I'm so good at what I do, I'm articulate, I'm competent, so I can take a risk here." And a risk taker is somebody who has confidence.

Those who rebel and "take a risk"—even by re-adopting a traditional model[4]—are less likely to be pushed around, a desirable quality in a lawyer.

---

[4] It is, of course, illegal to discriminate against individuals because they don't conform to gender stereotypes, as established in the case of Ann Hopkins. Ms. Hopkins sued her former

It suggests that the women who were previously cowed or bullied into looking mannish lacked the self-confidence to assert themselves.

Women resolved the contradiction between femininity and competence by having the self-assurance to look the way they liked and let their abilities appease the doubters. Roberta, who has always worn her thick black hair long, despite early warnings from a consultant, and even her husband, says:

> I thought they might be right, but it wasn't worth it to me. Even now, maybe I'll walk into a courtroom, and jurors will see my long hair and their reaction might be, "How could she be a real lawyer?" but they'll hear me and after five minutes they'll forget that I have long hair.

Women in other professions also use dress as an indicator of rebellion and identity, as business professor Debra Meyerson describes in her book, *Tempered Radicals*. A female surgeon in a male stronghold wears lacy socks under her scrubs and says, "I'm a woman and a surgeon at the same time." A black woman refuses to unbraid her corn rows before an important presentation, because her hairstyle is too tied to her sense of self.[5]

Tracing the way women have "changed clothes" indicates a path from timidity to confidence, from assimilation to a greater individuality than blue-suited uniformity. Women felt they previously betrayed their true identities with male-style dress, and now feel a stronger alignment between the inner person and the outer look. This came about because of thousands of small "ah-ha" moments—hearing a juror's remark, admiring a beautifully dressed woman, getting a makeover—that have changed the way women look.

---

accounting firm after being denied partnership, partly on the basis of her perceived failure to conform to stereotypical feminine modes of demeanor and attractiveness. Price Waterhouse v. Hopkins, 490 U.S. 228, 109 S.Ct. 1775, 104 L.Ed.2d 268 (1989). In that case, a male partner advised Ms. Hopkins to "'walk more femininely, talk more femininely, dress more femininely, wear make-up, have her hair styled, and wear jewelry.'" 490 U.S. 236, citing the trial court at 618 F. Supp. 1109, 1117 (D.D.C. 1985). The case established that discriminating against Hopkins on the basis of sexual stereotypes was impermissible under Title VII of the Civil Rights Act of 1964.

[5] Debra E. Meyerson, *Tempered Radicals: How People Use Difference to Inspire Change at Work,* at pp. 44-45, 66 (Harvard Business School Press, 2001). For a detailed discussion about how women assert power through hairstyle, see Rose Weitz, "Women and Their Hair," 15:5 Gender & Society at 667 (Oct. 2001).

Going Casual

Another factor, the trend towards casual dress, also helped weaken this stereotype of understated, conservative dress. Although casual dress isn't as popular as it was,[6] it opened up a new universe of dress options for both sexes. And it caused problems for both.

The dress-down movement meant fewer differences between males and females. "Casual dress has been a neutralizer," reports Margo Hasen, a fashion and image consultant in New York City. "There isn't as much of a distinction between what women and men can wear." For instance, the trend towards pantsuits for women is "genderless," states Hasen, "and has more to do with comfort. It's liberating [for women] because you can walk faster, wear a lower heel or a flat, and you don't have to worry about your skirt riding up when you sit down."

But casual dress also caused confusion. The dilemma of "what to wear," previously only female territory, now plagues men as well. Jim, a thirty-five-year-old male associate in a large Midwestern firm, says:

> I make conscious dress decisions. For instance, I do a fair amount of construction litigation. If I am taking a deposition from people on a construction site, and I want to play the role of a buddy, I would dress down. I would wear khakis and some nondescript long-sleeve shirt. I'll do the same thing with one of the key opposition players, if I want them to think I'm some kind of rube. If I want to scare you, I'll put on cufflinks, the power tie and the dark suit and I might shine my shoes, to look the mean, nasty lawyer type. And if I'm going to court, I don't want to come across as a big corporate suit-wearer kind of guy. If I wear the sport coat and slacks, mismatched even, I might be better received by a jury.

Jim's dress code sounds a lot like Helene's, a partner in a large Northwestern law firm:

---

[6] Leslie Kaufman, "Return of the Suit, Tentatively; Some Men Are Dressing Up Again, but Casual Still Lives," The New York Times at C1 (April 2, 2002).

> Most people, including me, dress appropriately for what is happening. If I'm meeting with corporate clients at their headquarters, I wear a very nice, stylish suit. If I know I'll just be working in my office with no likely client meetings, I often wear a nice sweater with a skirt. Of course litigators still have to dress up for court.

Many men believe women currently have less difficulty with dress because there is a greater range of clothing available for them, whereas men believe they must look either formal (in a suit) or not (in khakis and a polo shirt). "In the casual world, men have problems like women have always had," complains a male in-house lawyer in Colorado. Indeed, many articles and workplace policies have counseled workers about the do's and don'ts for spaghetti straps and golf shirts.

Casual dress also confused status and hierarchy. Hasen points out that sloppily dressed lawyers clash with the "brand" of a tony law firm. And informal dress for all employees erodes status distinctions between lawyers and staff. Lawyers who were interviewed said repeatedly, "It should be clear who the lawyers are around here." A female in-house lawyer said that casual dress at a workplace encourages too much coziness between lawyers and staff.

Not only did lawyers look less like lawyers in their jeans and sweater sets, but they also appeared less controlled and confident. Atlanta image consultant Lynne Henderson Marks, president of London Image Institute, says that informal clothing seems to take control of the person, rather than the other way around. Her unflattering critique:

> Their clothes look tired, there's no tailoring, no structure. Your body takes over the shape. At least in the tailored suit it was the suit that spoke, or the silhouette that spoke, which made your body look good and your shape improve. Whereas if you put yourself in a pair of wrinkled chinos and a worn-out three-button polo, your body takes over the shape. Men's casual clothes reveal their rounded stomachs, along with their wallets in the back of their pants. It's equally objectionable in men and women. Tailored clothing is usually made with more robust fabrics, which enhance the female body.

All these points, asserts Marks, means formal wear is better. "If you master your clothing," she argues, "you project an ability to master your client's problems. You are 'count-on'-able, you're organized, you know what you're doing, you have a professional attitude."

Casual dress accelerated the decline of dress as a gender issue because wardrobe questions for males and females overlapped. Men and women adopted a similar look and explored wider options with casual wear, but also grappled with the same concerns: what to wear, being mistaken for non-lawyers, looking "out of control." They learned what it was like to share an issue rather than be divided by it.

"Pit Bulls in Lip Gloss"

Although the stereotype about femininity and competence has eroded, there are some remaining concerns. A woman's appearance can still prompt fleeting questions about reliability. A female federal judge believes that "a man standing in a three-piece suit is instantly credible until proven not credible." But a woman, she says, "is not credible until you prove you are. You have to prove you're a serious person." She goes on:

> When a new lawyer appears before me, I try to say, "What is my reaction to this person?" If she's a new person, what do I think about her? If she's wearing a red suit, am I discounting her? It's not an issue with men.

The "risk" of a red suit means that a woman who dons it acquires a burden to "prove" herself. There are times when it's still safer to retreat to standard-suit anonymity, as one female partner concludes:

> Sometimes I think, "I've got to wear a navy blue blazer and skirt," like when I'm going to a large meeting with a lot of lawyers that I don't know. I probably want to observe them rather than have them observe me. If you're just meeting one person, you've got this instant impression of that person, but you then can give a full impression of yourself as well. They quickly see I'm articulate and smart. But in a large group you probably won't have much interaction.

The greater scrutiny that women receive can affect the outcome of cases in court. A woman who successfully defended a case talked with a juror afterwards. She learned that, out of forty-five minutes of deliberation, thirty-five minutes were devoted to discussing what she and the female prosecutor wore:

They said, "Did you see that outfit that first day? I didn't like her hair that first day, I didn't like her outfit." I don't know if they do that for guys. Most of it came from the women. "Did you see those shoes?" I really felt like I won that case because they liked my appearance and my style better than my opponent's.

Sue, a female litigator, did a mock trial before a jury whose deliberations were videotaped. They had unkind words for Sue's flowing, floral-print belted dress with a white bodice top:

They just ripped my appearance. They said if I was going to represent a Fortune 500 company that I ought to get a makeover. That brought it home to me that jurors today still very much look at women's dress and evaluate women lawyers based on what they look like.

Former jury consultant Kathleen Kauffmann says:

Although there are places in the country where respectable women dress in a very narrow range of clothing options, I've never in my life advised that horrendous banker floppy-tie look that was prevalent there for a while. I've talked some women out of it, because jurors would talk about that in a negative way. The look is dried up and sexless. It's Jane Hathaway on "The Beverly Hillbillies." You don't want to deny who you are by putting yourself in some gunnysack to make yourself look unattractive. Most social science research says attractive people are more persuasive than unattractive people.

Some people believe that women run more risks with relaxed dress standards than men. A thirty-six-year-old female partner in a midwestern firm objects vehemently:

I think casual day is a terrible idea. I think women have a hard enough time being taken seriously. Why do you want to sabotage it? We are a society that judges on looks. If you look professional you will be treated that way. If you see a man in a law firm you assume he's a lawyer. You're not likely to confuse the lawyers with the guys in the copy room. Would being mistaken for a secretary be the worst thing in the world? No, but I want to look like a partner.

Indeed, in a recent survey, 45% of female lawyer respondents said they had been mistaken for an assistant, in contrast to only 9% of the males.[7] A female in-house lawyer comments: "I think of casual dress personally because I'm a petite woman, and I don't look my age. So when I dress down I look that much younger, and people say, 'Oh, you're a lawyer? Senior VP of a company?'"

Very attractive women still are affected by the clash between femininity and competence, at least initially. An in-house woman observes:

> I still hear of men being surprised when a very attractive woman attorney is very smart. It's almost like a kneejerk reaction. I think it's also that the men get very intimidated. This one woman, she's very stylish, high-powered. My boss was completely wowed by her, because of the whole package, that she had the brains and she had the looks and she was well put together. It's almost intimidating. I have felt that at times directed at me. It's sort of this mix of admiration and resentment.

Another woman mentioned the pull between "admiration and resentment," saying that a male frustrated by the tenacity of two female opponents called them "pit bulls in lip gloss."

Just as controversial as women's attractiveness is how "sexy" women appear to be. For instance, in one of many "genderation gaps" identified in this book, older lawyers think that women shouldn't look too provocative. A forty-three-year-old female general counsel noticed that a younger colleague wore a top that showed her navel:

> We're here to work. That was inappropriate. She probably didn't think about it, but it was distracting to me, and I'm sure others noticed. And I think perhaps there's a part of me that still feels like, "I know how men are."

Some younger women, however, say they are wary of this "rule" and frustrated by it. A newly minted associate in a big New York law firm criticizes female partners in her firm who wear "shapeless clothing," saying they

---

[7] "Gender Equity in the Legal Profession," at 21 (New York State Bar Association, Committee on Women in the Law, 2002).

"suppress the female look of their body." Another young women, thirty years old and a sole practitioner in Texas, says that she doesn't want to look "too stuffy or too sexy," but isn't happy with what that leaves: "Usually, I wind up wearing the same old three or four outfits to court because I know they fall within those boundaries. It is really frustrating."

Some minority female attorneys were particularly concerned about this issue. A young African-American woman said she hesitates to wear tight trousers to work. And she always wears her hair in a ponytail at work, because when she wears her thick curly hair down, people ask, "Are you going out tonight?" Another African-American woman who works in-house on the East Coast believes that she has "to walk a narrower line" than caucasian women:

> My [white] friends are able to wear some things that I'm not able to wear, because they won't be perceived as trying to challenge some-body's authority. There's another woman in my office, she wears men's shirts, not blouses, and they look good on her. And white women can wear the pinstripe suits. But if I put them on I think it would send the wrong signal. I don't want to appear to be too masculine. Like I'm challenging male authority in a way. I wear pants but I have to pay attention to the jacket and the top, because I don't want to appear to be too masculine either. I'm trying to give reassurance to men I work with.

Overtly sexual-looking dressing in the courtroom is also suspect. A female judge felt she had to tell a younger lawyer who appeared before the court that her skirt was too short. The younger woman was embarrassed and upset. "But I felt like I needed to tell her," the judge relates. "If I was reacting to her that way, how would the other judges be?"

Many female lawyers say they dress modestly in court (although they note many younger women wear short skirts and look sexy). Virginia, a Texas family lawyer, in a typical comment, says that her aim is to have her own appearance recede and let the case take front and center. In the office she wears pantsuits and paints her nails, but before a jury she'll wear tradition-al skirt suits and leave her nails unvarnished. She stresses:

> I don't want to become the issue. If anybody sees me, I want them to say she's nice, neat, well-organized. I don't want them to say what a body she has, great clothes. I don't look bland, just not flashy. I don't

31

wear short skirts, especially in front of a jury. I know some women who do, and they're comfortable with it. I mean, if you wear a short skirt and you drop a piece of paper, you'll have to think about it.

The above concerns—still greater scrutiny for women than men; more downgrading or status issues with casual dress; suspect reviews because of an overtly sexual appearance—mean that some question marks still hover around women's appearance, but not as conspicuously as in the past.

How Change Happens

What happens when a stereotype crumbles?

First, options and choices increase. For instance, that women's dress has ranged from masculine to feminine to casual to sexy means that women now have many more options for how to dress than they did in the past. For men, too, because dress has shifted from all-formal-all-the-time, to casual wear or three-piece suits depending on the setting, options also have increased. As a result, even as people absorb a message about an individual's distinctive personality from dress style, they also evaluate someone's clothing mostly for its appropriateness based on the setting.

Second, the double bind that is often at the heart of a stereotype starts to unravel. At the outset an attractive woman couldn't gain professional respect. Now, the window of judgment—the time when people look a woman over and decide whether she can be trusted—closes more quickly and affirmatively.

Third, a more neutral image arises, in this case with the mental model of a "female lawyer." Deborah Tannen wrote that there is no "unmarked" woman. I asked many people to visualize a "standard" professional woman these days, and their vision sounded a lot like C.J., the press secretary on television's The West Wing. C.J. always wears an attractively tailored suit with a bright blouse, and has shoulder-length hair and understated makeup. There's no question she's a feminine-looking woman; there's also no question she's a professional. An "unmarked woman" look may be developing. The implication is quietly exciting: that it's possible for a woman who meets this description to take her place at the table and not get the inspection and scrutiny she once did, and for her appearance to send a neutral message. She wears what she wants and others don't notice, just like men have always done.

Indeed, this stereotype is not the only one related to women in the workplace that has lost steam over the years. For instance, I heard very little in my research about "overly emotional" women. Perhaps this is due to the widespread emotiveness in general in American society—the greater acceptance of therapy, and popular confessionalism in talk shows and television—where men are nearly as inclined to display emotional reactions as women. Other minor fixed ideas also have slipped away: that women talk too much, that they have trouble being on time.

So if women's dress has declined as a gender issue, why haven't other gender issues resolved themselves as quickly?

Part of the success formula included greater numbers of female lawyers, who collectively presented a more feminine look and were accomplished practitioners. This injected a fleet of smartly dressed women into the workplace who could counteract established notions about the supposed disconnect between looking womanly and being a professional.

But "wearing what you like" was a grass roots phenomenon, whereby scattered individuals acted on their own, regardless of rank, to challenge informal dress codes; it was not the result of changes in official policies. Change on more complex matters—compensation and work/life balance, for instance—requires larger numbers of women in management positions who can influence policy. In 1995, Kathleen Jamieson wrote that "women are at highest risk of stereotypic appraisal when they form less than 15 to 25% of a management level. When women move in large numbers into upper management, as in many professions they are now poised to, the evaluative norms will change."[8] Although women represent nearly one-third of the legal profession and half the law students, they are far from occupying 15 to 25% of managerial-type positions.

In addition, it's easier for people to act as role models on a relatively superficial issue such as dress. Innovation falters when men are afraid to advocate for more controversial matters such as work/life balance, and when

---

[8] Kathleen Hall Jamieson, *Beyond the Double Bind: Women and Leadership,* at p. 141 (Oxford University Press, 1995). See also Virginia Valian, *Why So Slow? The Advancement of Women,* at pp. 139 *et seq.* (MIT Press, 1998), for a discussion of studies reflecting women's increasing power, and the decreasing relevance of gender, when women form a larger proportion of a workforce.

women feel they have been shortchanged on such important areas as compensation, but don't feel empowered to complain.

Women succeeded with the dress issue because they reclaimed a familiar stereotype—the feminine woman—and used it for different purposes. There's a greater chance of quick success when one works within an established stereotype while claiming a new goal. Trying to alter the familiar outline of a traditional gender role takes longer and provokes far more resistance. For example, increasing the acceptability of an aggressive female is a hard sell. Stretching those bounds automatically results in a stiff challenge.

A critical point is that men's and women's dress options have evolved together. It's much easier for men and women to walk together on a new path, rather than reverting to parallel paths with no meeting point. The casual trend meant both sexes started wearing similar clothing; the guys wrestled with "what to wear," which had always been the women's worry; and both got low marks for not "looking like lawyers," lacking an appearance of confidence and control. Common ground is harder to find for other issues. Clashes about mixing parenthood and work, for instance, which appear to be "only about women," occur because of sharply divergent stereotypes about motherhood and fatherhood.

What we wear has evolved and changed, and the gender aspects of the debate have dissipated. The next chapter on sexuality shows that although radical change has occurred in some areas, familiar stereotypes continue to grip our imaginations.

CHAPTER 3

SEX AND THE BAR:
TWO STEPS FORWARD, ONE STEP BACK

The Power Shifts
Flirting for Success
Lawyers in Love
Is the Customer Always Right?
Still Hard to Sue
Underground Harassment
From Silence to Humor to Rebukes
Chatting Up the Wives
Lurid Scenarios
Avoid, Avoid, Avoid
Aligning Public and Private Voices

A thirty-six-year-old woman in the South looks back to her earlier days practicing:

> The guy I worked for, when I was just out of law school, he was very good looking, married, probably in his late thirties. An Ivy League kind of guy. His reputation was as a ladies' man. He was just constantly hitting on me. He would pressure me to go out with him. It wasn't like a sexual harassment thing, that I felt like my job hinged on it. But it was just uncomfortable—he was married! I have to admit now, I'm sure I played my part in it. I was single at the time, he was cute, the attention was nice. I'm sure I gave mixed messages. Maybe I did feel pressure for my job. I never really said, "No, stop it, get away." I think I just did the stupid chick thing.

What's going on in this story? Is it just harmless flirtation, a "ladies' man" chasing after a "stupid chick"? Or is a high-powered partner pressuring a low-status associate for sex, setting up a sexual harassment claim ("Maybe I did feel pressure for my job")? The line dividing casual, sex-tinged banter from outlawed behavior is fuzzy and hard to draw.

Not that anyone thought refereeing the sexual interaction between males and females in the workplace would be easy. Especially if one assumes that the categorical statement of a fifty-year-old male practitioner is even partly correct:

> There's always sexual tension when there's men and women, period. As long as there's men and women together, there will be romance, and there will be sex, and people will be thinking about it all the time, whether they act on it or not. Every day, all the time.

After a generation of the two sexes working shoulder to shoulder, there's good news and bad news on the sexuality front.

Some things have been settled. For instance, although men may have assumed that women welcomed sexual overtures in the past, because of a stereotype of the "available" woman, the whole area of sexual harassment law has developed so that women can say "no" without penalty. Another development is more room for women to express their sexuality positively, without automatically being stamped incompetent.

However, a backlash to the new rules about sexual harassment keeps negative sexual stereotypes about women alive. As a result, sexual harassment remains a significant issue for younger women, who fend off both clients and colleagues. Further, it's just as hard to complain or to bring a sexual harassment action as it always was.

And even though severe, overt sexual harassment seems to have decreased, "underground harassment" has filled the vacuum with leers, off-color jokes, and pornographic e-mails. Another complication is "story making," where the rumor mill assigns meaning to make sense of new scenarios: "She can't just be a good attorney, she's got to be sleeping with someone," or "He's spending a lot of time with that young associate; he must be harassing her." This culminates in the biggest problem: avoidance. Men figure they'll avoid a whiff of trouble if they simply don't compliment the new dress, if they work with John rather than Jenny, and leave women out of the golf game. Both men and women react to the sexual minefield by retreating to a same-sex comfort zone free of innuendo or ambiguity.

The Power Shifts

The dynamics of power and sexuality in the workplace have shifted dramatically. Before the 1960s women in professional workplaces were present only in small numbers, generally as support staff. They were assumed to be sexually available and to welcome advances. Men were the aggressors, pursuing women in the office. At that time there wasn't even a concept of sexual harassment. If a woman complained, society blamed her—by questioning her chastity and sanity—and gave the man a pass.

Today the picture is radically different. Women are professional peers, not just support staff, and are present in greater numbers and for a longer period of time. In forty years we've gone from a problem that didn't even have a name to the concept of sexual harassment, with which most people are well-acquainted.[1] Paul Buchanan, an employment lawyer with Stoel Rives in Portland, Oregon, says:

---

[1] The Equal Employment Opportunity Commission has defined sexual harassment, actionable under Title VII of the Civil Rights Act of 1964, 42 U.S.C. § 2000e-2(a)(1), as "[u]nwelcome sexual advances, requests for sexual favors, and other verbal or physical conduct of a sexual

The conduct that's being complained about is now frowned upon, whereas before it was more a slap on the back. Now a male is looked on with real suspicion, and even with a strong defense it's hard to erase the cloud of suspicion. So [a claim of sexual harassment is] a very strong weapon on the part of women.

People within legal workplaces have a greatly heightened awareness of the risks of sexual harassment. Dr. Ron Kimball, a psychologist in Washington, reports:

> My sense is that law firms are extremely cautious and put a lot of pressure on their lawyers not to be engaged in such things. I had a young male partner in a small boutique firm. The administration descended on him, forced him to go see a therapist and to do psychological testing before he could go back to work. All he had done was touch one of the secretaries on the shoulder without her permission. She went to the managing partner and complained, and that's all it took.

Indeed, today a harasser's colleagues are more likely to turn against him than in the past. An employment lawyer in New York relates:

> Men get angry that one of their partners has put the firm in this position. "How could you possibly be so stupid?" they'll say. "Now we've got to pay somebody some money, it could create bad PR, how could you put us in this situation? You should know better."

Increasingly male colleagues voluntarily confront transgressors, even in the absence of formal complaints. A managing partner told an egregious sexual

---

nature." 29 C.F.R. § 1604.11(a) (1985). See Meritor Savings Bank FSB v. Vinson, 477 U.S. 57, 67, 106 S.Ct. 2399, 91 L.Ed.2d 49 (1986). A more recent case summarized the concept of a hostile working environment: "When the workplace is permeated with discriminatory intimidation, ridicule, and insult that is sufficiently severe or pervasive to alter the conditions of the victim's employment and create an abusive working environment, Title VII is violated." Oncale v. Sundowner Offshore Services, Inc., 523 U.S. 75, 118 S.Ct. 998, 140 L.Ed.2d 201 (1998), quoting Harris v. Forklift Systems, Inc., 510 U.S. 17, 21, 114 S.Ct. 367, 126 L.Ed.2d 295 (1993).

joke in front of the whole firm, and other male partners cornered him later to protest. A man viewed pornography on his computer with the screen facing the hall; his partners told him to stop.

Severe sexual harassment, as a result, seems to be on the wane in legal workplaces. An American Bar Association Law Journal article concluded that much harassment is "subtle" in nature, and that reported cases in law firms tend to involve administrative personnel.[2] It also indicated that virtually all studies of workplaces in general indicate a decline in *quid pro quo* sexual harassment and overtly hostile work environments.[3]

However, legal workplaces—despite employing lawyers who presumably "know the law"—don't seem to feature better behavior than other settings.[4] In some respects they may be a little worse. Dr. Fraeda Klein, of Klein Associates in San Francisco, who works with professional service firms on issues of harassment, diversity and bias, conducted independent research in 2001-2002 on this topic. She says that the frequency of harassment in large, multi-office law firms is in some cases higher than that in non-legal

---

[2] Debra Baker, "Plague in the Profession," ABA Law J., at 41-42 (Sept. 2000). For a full discussion of sexual harassment and applicable policies, see Deborah L. Rhode & Jennifer A. Drobac, *Sex-Based Harassment: Workplace Policies for the Legal Profession* (American Bar Association, 2002). A recent overall survey of the American workforce in February 2001 reports that 21% of women and 7% of men have been sexually harassed at work. ". . . 21% of women surveyed in the latest national poll report having been sexually harassed at work," U.S. Newswire (Feb. 5, 2002) (online article at www.usnewswire.com). In a 1989 National Law Journal/West Publishing Company survey of 900 women lawyers, 60% said they had been harassed in some way, but few had raised a complaint. Mona Harrington, *Women Lawyers: Rewriting the Rules,* at p. 105 (Penguin Books, 1993). A 1993 survey of 553 female litigators conducted by Prentice-Hall found that 89% of them thought sexual harassment was "somewhat of a problem," "a large problem," or "a pervasive problem." And more than half of the respondents in that survey said that they had been sexually harassed in the course of their jobs in the last five years. Lorraine Dusky, *Still Unequal: The Shameful Truth About Women and Justice in America,* at p. 223 (Crown Publishers, 1996). Other surveys cited in one ABA report are all from the mid-1990s or before. Deborah L. Rhode, "The Unfinished Agenda: Women and the Legal Profession," at 19, fns. 104 and 105 (American Bar Association Commission on Women in the Profession, 2001).

[3] Baker, *id.* at 40.

[4] Even law firms that advise clients on proper labor and sex discrimination policies can get in hot water themselves. One article describes a lawsuit against one firm for failing to practice what it preaches. Paul Braverman, "Manhandled," The American Lawyer (Aug. 2, 2002) (online article at www.americanlawyer.com).

corporations.[5] A recent survey of New York practitioners showed that 5% of female practitioners were "offered professional benefit in return for sexual favors,"[6] which echoed results from the Kansas and North Carolina bar associations.[7]

Greater awareness has led legal workplaces and other organizations to expend huge sums to train employees to avoid engaging in illegal behavior. The balance of power, therefore, has swung firmly from the men's court to the women's side, at least when it comes to actionable sexual harassment. Change came about because far-sighted practitioners recognized early on that it would be impossible for women, especially in professional roles, to achieve long-term success if the old script of sexual availability were not rewritten. This involved addressing a "sexuality/competence" double bind. If women were considered sexually available, they weren't going to be as effective or considered competent unless they were legally protected.[8]

Although attorney Paul Buchanan represents management, and encounters abuse of the laws, he nonetheless concedes their value. He declares:

---

[5] Dr. Klein found that in law firms 9% of respondents complained of unwelcome pressure for dates, 18% reported unwelcome gestures, and 15% told of touching, pinching, and cornering. In non-legal corporations, 17% reported pressure for dates, 10% unwelcome gestures, and 9% said they experienced touching, pinching, and cornering. Interview with Dr. Fraeda Klein, May 13, 2002.

[6] "Gender Equity in the Legal Profession," at 31 (New York State Bar Association, Committee on Women in the Law, 2002) (hereinafter, "New York State Gender Equity Report").

[7] New York State Gender Equity Report, id. at 30.

[8] The courts were way ahead of public opinion, which was galvanized by the Anita Hill/Clarence Thomas hearings in 1992. One employment lawyer called those hearings a "national seminar on sexual harassment, an aberrational public education campaign." The trend to widespread acceptance of sexual harassment as a cause of action can be traced with Equal Employment Opportunity Commission statistics. In 1992 there were 10,932 sexual harassment charges filed ($12.7 million in benefits paid); in 2001 the number of charges had increased to 15,475 cases ($53.0 million). These figures are more remarkable for the nearly five-fold increase in payouts than for the 50% increase in claims. Jonathan Glater, "Software Trains Employees and Limits Liability," The New York Times, at C-1 (Aug. 8, 2001). The cause of action is now so entrenched that males are suing, claiming sexual harassment by both women and by other men (with mixed results for the latter at the trial level because some courts maintain that the current statute relies on sex discrimination as a rationale and therefore prohibits suits by men against men). There were 483 such charges in 1991, which climbed to 2,172 charges in 1999. Reed Abelson, "Men, Increasingly, Are the Ones Claiming Sex Harassment by Men," The New York Times, at A-2 (June 10, 2001).

> I really think it's good and important, if we're going to have men and women working together, that employers have a certain measure of fear about liability, because it motivates employers to deal with bad conduct in the workplace. That's the best thing about the law.

Flirting for Success

Along with legal protection to fend off advances, the other side of the coin is that females are allowed more space to decide affirmatively how they want to assert their sexuality, if at all. For instance, some women use flirting or charm to facilitate relationships with colleagues and clients and to advance their careers.[9] A male in-house lawyer describes how his female boss interacted with a company client:

> The man was obviously smitten by our boss, who's an attractive woman. Instead of failing to use all her weapons in her arsenal, she leaned in close to listen to him, touched him on the arm, went on a major charm offensive. It was an effort to close a deal. She has the credibility—academically and professionally—to overcome stereotypes.

A litigator in Virginia observes his female peers in court:

> Some women, rather than be tough, will use their little girl charm, just like some men will use their old boy charm. Women using their feminine wiles, that's okay, that's fine. If some woman were up against me in court and she's got a flirtatious relationship with a judge, I would be envious that she's got that advantage.

---

[9] One survey reported that although 26% of Canadians have flirted at work, 56% believe relationships and flirting have a negative impact on the quality of life in the workplace. Donald Mackenzie, "Workplace Flirting Has Negative Impact on Life at the Office: Poll," The Canadian Press (July 21, 2002) (online article at www.cp.org). A survey in 2001 found that 86% of United Kingdom workers admit to flirting with colleagues. Ninety percent of men and 75% of women said that it "makes for a more pleasurable workplace, makes the day go faster and is a bit of fun." "Flirting the Key to a Pleasant Working Day," The Times (Nov. 7, 2001).

A racier story comes from a female former criminal defense lawyer, who talks about her days in court:

> I wore short skirts all the time. Certain judges I would be conscious that, "If I have to go to Judge X tomorrow and I'm asking for a really big thing, I'm wearing a really short skirt." I noticed a correlation in getting what I wanted. There was a woman in my office, she was beautiful, with long hair and she was a very good lawyer. She would be on trial, she'd say, "Juror number 6 is looking at me so I'm going to lift my skirt a little."

Recall from Chapter 2 that many women dress attractively and fashionably not to attract a mate, but to project confidence and professionalism. Here, a familiar model—the coquettish female—is wheeled out as the woman flatters a man in order to close a deal or get a favorable ruling.

Many people view sexualized behavior aimed toward workplace success pragmatically, a "weapon in the arsenal" that a woman can deploy to gain an edge. The male in-house lawyer whose female boss charmed her way to a deal says, "There's nothing wrong with women using sexuality in the workplace, if it's used properly." A fifty-two-year-old female courtroom lawyer says:

> I can be very disarming. I tell opposing counsel they have nice ties, they look cute. I just think that women have tools that they can use. We should not be deprived of using those tools, especially if those tools include the ability to develop collaboration. So I'm charming rather than adversarial.

A thirty-year-old male associate in Washington, D.C. remarks:

> If I were giving advice to a new young female associate, I'd tell her to use her sexuality, use her attractiveness. Some people who master it, succeed. It works for men in some fashion as well. I've seen older woman who flirt away; it's just one of those benefits of power. I'd tell them to go ahead. It works.

This approach isn't without controversy. Many think those who use sexuality as a career advancer will slide down a slippery slope. In their view it de-legitimizes a woman by reawakening the stereotype that a woman's mere presence is overwhelmingly sexual rather than professional. A female partner in a large Midwestern firm is adamant:

> You don't want to talk about sex at work, period. You might talk about your husband and what you're doing for the weekend, but that's it. Men are very likely to be perceiving women sexually and you don't want to do anything to add to that. There are women who get ahead that way, but I don't think that's a long-term career strategy. You get old, you gain weight. It's sort of all comes down to the rubric that it's so hard for women to be taken seriously anyway. Why go there? I can certainly imagine people taking a different view, it's really helped them get ahead, you play up to him a little bit, but you have to be very skilled at it.

A forty-year-old female partner in the Southwest avoids even a hint of sexualized conduct:

> I don't physically touch a male client. It's too risky and it's sending the wrong messages. I would never touch his shoulder or touch his arm or anything, particularly a business client. I wouldn't talk about family or kids. I would never initiate those conversations. If they talk about their children or their wives, I would talk about where my kids go to school.

Another woman thinks it's acceptable to be flirtatious if it suits one's personality, but not if it's calculated:

> If the person is that way anyway, it's okay. The ones that I cannot tolerate are the ones that are not that way and then go in and use it at work. It's blatant, it's really a put on. But it works with a lot of these guys.

One woman defined different kinds of flirting:

> There's good flirting and bad flirting. Somebody might look at what I did and call it flirting. I wanted to let people see who I was, get to a comfort level. It was completely non-sexual. I would joke around, I would try to enjoy working with the person. Bad flirting is a way to compensate for shortcomings, a way to get to the top without showing substantively that you can get to the top. I know there is this

image out there of women who use that to get to where they want to be.

The in-house man with the flirtatious boss agreed that flirting without substance wouldn't work: "If it's your only weapon you'll be discredited. Like, when all else fails, try some lipstick." His comments quoted above noted that his boss's "credibility" overcomes stereotypes, as if a woman's professionalism is an answer or antidote to what might otherwise be unjustifiable behavior.

Psychologist Dr. Ellen Ostrow, who coaches women lawyers, believes that it's "absurd" to say that sexuality has no place in the workplace because it leads to an "alternative stereotype that we have to become asexual." Rather, she advises, it's important to be sensitive and use one's sexuality carefully:

> I don't think there's anything wrong with flirting per se, for either gender, as long as people know what the boundaries are. I think it's a slippery slope if you don't know what you're doing. This is where emotional intelligence comes into play. You have to know who you're flirting with and how they're reacting. Somebody who knows that on some level you're playing, it's okay, if you're comfortable with it, and as long as you don't experience it as debasing yourself. I don't think that the goal is to come up with an alternative stereotype, that we have to become asexual. In my mind the goal is that everybody has the greatest range of options, as long as you're making choices and not losing self-respect.

It should be noted that for some members of racial or ethnic groups, options for sexualized behavior are greatly reduced due to prevailing stereotypes. Professor David Wilkins, Kirkland and Ellis Professor of Law and Director of the Program on the Legal Profession at Harvard Law School, points out that both male and female African-American lawyers face far more scrutiny about sexualized behavior than do white lawyers. They are "constantly having to negotiate complex fears and taboos having to do with sexuality," he comments.[10]

---

[10] See David B. Wilkins, *The Black Bar: The Legacy of Brown v. Board of Education and the Future of Race and the American Legal Profession* (Oxford University Press, forthcoming).

Whether using sexualized behavior as a career facilitator is advisable or not, the point here is that it's allowed in some circumstances, instead of being completely taboo. If at first women were expected to be severe and asexual to be "taken seriously," now there's a bigger entry for "feminine wiles" in the lexicon of permissible professional behavior.

Lawyers in Love

Another arena where the range of sexual behavior for women has broadened is workplace romance.[11]

Today many studies show that romantic relationships at work are not unusual.[12] Although there are no statistics on lawyer workplace romances, one can assume from the overall data, and from widespread anecdotal reports, that romances in legal settings are about as frequent as in other workplace settings. Indeed, some law firms are described as cauldrons of lust, especially large, multi-office firms. Said one woman:

> My firm was a hotbed, a Peyton Place. Married people all around were having affairs with other married people at firms. The Christmas parties were something to see. You never missed the "after" party.

A male employment lawyer says:

> In the major firms, the 24/7 settings, where people don't have a life, they look to their cohorts. There's sexuality there, not sexual harassment. [One New York City firm] is a hotbed of sex, you need a scorecard. It's unbelievable. I've never seen anything like that. It's just sex.

---

[11] The unsentimental definition of workplace romances is "mutually desired relationships involving physical attraction between two employees of the same organization." Charles A. Pierce, Herman Aguinis & Susan K. R. Adams, "Effects of a Dissolved Workplace Romance and Rater Characteristics on Responses to a Later Sexual Harassment Accusation," 43:5 Academy of Management J., at 869 (Oct. 2000).

[12] One study reports that 71% of employees have either observed or participated in a workplace romance, 24% of managers have been romantically involved with a co-worker at least once, and 33% of all romances develop at work. Pierce et al., id. at 869. Another study determined that 80% of American employees have experienced a romantic relationship at work. Cindy M. Schaefer & Thomas R. Tudor, "Managing Workplace Romances," 66:3 S.A.M. Advanced Management J., at 4 (Summer 2001).

Widespread affairs and romance have resulted in more equity between the sexes and a softening of stereotypes, such as the double standard that historically permitted male sexual escapades but shunned sexually active women. Personality and likeability can triumph over those traditional gender roles. One young woman reports that she had a high-profile relationship. When it broke up spectacularly, she fared better than the male, because he was cocky and arrogant whereas she was well-liked:

> I've been involved in scandalous things, and people still really respected me. I've never been affected. I'm thinking of other people I've known who've dated people at work, I've never been aware that partners think about them differently. If you do good work, and you handle yourself with class and decorum when you're discussing work things, you'll be fine.

When another associate arrived at her current law firm, she heard discussions about relationships between male partners and female associates, and said that the women weren't denigrated. Although it was "obviously interesting enough for people to talk about," she says, the relationships weren't big news: "It wasn't discussed as a scandalous thing, but was just matter of fact. I have not gotten the sense that it's totally taboo."

And a male can suffer from sexual exploits if he's carelessly arrogant. "There was a summer associate who had sex with his secretary on his desk," one person reports. "He didn't get an offer [to become an associate with the firm]. 'Of course he didn't,' people said. It's not something to be proud of. He was treating the firm with disrespect. I think that if you command respect otherwise, then you're okay."

Not only are women less tainted by romantic exploits, but increasingly females approach males for romance. One lawyer, talking about the big firms that are awash in romances, says, "It's not harassment, the most aggressive ones are the females." And a young male associate in California got a taste of the social awkwardness that women are familiar with:

> I've worked with one co-counsel who hit on me. We were representing different defendants in a lawsuit. She would call me late at night, sometimes from home, and asked to meet for drinks constantly, to "talk about the case." I was not interested. At first I wasn't sure where she was coming from, but she called me once at the office at about

12:30 at night, and she had been drinking a little bit. Ostensibly she called to talk about the case, but she was trying to get me to meet her. I put her off, said I had to work. There wasn't a power differential, but it was still a pain. The case settled so that was that. People eventually give up on these things after they've been rebuffed a few times. It gives you some empathy with women, feeling uncomfortable talking to people who you have to talk to for professional reasons. Since she was not a client it was not as difficult, but I certainly felt a lot of discomfort, and if the case had gone on, I could have seen it as potentially something that could be detrimental to our client.

Another male lawyer, who is married, had to be more adroit in his handling of a come-on:

There was one situation where a young staff woman was asking me out to lunch. I knew it wasn't right. I sat the person right down and said, "I can't do anything, I'm not going to do anything. I like you, I think you're cool, we can be cool, but that's it. If it makes you feel any better, maybe you should leave here and we can get together." Then we laughed, which made the let-down that much easier.

Some women in positions of power are also approaching men. A young female associate says:

One thing that's interesting that I've seen here, which I haven't seen before, there are one or two female partners who have taken on that drunk-guy-at-the-party role. You know, inappropriate flirting or touching at the office Christmas party. That's totally not appropriate but almost refreshing to see women getting to that level of power. Others were more amused by it, they think it's pretty funny. Kind of ridiculous, a woman making a fool of herself. It's definitely seen as less threatening than if a man was doing it. An older desperate female partner, they think. When the story's told it's also told in a surprised way, like, "Wow, the tables are really turned. Hmm, now male associates might be subjected to these things."

Although the workplace is more open to new modes of behavior, old stereotypes have not completely evaporated. A male partner in a Southwestern firm warns:

One of the remaining issues is that in a large place, if you have a male attorney who does a little bit of sleeping around, he can get away with it, whereas if a woman attorney does, the ramifications are much harsher. The woman gets a bad reputation, and then people attribute it to work, people say she's not really serious, because she's had these frivolous affairs. Whereas a guy, they have a grudging respect for him: "That guy's a stallion." There's still a big difference between how you view a guy in the firm who's slept with five female associates and a woman who has slept with as many male associates.

A female partner in the South says observers are "judgmental," and adds:

I know of a young man who ultimately married a paralegal, but in the meantime must have dated eight or nine women in the firm. Nobody ever said anything. He's now a partner and very bright. I don't think a woman could have gotten away with that. It would trickle into the perceptions of the people who are giving assignments.

The door isn't swinging wide open for women's sexuality. The double standard is still around; males can view female come-ons as distasteful or laughable, and women still have less maneuverability than men. But that door is open a few inches wider than it was. The overriding credential of a "good lawyer" helps to counteract attempts to marginalize women for sexual behavior that is tolerated or admired in men.

Is the Customer Always Right?

Although sexual harassment has been unequivocally established as a credible cause of action and, at the same time, women have acquired more freedom to assert sexualized behavior, other problems have sprung up. For instance, clients are responsible for 18% of the harassment of attorneys, according to Fraeda Klein's research. A man with friends who have to handle harassing clients says it's tough:

Women have gotten calls from clients long after cases ended, trying to get them to go out with them. For the most part the cases don't last forever and they ended up trying to balance keeping at arm's length with the client and not blowing things with the firm. The women have tried to be as polite as possible, they've tried to be diplomatic about it. Nobody wants to cause a scene with a client.

A Midwest female practitioner confides:

> I have one client, he's both a client and sends me business. He's constantly asking me out for dinner, sending candy and other gifts, and he's married. He keeps saying it's on the up and up, but it's a constant thing. He's stopped the candy and gift thing, and he's cooled off a bit. I had to face how not to screw up the business relationship and at the same time get him to stop. I stopped returning phone calls for a bit, and I wasn't really very effusive in terms of my thank yous. I told him that people in my office were starting to remark and I told him that he should spend the money on his wife.

This strategy seemed to work: the behavior stopped and they now have a good business relationship.

Client entertainment can result in awkward situations. One woman in New England reported that a female partner went to dinner with a client, who slipped his hotel room key into her purse. "She just ignored it," the woman said. "She's not a very confrontational person. The case settled and so he disappeared as a client. We were glad to see him go."

An employment lawyer says law firms are good at controlling harassment within their own four walls, but are "behind the curve" about client harassment. Women are expected to "put up with a fair amount from a client," he reports. Clients call women and ask them on dates, whereupon the women complain to their supervisors. The partners then say, according to this lawyer:

> "Would it really kill you if you went out for a drink with the guy? Can you find a way to appease him but not upset him so he doesn't not do business with us anymore?" The reaction is not anger or frustration, but it's, "Boys will be boys," or "You should feel complimented that he thinks you're attractive." The women are frustrated that they're left to their own devices.

Fraeda Klein comments:

> This is a problem that law firms do a particularly poor job of handling. They're afraid of losing the business. Also they minimize the impact. "What's the big deal? You should give the client a little more room. You don't interact with this person all the time, like if it were someone here." This is a misunderstanding of proximity versus power.

> I hear over and over this sort of overreaction from partners in smaller firms who say, "Great, we'll confront our largest client and they'll take their business, and we'll have to lay off 40% of our people."

Hence, although managers feel confident confronting sexual aggressors within the office, they are reluctant to educate clients when this can jeopardize business. The rules outside the four walls of a workplace are more shadowy than those within, leaving women to figure out the awkward balance between maintaining their self-respect and not "losing the client" on their own.

Still Hard to Sue

It's also not easy for women to decide how to react to sexual harassment—to complain, sue, or keep quiet. One study showed that 60% of people who are subjected to sexual harassment don't complain. A female judge, formerly a practitioner, laments:

> It's still a difficult issue to raise. It's your word against his word. If you raise it, are you then colored every place you go? Will you find another job? Is it better to leave and move forward somewhere else?

A female employment lawyer concedes, "It's still extraordinarily difficult. If somebody is still working someplace and wants to stay, the possibility of retaliation is still high." They won't get fired, she says, "but sometimes it's worse to face retaliation that's more subtle. Like being excluded, being shut out, the assignments are not as good. It's not as blatant." She counsels people in their first job to think long and hard before bringing an action, because they don't have the contacts and track record to get anther job.

Some people sift through the possibilities and decide to bury their complaints. Many stay silent out of fear. One female partner muses:

> Should you speak up in the workplace? It's hard. If you're dependent on someone for work, and something like that happens, maybe you won't get any more work, and that's going to affect your job.

Others believe they brought the problem on themselves and wait the harasser out. One woman reported for a "working dinner" to a hotel suite only to find the male partner offering roses, champagne, and an invitation to sleep together. She refused, and was dogged for months by the man's negative reports about her work. She never revealed what happened to her superiors, blaming herself, and eventually the harasser left the firm for unrelated reasons.

Some keep mum out of loyalty to fellow members of a racial or ethnic group. Lucia, a Latina woman in a government office, talks about a Latino man who acts inappropriately:

> Because of the bond of being Latino he feels comfortable with me, but he then will cross over. He says, "Can I smell your hair? Oh, my God, it smells great," or "Oh, wow, your shirt looks really great on you." It's textbook 1950s stuff. Even telling you right now I can't believe I didn't sock him. But I don't want to blow the whistle on him. If this were an Anglo guy, there probably wouldn't be this relationship. I would have screamed at him, gone to somebody else above him. I don't want to get a Latino guy in trouble. There are not enough of us in the first place. All we need is another example of someone doing something wrong.

And those who have been through sexual harassment situations—where the matter was resolved quietly, formally settled, or litigated—say the aftermath can be nerve-wracking. Joan, from the Midwest, was a new associate when her sixty-year-old boss started making sexual comments when they were alone. They were often couched humorously, "to give him deniability," as she put it. "He was very vulgar," she recalls. "He would talk about oral sex, about buying me sexy underwear. At first it was kind of subtle and I'd think, surely he couldn't have meant it that way, but then he got more and more blatant." She left the firm, brought an action for harassment, and settled in her favor. She now says:

> I worried about it being made public. Here I am a brand-new lawyer, I didn't want a taint to my name. But I have never heard anyone mention it. And I've never mentioned it to anyone. Sometimes I feel like I have this little secret, because I don't know how some people would react. I still worry about the stigma. I'm really glad that I litigated it, but if this happens again, I wouldn't want to litigate it again.

Another woman, Serena, practicing in the Southwest, was pressured for months by a partner who was married. He would book flights and lodging for them to take a continuing legal education course together. Eventually the other partners got wind of it, sat him down for a stern talk, and the harassment ended. Serena stayed on at the firm, but noticed a distinct chill in the air:

> Now I'm not one of the guys. They censor their talk, they censor their actions, and I don't know which is worse. They're a lot more aware. Part of it is, we used to go out have drinks after work. They would always tease me about being single and say, "We need to find you a boyfriend." They don't do anything like that anymore. I feel like they look at me as a whiner, like I couldn't handle it. I'm now feeling a little out of the loop.

Indeed, complaining or bringing an action can breed rumors. A West Coast male states:

> I've heard stories of women who were harassed and who stayed on at firms for years without doing any work, in a position where they had some leverage. They're coasting because the partners are scared.

Actions for sexual harassment remain more useful to women as a threat in the air, a way to regulate behavior on a global basis and prevent it from happening in the first place. When a real problem comes up, deciding how to proceed is still fraught with anxieties. As a result, although sexual harassment actions have more currency than they did previously, they still prompt charged, complicated emotions and consequences for the individuals who are directly involved.

Underground Harassment

Even though severe sexual harassment is on the wane, "underground harassment" is far more prevalent on a day-to-day basis. This includes calculated behavior that is "close to the line," such as off-color jokes, leering remarks, uncomfortable body language, and bawdy e-mails. In some cases these incidents could constitute actionable sexual harassment under the "hostile environment" theory,[13] but women typically don't run to the court-house over such behavior.

A 2002 New York survey of practitioners showed that this is an omnipresent feature of female lawyers' working lives. Sixty-six percent said they were called names like "sweetie" or "dear," 65% said they were subject to "sexist or demeaning jokes," 53% fielded "inappropriate comments" on their appearance, 47% complained of "sexual teasing," 42% reported "sexual looks or gestures," 30% said they were subject to "verbal advances," 14% told of "touching, pinching, cornering," and 15% experienced a "pressure for dates."[14] And this is only what they personally hear and see. As one litigator said about males regarding females in the courtroom, "Male lawyers will talk about them all the time. 'She's not bad looking, I wouldn't mind screwing her, too bad she's a lawyer, she's probably frigid.'"

Examples of this behavior abound. A young woman in Texas recalls episodes from her first days in practice:

> The name partner, who had taken me on as a baby lawyer to train, would periodically tell me how men practice. He was very careful, he in no way sexually harassed me because he knew sexual harassment law, he knew what all the boundaries are. He'd say, "You're going to have to be tough, you're a young and very attractive young lady, it's going to be very helpful in your career, take that for what it's worth." It was nothing overt but I thought it was inappropriate. He would say it's just a compliment.

Lisa, a clerk for a trial judge, heard similar remarks:

---

[13] Under the" hostile environment theory, "'bad behavior' can also constitute unlawful behavior. Simply put, when it is directed against a coworker or subordinate on the basis of membership in a protected class, bad behavior is illegal discrimination." Wanda Dobrich, Steven Dranoff & Gerald L. Maatman, Jr., *The Manager's Guide to Preventing a Hostile Work Environment: How to Avoid Legal and Financial Risks by Protecting Your Workplace from Harassment Based on Sex, Race, Disability, Religion, or Age,* at p. 3 (McGraw-Hill, 2002).

[14] "Gender Equity in the Legal Profession," at 31 (New York State Bar Association, Committee on Women in the Law, 2002).

In the courtroom, people come up to me and say things like, "What's a pretty little clerk like you doing you in a place like this?" It's not like really harassment. Not *quid pro quo*, nothing to sue for. It registers, it's kind of funny, it makes me laugh at them, but it's still surprising. One of the attorneys in a recent case, I was taking the elevator down outside the courtroom, and I said something about "going down," and he made some comment, "Oh, I wish." The doors closed, and I said to someone else, "He didn't mean that in a gross way," and he said, "Yes, he did." The man was as old as my dad. It's joking but really lame joking.

A man in a Western firm says many of his female colleagues from law school have been subjected to mild harassment:

Some women have had partners constantly comment on their appearance, like "You look hot in that skirt, I love it when you wear that." Or putting a hand on the associate's leg, touchy/feely type of things, a woman bending over a table and a partner making a lewd comment about looking down her cleavage or that she's looking good bent over a table.

A female senior partner remarks:

We're pretty good about clamping the lid on a racially inappropriate statement. But you still have men left and right making [sexual] jokes or innuendo, at the beginning, middle, or end of a meeting. I find that happens both by the client base and your colleagues. Recently everyone was passing around a photograph of [a celebrity's] new girlfriend naked by office e-mail.

Some underground harassment includes comments on the "exoticism" of people of different ethnicities. Lucia, the young female Puerto Rican practitioner quoted above, says she has worked with men who are fascinated by her ethnic background and make repeated references to it. "Is this how you do things where you come from?" they ask, along with mild sexual references. Lee, an Asian woman, bristles about "Asia-philes," as she calls them:

They love to tell me they've been in the Hong Kong office, they've had a Chinese girlfriend, as if that will make me happy. A lot of times

55

they get my wrath the most. Certain things will tip me off to those things, like if they're mentioning that my hair is like silk. The whole exotic thing—that's just out the window.

That underground harassment exists at all was an issue for some younger attorneys, another "genderation gap." They were surprised at sit-com situations, episodes they thought were old-fashioned and a thing of the past. Lisa, the law clerk quoted above who says people call her "pretty law clerk," relates:

I feel like these are kind of clichés. But I've had a lot of cliché things happen to me that I thought didn't happen. I thought of these as passé. And it's not. I thought it was like stories you heard about what used to happen. Ha, ha, ha. And they still are happening.

Young men were taken aback as well. Joseph, a thirty-year-old West Coast male associate, recalls:

When I first started at a large law firm, my grandmother called up and talked to my secretary. Then my grandmother got on the phone with me and said, "Oh, you have a secretary! Does she sit on your lap?" I couldn't believe that she was saying that. But I can only guess that at an earlier time that's what a secretary did.

Jeannine, a senior female partner at a big firm, says young women are flabbergasted that they have to put up with such behavior:

They went through college and law school as complete equals. So they've never experienced discrimination in their lives. They came up in an environment where they don't have to put up with that crap. Now they're in a situation with a client or senior lawyer, and they've lost their bearings.

It's almost as if the lessons about sexual harassment have been learned too well. Lawyers know that the real thing can cost them big, so they (generally men) are more careful than they used to be, not saying anything that can land them in hot water but skirting close to the edge.

From Silence to Humor to Rebukes

Women respond to underground harassment as best they can: by joining in, ignoring it, or putting up with it, laughing along, joking to make a point, getting a superior to handle the situation informally, and sometimes confronting offenders directly, without humor.

Some lawyers who are subjected to overt harassment say nothing out of fear. They don't want to offend a partner or a client, get a reputation as a troublemaker, or affect their chances for advancement. Jeannine's advice to young women when they are harassed by clients, which is "conservative and a lot of women don't like it," as she says, is to distance themselves and keep their eye on the ball, because the client's interests outweigh taking offense at the sexual byplay. She gets a split reaction: "Some will say that's good advice. Others, because they've grown up in a generation where they didn't have to put up with this behavior, think that it's kind of an Uncle Tom thing."

Others just ignore the buffoonery or laugh it off. A woman in the South says, "If you don't feel like you have to call everybody's attention to every example of politically incorrect language that's used, if you go along and get along, you're easy to get along with." Another is more pointed about not joining in: "I don't participate in some of the jabbing, joking stuff among the men attorneys. I just walk away. You kind of let everyone know where your line is."

In other cases, rather than taking offense, younger women simply write off the remarks as an unbridgeable generation gap. One says:

> You're not going to change the ways of someone who would make a comment like that in the first place. It doesn't really bother me or affect me except that I was surprised there really are people in this day and age who still feel that way.

Some weigh the offense, on the one hand, with their relationship with the person involved, on the other, to decide how to proceed. A young woman says:

> I have been surprised to see that so much inappropriate behavior is still prevalent at law firms. You'd think that lawyers would be aware more than anyone that you just don't go there. Like at the office Christmas party, the partner is getting a little drunk, his hands are on

your waist, or on the hip. And they're people that I like, partners that I work with, good personal relationships, I know they love their wives. They get a little bit drunk and they're all over you. It's really weird. I've never felt really threatened, more uncomfortable and shocked that they're doing it. I've really just laughed it off. I've sort of tried to pretend that it wasn't happening. I didn't want to call attention to it, didn't want to embarrass them, they're drunk and this is making me uncomfortable and I know that they don't mean anything bad by this. I would step a little bit to the right so that they weren't touching me that way. I would continue on in the conversation. I would treat the man like a friend or an acquaintance who had had too much to drink. I think that's because the two partners that this happened with, I got along with them really well and I knew that they respected my work. My reaction would have been very different with partners I didn't like or didn't work with. I would be more insulted that way.

This story includes surprise, shock, and embarrassment, but basically the attorney quoted above gives these men a break because she likes and respects them. Maintaining valued relationships can trump an episode of drunken groping, if it is not too severe.

Some say if you can't stand the heat, get out of the kitchen. A woman in the Midwest remarks:

In my firm, there's a pretty high tolerance level for language that some people might find offensive. It's a little bit of, "We're important, we're busy, we can say 'fuck' whenever we want." It seems to be the case for women as well as men. Sometimes people will object, and there are times when this behavior crosses the line of acceptability. For example, my first firm had an annual party where the male lawyers would watch stag films and football. That's unacceptable and so is any kind of sexual harassment. But to some extent, I do think if you can't take some level of high-stress irreverence, you oughtn't be in a law firm. It goes with the territory. It's not necessarily good or bad, but it's a fact.

I heard many accounts of women who were bawdier than the guys. People call them "characters" with "a mouth like a truck driver," oddballs who are funny rather than sexually threatening.

Rather than ignoring the antics, clamming up out of fear, or joining in, others are quiet change agents, joking in response to inappropriate comments. A young female lawyer says:

> One day after a luncheon meeting I finished my lunch and put the plates in the kitchen. A partner made some comment, "Oh, I guess you're comfortable doing that." I looked at him and I said, "You mean, because I'm a woman I'm comfortable bringing plates in? You know, you should enter the 20th century." I said it with a smile. He didn't say anything, he just sort of stood there.

Another woman repeats sexist comments back with a sarcastic grin, such as "Good morning, honey." Says she: "They usually get my message." This approach communicates a message with a minimum of alienation. Another woman counsels:

> If it's sort of borderline, humor is a very good way to get a point across. Short and sweet, you're in, you're out. It gets the point across without unduly embarrassing them, because you want them to work with you.

Yet another approach is to spread the word informally against a transgressor. A woman now in-house recalls an incident in her former firm:

> A male partner asked me if I was pregnant again, because he said my boobs looked bigger. It was unbelievable. It still makes me sick to my stomach. Hindsight is 20/20. I wish I could have anticipated that comment and crafted a response. But when it happened I was so incredibly caught off guard. I didn't say a word. I stood there with this shocked look on my face, and I turned around and I left. Every day after that, I remember in the morning getting ready for work I stood in front of the mirror, and if I thought my outfit showed my breasts, that outfit was back in the closet. After I got over the initial shock of it, I told everybody. I used his name, I told everybody. I thought, "This is my revenge. My revenge is that everybody in this community that asks me, I'm going to tell them. If he's willing to say such a godawful thing to me, then everybody ought to know."

An Asian woman said that in cases where minority group members harass others in their minority group, one approach is to voice distaste or anger to other people in the community. She says:

> I know that there was a black associate who kept on hitting on a lot of the female associates of color. And rather than report him, what a lot of the women did was they talked to other junior female associates of color or male associates of color, to embarrass him.

Others seek change by directly challenging people, minus the humor. Higher status makes it easier. A senior female partner says she got a "very sexist e-mail, in the form of a joke." She shot it back with a statement that the "joke" violated the firm's e-mail policy. A thirty-one-year-old Colorado male lawyer, now working in-house but formerly at a firm, says:

> I've been in meetings where perhaps the secretary will come in, and she'll be attractive, someone will make a comment and there's a woman in the room, and I have seen the female speak out and say that's not appropriate. Usually female associates don't say anything, they don't want to challenge the structure. But as you move up the power chain, you get women who are partners, heads of practice groups, who say, "Don't say that around me at all, it's offensive."

A partner in her forties says she is now more likely to take a stand because she has more power:

> At a partnership party two years, a partner was fairly drunk. He was giving out awards and told a sexist joke that was stupid. I didn't feel any problem with saying something to him about it, which I would not have done years ago. I said, "That was just incredibly stupid." And he was very embarrassed. If somebody said something like that now, I wouldn't hesitate to say something. There's a difference between being an associate and a partner.

Although underground harassment seems less of a concern than more severe harassment, over time underground incidents can be like a thousand pinpricks that add up. This syndrome is complicated by the facts that the episodes often are fleeting, masked as humor, and involve people one otherwise likes and respects. Responding can be difficult; women often bite their tongues because they don't want to cut themselves out of the informal office politics by being labeled humorless or overly sensitive. As a practical matter, these fleeting remarks and ambiguous looks represent far more of the reality that goes on every day than does actionable sexual harassment.

Lurid Scenarios

Another syndrome is "story making." It is making sense of unaccustomed relationships (like a male partner meeting frequently with a young female associate to talk business) by assigning stereotypical story lines (that they're having an affair). Story making is more insidious than underground harassment because it's usually composed of back-channel whispers. It's the rumor mill that cranks up in response to situations that are susceptible to scandal. This causes onlookers to embellish the scenario, often without any real proof. Moreover, speculation about competence and credibility accompanies these lurid scenarios.

To be sure, many people reported that they and their colleagues are less likely than in the past to automatically assume something is "going on" between men and women who work together. There's a broader array of examples where it's clear that the relationships are strictly about business, which quiets the rumor machine a little. Says one woman: "We've made huge headway in that regard. It's more natural to see male and female colleagues working together, traveling together, without that instant presumption."

But story making continues. For instance, I talked with many interviewees who—while not knowing the actual facts in a situation—speculated that women involved with higher-status men were cynically sleeping their way to the top, and were actually incompetent. A young female practitioner comments on some "odd relationships" she's seen:

> There was one female litigation partner who was the protégé of the most powerful litigation partner. She was happily married and had a baby, he was married too. Everybody was always convinced that she had to be sleeping with him, nobody really bought that she was his right-hand woman, because it was not based on merit, they were a little too close. She didn't seem that great an attorney. It seemed that they spent a lot of time together, on almost every single deal together. Everyone assumed that she encouraged it in some fashion.

Note that speculation abounded even though the perception was that the woman was "happily married." More generally, says a young male associate in Los Angeles:

> Where the man is a partner and the woman is an associate or para-legal, I think a lot of people make assumptions about the woman in the relationship, that she is incompetent and is sleeping with the part-ner in order to keep her job or to advance in her career.

This can carry on throughout a woman's career. One now-senior female partner had long since ceased working with a particular male partner, but other partners in the firm still assumed the man was "ghostwriting" her work because of his earlier mentoring and speculation about a (nonexistent) romantic relationship. There was an "explicit suggestion that I got there on my back," the woman said.

Some perceive that the reverse situation, an older woman supervising a younger man, wouldn't invite commentary. A female litigator in her fifties has a male junior partner on her team. She says that people don't ascribe any sexual content to their relationship:

> Nobody thinks there's a sexual connotation when the mentor is an older woman. People are trying to put in a familiar box a set of rela-tionships that they don't understand. So people reach for the familiar construct: "It can't be sex because she's old and he's not. It can't be anything that we're familiar with in terms of male/female relation-ships."

Her example involved an older woman and younger man; a similar dynam-ic can occur when people of different races are involved. Says one black female:

> Being an African-American female works to my advantage—I'm not perceived by white males as a threat. If I were a white female, I prob-ably would be perceived somewhat as a threat, because of the sex relationship. Good-looking [white] women have trouble because there's always a sex overtone in the relationship. But I think as an African-American woman I don't have that because I'm not normally perceived as sexually attractive.

But as with so many assumptions, the boundaries are changing a little. A male litigator on the East Coast tells a story about an older female boss:

> If somebody's attractive, and my old boss was, people made comments. I'm an attractive guy and she was introducing me to some guys. One of them remarked, the reason she hired me was because I was this young, good-looking guy, a little sex toy. Everybody brushed it off, the guy was just trying to be funny. I just smiled, and thought, the guy's just an asshole. [My boss and I] tried a case together that was four hours from home, and we had to stay in a hotel. My buddy lawyers said, "Hey, did you have a good time? Did you guys get together?" Of course you say no. It opened my eyes about what she had to deal with in the law.

As with underground harassment, it's hard to counteract or respond to story making. Without contrary evidence, the urge to interpret new-looking relationships in familiar, stereotypical ways is strong.

Chatting Up the Wives

All the talk about sexual harassment, along with widespread fear of lawsuits[15] and story making, causes second-guessing and worry. As a result, many people take affirmative steps such as making strategic alliances so that rumors don't swirl. A young female associate in Texas says:

> We have parties with the wives, and I make a point of speaking with them and make them feel comfortable. I'm here on my credentials and I don't want to have anyone think otherwise. My boss's wife is a little uncomfortable. I'm half his age, single and unattached. I definitely wanted her to be comfortable. We work late hours and we are here alone. That is always in the back of your head. You don't want to be part of an ugly rumor.

---

[15] Fraeda Klein has done research showing that false claims constitute only 1% of the total claims made. One survey of workplaces generally that was conducted in 1999 by the Society for Human Resource Management showed that, after investigation, two out of three complaints were substantiated. The remaining claims are not differentiated between substantiated and unsubstantiated. "SHRM Survey Finds That the Number of Sexual Harassment Complaints Is on the Rise," Society for Human Resource Management (March 15, 1999) (online article at www.shrm.org).

An older woman joined the board of a legal organization and asked a long-time female board member for some tips to increase her effectiveness. To her surprise, she says, "The advice wasn't to be on time, or read your materials five times over." Instead, her friend urged, "Take your spouse. You will be ten years younger than the average male on the board, they all bring their spouses. The best way to endear yourself to the spouses of these older men will be for them to meet your husband."

Other lawyers, when they must work closely or travel with someone of the opposite sex, publicize the reasons widely. A male partner in his fifties says:

> You may go out of your way to make clear why [a female] is going traveling with you. I had to go to Chicago to take depositions. One of our female associates was working on the case with me. We went, and I do recall feeling that I had to make sure that people understood that she was there as a part of the prosecution of the case. Whether I said anything differently because she was frankly an attractive blonde as opposed to a young male associate, I'm not sure. It was in my head. I felt a little uneasy because we had to meet the night before the depositions to review, and the only place we had available to meet was in the hotel room. It would have been easier if it was a guy.

Another way to avoid misunderstandings or rumors is to think carefully before acting. A young male in Colorado describes his mental gymnastics before giving a compliment:

> With internal office flirtation, you're just trying to be nice and make somebody feel good because they may look good. It's tough to have those conversations until way down the road, when you get to know someone. It would take some time, so that she knew me, and knew that my compliment was strictly a compliment, and not an advance towards her. At the same time, if that person gives compliments in her own right, that's a green light that it may be okay. I still don't respond though for a while. A woman can make an advance to a male just as easily as a man can make an advance to a woman.

People hesitate about even friendly physical contact. Recalls Vera, a female partner:

> At a Christmas party a couple of years ago, my husband saw a young associate, and he went over and hugged her. I watched her body language and thought, "He can't do that." He felt mortified when I told him. A man I've known forever came into my office and shook my hand. I had to say, "John, you don't have to shake my hand, give me a hug!" I put my hand out and then I hugged him.

Men sometimes censor their talk or hesitate to bring up personal topics, for fear of being misinterpreted. One woman recalls that her lawyer husband was hesitant to follow up with a female colleague about a recent medical problem, thinking he might seem too personal.

Even office perks can be fraught with complications. An in-house woman agonized for an hour and a half about what to do with four tickets to a professional football game. Part of her concern was about general office politics, but she was just as worried about gender politics. She didn't want to offer the tickets to men, because she didn't want them to think she was coming on to them. She couldn't ask men who were married, because there weren't enough tickets to include their spouses, who might be offended if they weren't asked along. If she only invited women, she would be safe from upsetting the male attorneys' wives, but might then upset males and be accused of distributing the tickets based on gender. Eventually she gave up and offered them to someone outside the company.

Avoid, Avoid, Avoid

The above tactics attempt to combat rumors and regulate behavior so that the sexes can still interact and continue working. But another way to squelch rumors is all-out avoidance. Reports Dr. Ellen Ostrow, a psychologist/coach in Washington, D.C.:

> Men who are very supportive of women attorneys have an increasing amount of concern about being P.C. I talked not long ago with an attorney who is a senior partner in a firm, and he's very much an advocate of diversity of all kinds. But he said he's started worrying, and I think what started him worrying about it was a comment his wife had made: "What's really going on with you and that associate?" She said it teasingly. It made him realize that every time he shuts the door with a woman because he wants to discuss something confidential, there's a risk.

It's a short step from that discomfort, the sense of risk, to avoid giving compliments, being alone, or going to dinner with a member of the opposite sex. "Sexual harassment, that whole issue just had some negative consequences for women in the profession," a male points out. "Everyone is a little more cautious than they used to be. There are some good and some bad results." Ostrow continues:

> The risks involved for men inhibit their straightforwardness. There are men who are afraid to say the caring, concerned things that a woman might say, for fear that it might be interpreted as coming on to them. Or they're afraid to mentor a woman, for fear of their wives' reactions, misinterpretation on the part of women, potential liability, and because not everybody is sued for good reason. And these are really good guys.

Fraeda Klein agrees:

> The rules have changed, the practice of law is completely different than it was on all fronts, including the culture of law firms. I certainly have some empathy with the men partners who are genuinely confused about whether or not or how to approach mentoring a young woman associate.

The repertoire of avoidance is broad. A young male says compliments are a "no-no": "For me I tend to stay away from that altogether on both sides. Any compliment on appearance, I wouldn't say it to a guy or a woman, I don't think it has a place in the workplace." Women avoid men who are younger to sidestep sexual overtones. Vera, quoted above as concerned about hugging, says:

> I've realized that with some of the younger guys, I'm backing up and just shaking hands. To make them feel more comfortable. I'm senior to them and I'm not going to put them on edge. I'm a big hugger so that's hard.

A mid-level female associate says:

> I'm thirty-one and I'm supervising guys who are twenty-seven. You don't want to give them the wrong impression, seem like you are

flirting, you don't want them to think you are interested in them. So you just give them the assignment and tend to chat less.

The most significant avoidance effect is when people try not to be alone with members of the opposite sex, especially when there's a status difference. A male partner says:

> I think that it takes longer for a male partner, me specifically, to let my hair down when supervising a woman associate than with a man. You kid around in a different way, talk about different things. While you're sitting there waiting for the ninety-eight-page brief to be faxed to Utah, you talk about different things. The fear of lawsuits is in there at all times at some deep level. We don't want to create a hostile workplace so we create a stultified workplace. A guy is more easily prone to ask a guy who he was seeing, but I wouldn't ask a woman that unless I knew her well enough. I would be less reluctant to ask what a guy did over the weekend. I'd be more careful in my language, I'd swear a bit with a guy. I wouldn't do that with a woman. I sort of regret that I have to be that way.

This can happen with women as well. The young woman quoted above who says she doesn't want to appear to be flirting with younger male attorneys observes that, as a result, "I subconsciously tend to favor the female associates. I have an easier time chatting with them. Once I've said here's the research and the deadline, it's easy to slip into personal conversation."

Seemingly small adjustments can morph into bigger avoidances. Fraeda Klein remarks:

> There's the issue of men partners who flatly refuse to take a woman associate to dinner. The way they solve the problem is to avoid it. They minimize travel with a female, they minimize drinks or dinner after work with a young women associate. I heard a partner in a law firm say recently, "I don't care what anyone says, I'm never having a woman in my office with the door closed."

A male in the Southwest points out the problem with this approach:

> I was at a seminar, and a defense lawyer, a partner in a huge law firm, said the advice he gives is, do not interact with women subordinates

socially, period. Don't ever go to lunch one on one, don't ever go for drinks after work, don't ever do stuff on weekends. I knew this guy. I knew he's a real social guy, a party guy. I raised my hand and said, "Isn't social interaction helpful to one's career; aren't you more apt to give [an associate] work if you go out to drinks with him?" He said, "Yes, that's true." So I said, "What you're saying is that to avoid sexual harassment you're going to have to engage in conduct that's discrimination."

A male partner points out, "You don't want to get into the situation that you don't take an associate traveling because she's a female. You should travel with her because she knows the case. Why should she lose the opportunity just because somebody is trying to avoid a rumor?"

One male partner in a Midwestern firm took a younger female associate with him on a nationwide trip to interview witnesses. She said to him, "You know, a lot of people wanted to know whether you would do this, and whether you would take me along." The partner was "floored," and says:

I just had never thought about that. It made me realize how stupid I am. It never crossed my mind that anyone would think of that in our office. Now after she told me I felt so stupid. Once I resolved in my mind that she's got to come and we're working together, I never thought beyond it. She was glad that she got the opportunity. That was the surprising thing to me. She didn't say it in these words, but the way I read it, the talk among the associates was she wouldn't get the chance, because it's a guy thing, a man would feel uncomfortable with that.

This concern for appearances can affect business development settings. Women say they have to be careful about the venues they choose when socializing with clients. A woman in the Midwest warns it can look improper:

A woman who would do a lot of socializing after hours with clients who might predominantly be male, people might wonder about that person, whereas it's completely standard behavior for a man.

A female partner in a big firm contrasts her networking with her lawyer husband's:

Right now Bob is on a plane to New Orleans, going out to dinner with a bunch of guys. With women there's still some underlying "it's a date" kind of thing. It's hard to make it completely business unless you happen to hit women in-house counsel and the whole group is women. I don't think my husband would be comfortable with me going out to the kind of dinners he goes on. It's an ambiguous social occasion. It would give the impression that I'm interested in more than business if I'm having a glass of wine with a bunch of men.

Another form of avoidance is segregation of the sexes. This is a pattern that is discussed throughout this book, for a variety of reasons. In this instance, the motivation is the awkwardness of mixing the sexes due to ambiguous sexual overtones. Women say they are comfortable with women, men with men. Says Ida Abbott, an Oakland, California-based consultant to law firms: "I don't think that that has changed or will change. Really, it's a matter of comfort." A female who formerly was managing partner of her firm says, "I do think that there's an element that people like to be with people who look and sound like themselves." A male lawyer in Colorado says it's just easier to spend time with other guys:

It's all about everyone finding their own comfort zone. There's a certain level of rapport. I keep going back to the word comfortable. You see it every day, the guys go out to lunch, the girls go out to lunch. If you call up somebody to go play golf, typically it would be a guy, you don't invite the gals.

A female partner says workplace relationships between the sexes follow a clear pattern:

My friends are either the same gender or colleagues I worked closely with. It is very hard to cross the gender line on a casual basis when you're not working with people. We had a young male associate, and the head of the team would ask him to go out with him for a sandwich. On the way to ask him he would walk by the offices of females who had worked for him for ages, and we had never gone out to lunch with him.

An in-house woman says there's more mixing in her legal department than in law firms:

> I still find very much that with your firms, the golf outings, the guys still generally go to lunch together, and the women go to lunch together. This is more in firms, whereas I find more of a mixing in the corporate legal structure. I think it has to do with the lack of competition in-house. I think competition really breeds a lot of ugliness.

Informal patterns of pure friendship based on sex don't incite controversy when the participants are peers. But when gender-based friendships spring up between people of different statuses, they can systematically prevent members of the opposite sex from enjoying the benefits of close contact with people in positions of power.[16]

Aligning Public and Private Voices

The workplace is "two steps forward" in that sexual harassment has been unequivocally established as a credible cause of action and women have more freedom with sexualized behavior. Stereotypes have softened, resulting in more options. Sexualized conduct by women, which used to be completely off limits, is permitted within limits. Some options for men have decreased, such as the automatic assumption that women welcome sexual advances. And suspicions about "predator males" may be stronger than formerly. However, men are seeing and experiencing different scenarios, such as powerful women exerting sexual power. This suggests alternative ways of relating in the workplace that ultimately can blossom into greater flexibility about perceptions of sex roles.

Thus the double bind surrounding "sexuality versus competency" has started to unravel. It has not almost vanished, as with the "femininity/competence" contradiction discussed in Chapter 2. But men and women can work and travel together with less of the "instant" presumption that they have an inappropriate relationship. Women can have relationships in the workplace without paying an automatic penalty in credibility and perceived competence.

We are also "one step back." Some issues have been resolved, but others have sprung up that the "solutions" have helped to create. Psychologists Dr.

---

[16] This is explained in more detail in Chapter 6 *infra*.

Wanda Dobrich and Dr. Steven Dranoff conduct sexual harassment training, investigations, rehabilitation of offenders, and organizational recovery programs. They discuss hostile environment situations by contrasting "public voices" with "private voices." Says Dobrich:

> We have trained people to be socially correct. But with that comes a huge backlash. And when a behavior is underground, it is much harder to change. What we have in this culture now is an oversocialized public voice, but a very resistant private voice. When you get an overtrained public voice, you get a lot of kickback and resentment. People just get sick and tired of the public voice.

Dobrich and Dranoff claim that when the public and private voices are out of kilter, that's when trouble in the workplace begins.[17]

Some wish fervently for the well-trained public voice. A woman was repulsed by a graphic remark from a colleague, which made it clear that he was scrutinizing her body. She says:

> That colored my feelings from that day forward. I thought, I don't want to work for people where that's how they view the women who work here. They're checkin' us out. I know that this is how men are, look, I understand. But you don't say it. Let me live in my ignorance-is-bliss world and let me think you're not checking me out. Let me delude myself. Don't ruin it for me.

This plea for good behavior is understandable. But fashioning the public voice while ignoring the private voice is risky. Aligning the two will be key to narrowing the gulf that now exists. So long as people profess one attitude but think the opposite, the office will be a subtly poisoned well. Both underground harassment and story making are unintended consequences of well-meaning laws, the fine print of the contract outlawing sexual harassment. Stereotypes have retreated a little, but they still lurk beneath the surface and emerge in countless covert ways. The debate must permit a broader, more candid discussion of attitudes, rather than eschewing them in the hope that they will somehow disappear.

---

17 Dobrich et al., N. 13 *supra* at p. 6.

At this crossroads, we can ask whether this is a transitional time, in which the complexities of gender politics are gradually worked out, or whether a wedge is being driven between the sexes that will widen over time. There are signs that the workplace threatens to become balkanized, where the avoidance strategy for both sexes pushes males and females to their separate corners.

Why should this concern us? First, however innocent or understandable avoidance on the basis of sex might be—a male assigning cases to males rather than females, a female partner preferring to travel with a female associate—it is sex discrimination all over again. Second, the long-term effect of this kind of resolution of sexuality issues is not the best thing for workplaces and clients. It does not help build great working relationships, and it does not maximize the power and talent of the organization. Clients need the maximized power of organizations, not a fractured group organized by sex rather than brains, practice area, and people skills. Increased segregation of the sexes due to fear can cheat individuals out of development opportunities and clients out of the best attorneys for the job. A starting point to ameliorate this situation, therefore, would be to suggest a goal for a healthier workplace, specifically addressing the trend towards avoidance, such as the intelligent balancing of responsible, unthreatening forms of sexuality in the workplace, on the one hand, and simultaneously maximizing performance and excellence, on the other.

The line drawn between acceptable conduct and unacceptable conduct will never be precise. As with the opening anecdote to this chapter—the ladies' man and the stupid chick—these scenarios are susceptible to rumor, and feature limitless potential for misunderstanding, fear, and gossip. We've resolved this issue to date only by using a blunt instrument—lawsuits—and haven't developed many sensitive ways to resolve the dilemma. It's been every person for himself or herself to lurch along, stanching rumors, fearing scandal, often taking the path of least resistance and avoiding the opposite sex. It will never be easy, but a more nuanced approach that acknowledges how people really feel may help get beyond the crossroads and on the way to a thriving workplace.

The chapters on dress and sexuality have explored stereotypes relating to the clash between sexuality and appearance, on the one hand, and women's perceived competence, on the other. The next chapter examines the subject of women's perceived competence in more detail.

CHAPTER 4

Question Marks and Quizzical Looks: Closing the Competence Gap

Male Dominance
The Underdog
Strict Scrutiny
Male Backing
The Dedication Factor
Trouble at the Top
Leader of the Pack
On the Outside Looking In
Closing the Gap
Can-Do Attitudes
Reaching Out
Mind the Gap

A female partner in a Southwestern law firm in her forties is at the top of her game. She has a big book of business and has served on her firm's management team. Nevertheless, she reports:

> It surprises me that people still see me as a woman first, rather than, "Here's my lawyer." Now, has any client told me that? No. But do I sense that? Yes. I still feel like women have to prove themselves. I feel like I have to outpace and excel my male counterparts, my male opposing counsel, to attain the equivalent level of respect.

Shouldn't this story be a thing of the past? This made sense in the 1960s, when the "pioneers" of female law practice uniformly asserted they had to work harder than a man to succeed.[1] They looked forward confidently to the day when, with more women in the ranks, the "work harder" dictate would disappear and they would be judged to be equally as competent as their male peers.

Fast forward to the present, forty years later, with the ranks of women nearly 300,000 strong, as compared to only 7,500 in 1960. A generation has passed, and the numbers are in place. But what's happened to that prediction? Are women viewed as equally competent? Can they put in the same effort as their brothers in the law and succeed?

There seems little question in people's minds that women are *capable* of doing legal work as well as men. Indeed, many men and women lawyers state promptly and decisively that the competence gap is closed. When asked whether there are remaining questions about the performance of female lawyers, this male from Wisconsin replied:

> Only in the minds of the troglodytes. That's behind us. There are enough women out there now, very competently practicing, that while it's probably true that that image has not been entirely gotten rid of, we're well on the way to getting rid of it. There's a growing number of women on the bench, a growing number of women who are partners.

---

[1] Cynthia Fuchs Epstein writes that they felt "overwhelmingly" the "need to prove their performance." *Women in Law,* 2d ed., at p. 278 (University of Illinois Press, 1993).

"Thirty years ago, the question was, could women really be good lawyers?" declares Martha W. Barnett, past president of the American Bar Association and a partner with Holland & Knight. "Would clients accept them? Today we talk about women as managing partners and very significant rainmakers."

Many express the remaining issues as a "genderation gap": older male lawyers and clients, they say, may cast a dubious eye on women, but the younger ranks of men think their female colleagues are equally adept. A young male lawyer in the South, for instance, says that many men in the older generation still see women as intruders and outsiders, not part of the club:

> The bar in general is pretty aggressively anti-woman. Under the surface. It's politically appropriate to say otherwise. But at the bar, drinking a glass of scotch, or on the golf course, I don't think it's good for women. The older guys probably feel like, you know, it's humorous to have women around. It's sort of a novelty. I don't think they take them seriously. For example, there's a female federal judge. These guys will be nice to her and shake her hand, and behind her back, they'll try to take her down. "She only got the job because she's a woman. She can't do legal work so she's a judge." That kind of viewpoint is rampant.

But others say that even older clients and practitioners are persuaded once they see an accomplished woman in action. Says a male partner in South Carolina:

> Quite often, particularly with older male clients, all of a sudden they see a younger female lawyer, there's a guarded approach at first, but when they see the competency, if you can do the job, they want to go in the foxhole with the female lawyers. Competency overcomes gender issues real quickly.

A thirty-seven-year-old female practitioner from Washington, D.C., like many others who commented, is unequivocal:

> I think it is a total non-issue. I perceive that people do not have any negative ideas about women's competence to be lawyers. Every once in a while you read about some stupid judge somewhere. That is something you read about in a newspaper every once in a blue moon.

These comments sum up the prevailing view: questions about women's competence are a thing of the past, relegated to a small minority of oldsters and "troglodytes," and it's only a matter of time before all misgivings disappear.

However, that day has not yet arrived. Although the basic question of whether women are able to perform well may have been settled, other dynamics have kept the perceived competence gap open. In fact, women today are at least as likely, and according to some data, *more likely* to believe they have to work harder than men to succeed than they did previously. Even a practitioner as prominent as Mary B. Cranston, CEO and Chair of Pillsbury Winthrop in San Francisco, declares flatly, "Women have to be objectively better to be perceived as equal."

An American Bar Association poll taken in 1983 revealed that 38% of women lawyers said they believed they had to work harder to prove themselves. By 2000, that figure had zoomed to 60%.[2] A survey conducted in 2002 by the New York State Bar Association showed similar figures. Forty-four percent of the women overall agreed with the perception that "female lawyers have to work harder than male lawyers to get the same results." For private firms and in-house women, the numbers were higher still: 50% and 57%, respectively. Although the figures for public interest lawyers (34% of those females said they had to work harder) and for the judiciary (39% of the female judges concurred) were lower, they were still significant.[3]

Even more striking is that the same survey revealed a perception of less respect for women. Sixty-four percent of the women and 34% of men agreed that "female attorneys are accorded less respect than male attorneys." And a whopping 70% of the women, and 39% of the men, said that women are treated condescendingly by their male colleagues.[4] These figures—and

---

[2] Hope Viner Samborn, "Higher Hurdles for Women," ABA Journal, 31 (Sept. 2000).

[3] "Gender Equity in the Legal Profession," at 27-29 (New York State Bar Association, Committee on Women in the Law, 2002) (hereinafter, "New York State Gender Equity Report").

[4] *Id.* at 31.

accounts from my interviews—directly contradict any notion that questions about female abilities and performance are relics from the past.

Why is this? There are many explanations, but the answer starts with the fact that most lawyers are still men.

Male Dominance

As discussed in Chapter 1, the flood of women into the legal marketplace has gotten so much attention that it's obscured the fact that women are still a distinct minority. Men continue to dominate the profession, in numbers and attitudes. Although females constitute nearly one-third of the profession, and their share of the workforce increased dramatically in a very short time, they remain younger and less experienced, and many take time out for raising children.[5] As a result, women's very "female-ness" is conspicuous, an exception to the general rule of male dominance. (For instance, many women said that being a woman was an advantage because they stood out and people were more likely to remember them. This is only the case because their numbers remain lower.) A woman in Virginia remarks:

> Some men look at you or refer to you as the "lady lawyer." Some people automatically assume maybe that you don't know as much as you do. What does "lady lawyer" mean? It's kind of a negative. Like you're odd for being a woman and being a lawyer.

Women feel this sense of "oddness" when men try to pigeonhole them, baffled because sometimes it isn't clear how to categorize them. A real estate practitioner says:

> They're not exactly sure where you fit. That happens to me a lot. I'm 5'10", I'm a woman, I'm Hispanic. They always are surprised. They just don't know how to figure you out.

When I asked the lawyers I interviewed how often they have faced a female opposing counsel, most reported it was only 10% to 20% of the time.

---

[5] *Id.* at 6-7.

Many of the women mentioned that they are frequently the only woman in the room. As psychologist Virginia Valian writes: "The sheer numerical imbalance leads us to associate men with successful performance and women with its opposite, and to see successful performance as a masculine characteristic."[6] The quick image that is likely to come to people's minds when they think "lawyer" is still male.

Because of the male-lawyer paradigm, there is an assumption that women lack power and therefore don't need to be taken as seriously as men. For instance, many people avoid eye contact with women. Making eye contact is validating; avoiding it is dismissive. A thirty-year-old female government lawyer in Colorado who often goes with a more junior male to meetings with parties says:

> You go into a meeting and say, "Okay, look, we have this case, we'll inform you of the evidence gathered, we'll probably file a complaint against you. Do you have defenses?" I'm there with someone who's assisting who's male, who may have played no role, and he gets the only eye contact. You're always trying to redirect, like, "Talk to me! I'm over here!"

A woman who was managing partner of her firm watched outsiders do an about-face as they realized her status:

> Sometimes with vendors and other people coming into the firm, this would happen all the time, all their body language and attention would be centered on the male partners of the management committee. There would be very little eye contact with me, all of their eye contact was towards the male partners, their seating position, the way they shifted their whole body would be faced towards them and away from me. It was really quite stunningly obvious. It did irritate me, but it was also amusing, because I would just pick the appropriate time to drop this zinger, in a subtle way, that I was managing partner. All of a sudden their body language would switch, they would be avid, these bells would ring.

---

[6] Virginia Valian, *Why So Slow? The Advancement of Women,* at p. 167 (MIT Press, 1998).

Many women said that men who are junior to them give them less respect and deference than might be appropriate. A mild-mannered woman complains that a male associate who is far junior to her frequently talks over her when she tries to speak. "I think, 'Do you do that to Tom?'" she says, referring to another partner who is on her level. "I've never said anything about it. But I think about it." Another variation is men who are overly casual and familiar, due to their lack of respect for women's status. Rhonda, a female senior associate in New York, says:

> I have definitely had a sense that some of the male law students who are interviewing don't seem to regard me as someone they need to make an effort to impress. I've had them meet with me, slouch in their chairs, pick up things on my desk, talk about the baby pictures in my office. They'll ask about the next guy they're going to meet with, what's he like, that sort of thing.

When the hiring attorneys meet to compare notes, Rhonda says the women criticize the casual male candidate, whereas the men are enthusiastic:

> They'll say he was very polite, very deferential, he listened, he maintained eye contact, he answered my questions, he wasn't casual at all, sat upright the whole time, and didn't seem relaxed.

Her conclusion is that the male law students see her and other females as less threatening and less important in the hiring process. The male law students see the women as allies, who can give them inside information and will be sympathetic and understanding, rather than judging them and exercising power negatively.

Another sign of lesser status is that women still are more likely to get administrative or housekeeping tasks. A female partner in her forties on the East Coast says:

> I was at a meeting with a bunch of judges. There was an older judge there and something needed to be photocopied, and he handed it to me. I've been in meetings with partners who've said to me, "Can you serve everybody the lunch?" That happens to me and [her female partner] more than it should. You're in meetings with clients and somebody has to go get the coffee, and it's you. One could

argue that these tasks often fall to the person who is chronologically the youngest. I don't buy it.

A female litigator in New York observes:

> There are definitely instances where I have seen women doing things that I really question whether they would have a guy do. There are three people on a case, the most junior attorney is a woman. She's ordering dinner and organizing delivery of the documents. Would three men have the most junior guy do that? I have never seen a male attorney tell a junior male to order dinner. I have routinely seen a male attorney order a younger woman to do that. I also have seen situations where the most junior person is a woman, and she's doing paralegal tasks, making sure the expert gets the documents, doing the exhibit books, redoing the tabs. If the most junior person is a man, I don't think he would do that stuff.

Without knowing who's in charge, individuals make the shorthand assumption that it's probably the man over the woman, undermining women's perceived status and competence. When women are ignored, patronized, or placed in lowly situations, they have to assert their status just to get to the starting line.

The Underdog

A direct result of their lower status is that women are also often perceived as being weaker than men or incompetent until proven otherwise, especially for men who exploit this possibility as a possible advantage in prosecuting a case. One outcome of this perception is that women repeatedly say they are underestimated. An in-house attorney in Washington, D.C. says:

> When businessmen meet me, they underestimate me, which for me is good. I love it. "Please underestimate me," I think. Because it gives me the advantage of surprise. When I finally do deliver the punch, it comes from left field, they never saw it coming, which is great.

A Texas family lawyer says the same thing happens to her in court:

> I've dealt with some really jerk lawyers who think every single woman on the earth is an idiot. I enjoy that. One of my favorite things to do

is to get a man on the stand and be absolutely killing him with evidence, and be very polite, and they just don't know what to do. If you go into it, you can just kill 'em. They don't believe that you're smart enough to figure out real questions and real evidence. Let them underestimate that!

A female litigator in New Mexico assumes she will triumph:

When I first started practicing law, men always underrated me, which was a terrific advantage. You are somebody's champion in a battle, so you always want the enemy to underestimate. I'm going to kick their butt in the courtroom.

And a corporate lawyer in Louisiana relates:

A lot of guys underestimate me, they assume they're just up against some intelligent girl who doesn't try cases. It's like a stealth attack, they get screwed because they're not expecting it.

These women converted a supposed obstacle into a success factor. Their bellicose words—she "delivers a punch," "you can just kill 'em," "I'm going to kick their butt," "they get screwed"—show hostility towards the skeptics and glee at proving them wrong. But women wouldn't have this weapon in their arsenal or feel so triumphant absent assumptions that a female opponent is not as challenging as a male.

Strict Scrutiny

In addition to being underestimated, some women believe that their performance is more closely watched and with greater suspicion than the performance of men. Twenty-five percent of women in a recent survey agreed that "the work of female lawyers is more scrutinized." In private firms the percentage was 32%.[7] The same survey revealed that women are much more closely supervised than men: 38% of male attorneys reported that they

---

[7] The figures for in-house women were 26% and for public interest lawyers, 15%. "New York State Gender Equity Report," N. 3 *supra* at 27-29.

worked unsupervised, versus 17% of females, and these results were consistent regardless of experience levels.[8]

Close observation occurs in ways large and small. A female general counsel in her fifties, on the East Coast, reported on the handling of a crisis situation to the management team. Men at the meeting repeatedly pressed her about whether the matter was being handled properly. A woman who attended the meeting said afterwards, "This line of questioning would not have occurred if the general counsel were a man."

Not only does the work of women get more scrutiny, but women also are tested more, as colleagues, clients, or opposing counsel push the boundaries more than they would with males. A female judge in Missouri has to set limits in her courtroom:

> I do think that men attorneys say things to women judges that they would never say to a male, like "I just can't get a fair trial in this courtroom." I stop the behavior. I had a guy who was just spitting questions in a woman's face, and I said, "That's inappropriate," and he didn't back off. "Now," I said, "you'll continue questioning from counsel table." He kicked the chair and said, "It doesn't please me to sit down," and I said, "That's good, I wasn't trying to please you." I don't think that it would happen with male judges. I think women judges have to set limits. With some people I have to set the limits all the time. These are males. I won't say that I haven't had an unruly female, but when I have it hasn't been directed at me. The men are more out of control.

A woman who is now in government says that at her old firm, women who wanted to make partner had to jump through more hoops than the men:

> Right as I was leaving, there was one woman in particular who was just going through the wringer because they were saying, "We don't know about her book of business," yet they let the males slide through. Then she wound up with the biggest book of business. She had to suffer to make it. It's harder to make partner for a woman than a man. The scrutiny of a woman's book of business is harder.

---

[8] *Id.* at 20.

A female in her mid-thirties in Maine felt on the spot while in a deposition. She was questioning the deponent with a stack of exhibits in front of her. At some point she began questioning about a particular document, without showing the exhibit to the deponent. She described what the male attorney defending the deposition did:

> He started saying, "You should let her look at the document." I ignored him. He reached across the table and started going through my stack of exhibits. I stopped the deposition and said, "Can I help you?" He said, "I'll find it." And I said, "It's incredibly rude and unprofessional to grab someone's exhibits." He rolled his eyes and pushed the exhibits back across the table to me. I left abruptly right after the deposition was over. The next morning at 8 a.m., I got a phone call from that attorney apologizing for his behavior. It was definitely a test. I definitely passed. It pissed me off that I got tested in the workplace. Everyone in the office said he would never have done that to a man.

A New Jersey male litigator consistently observes more aggressive questioning of female lawyers in depositions than of males:

> I have seen what I would characterize as older male attorneys who attempt to aggressively defend, be more in your face, attempt to browbeat the inquiring attorney back during the deposition, more so when it's a woman than a man. I now look for it. [The attorney] will start with the baseless objections right away, belittling their questions, making speaking objections, "Didn't you already ask that, can't you move on?" It's very interesting to watch the response. Some women are very good, they very ably and casually, without being aggressive, just brush it off, and just say, "Just answer the question." They don't get upset. But I have seen one or two young female associates who allow themselves to get emotional and disrupted, they lose their train of thought, they are drawn into this game.

A male trial associate reports that, although he tests everyone in the litigation arena to try to unnerve them, he has a working assumption that women are easier to bully and that he can knock them off their stride more easily than a man. For instance, if he has information about a woman's child care responsibilities, he will try to push depositions and their timing to the last minute, knowing that it creates a time crisis for the woman.

Depositions in general are a focal point for testing women. As one article written by female litigators about depositions noted, "While facing an antagonistic and aggressive adversary is not uniquely a woman's problem, it does pose special difficulties for women. Women may elicit more challenges than men because women are perceived as being weak. . . . Frequently, the male lawyer will attempt to bully and intimidate his female colleagues. This is done in a number of ways. He will interrupt her continually or attempt to engage her in interminable colloquy or argumentation. He will try to undermine her confidence by objecting to every question she puts forth, or by suggesting that she does not know how to ask a proper question, or by instructing his client not to answer."[9]

Minority women say they get even more inspection. An African-American woman who has worked in firms and now works in-house in Florida says:

> I have noticed that there tends to be a closer eye to how I behave, and less scrutiny for white females. I've seen it more often in depositions. There's like a hush when I speak. And then I get a lot of comments about how extremely articulate I am. My white female colleagues who are equally articulate don't get those compliments. I've had judges say, when I am about to make an argument, "Yeah, I really want to hear what you have to say." I never hear anybody else preface their argument that way. I've observed it so many times that it's not an aberration. I think there is an extra challenge of trying to behave above and beyond reproach that is a burden of African-American females. To articulate ourselves a little more clearly than most.

Indeed, according to Harvard Law School Professor David B. Wilkins,[10] the competence issue is a complex one for black lawyers. "Whites sometimes may have subconscious images of black women as 'supportive,' 'warm,' or 'trustworthy' as a result of prior contact with black nannies or housekeepers,"

---

[9] Jean MacLean Snyder & Andra Barmash Greene, eds., *The Woman Advocate,* at pp. 177-179 (American Bar Association Section of Litigation, 1996).

[10] Professor Wilkins is Kirkland and Ellis Professor of Law and Director of the Program on the Legal Profession at Harvard Law School, and is writing a book on African-American lawyers entitled *The Black Bar: The Legacy of Brown v. Board of Education and the Future of Race and the American Legal Profession* (Oxford University Press, forthcoming).

Wilkins notes. "On some occasions, this visceral connection allows older white male partners to form connections with black female associates that they do not form with black male associates, who these same partners may often equate at the subconscious level with pervasive images of crime, fear, and intimidation."

"At the same time," Wilkins continues, "the very images that make possible the connection between older white male partners and black female associates may also limit the partner's ability to see his black female protégé as sufficiently 'tough' or 'commanding' to assume a leadership role within the firm. On the other hand, while black men are often perceived as 'threatening,' they also have an easier time than their black female counterparts in using the traditional avenues of male bonding within corporate workplaces—sports, competition (within limits), and sex (as long as it is not interracial sex)—to forge connections with white male peers. They are, after all, 'boys' in what has always been—and in many ways continues to be—a 'boys' club.'"

As with being underestimated, women lose as soon as the scrutiny tightens, the skeptical question is asked, or the extra hazing delivered. Responding to critical oversight keeps women on the defensive, reinforcing questions of competence and effectiveness.

Male Backing

Women sometimes find that they need male colleagues to step in to grapple with unruly opposing counsel, or endorse their advice to clients to get them on board. A powerful female partner in Washington, D.C. reports:

> Sometimes clients don't listen to anybody, or they won't listen to me. Sometimes I'll draft a guy to say the same thing I did. If it's a $150 million case and I'm not sure this person's listening, I'll go get someone else, I'll get some reinforcement. It could be gender, it could just be brain damage. It doesn't always do the trick. It is better to have somebody male to reinforce it. And I do it, because I don't want anyone to say the advice wasn't taken because I didn't do this. I do risk management. People are not gender neutral in society, and if you can get two people to say it, who cares? When we have to deliver a message, sometimes that's based on gender.

Another woman also asks her male partner for validation, especially at the outset of a client relationship:

> Lots of times with a new client, it's a new situation as a result of a preexisting friendship or acquaintance. And they come in and they're expecting John [her partner], who's well-known, and they're getting me. And I'm also only five feet tall. And they're like, "Oh, well, where's John?" Even now as a fifteen-year litigator, I have to convince them that I can do it. We have this routine down. Lots of times, John and I will meet with them together, he will say a few things about my background to convince them that I have the experience. He will talk about his unavailability. And when I start giving advice to them that I know will not be well-received, instead of waiting for them to say, "What does John think?" I preface it with, "John and I talked about this." It's both a gender thing and a superior/inferior thing.

An in-house woman in Wisconsin says:

> Our customers, when dealing directly with me, it's almost like they don't believe me, because they'll turn around and talk to someone else and confirm that I have support. If we come to loggerheads, I've found some occasions where the person will almost disregard me. They'll say, "I'll talk to Jim [the president] about that."

An employment lawyer in the Midwest comments, "A lot of male lawyers treat women lawyers differently. Aggressively, sort of intimidating, ridiculing." She dealt with one opposing attorney who was obnoxious to her but not to the other men in the firm. At first she ignored him, but in depositions he would comment sarcastically on her objections, or use disrespectful body language. Eventually, she says:

> I had one of the guys deal with him, to take a deposition, because it was so important to our case. That sounds like a cop-out, but it was the right thing to do for the client. With my male colleague in the deposition, the hostile guy was really mild. If there's male supervision he doesn't do it.

Marcia, a female in-house counsel in the Midwest, says that gender is regularly considered to determine who will deliver a hard message to a demanding committee of male clients within the organization:

> When we have to get [the male committee] to change the way that
> they provide a service, we will sit around the table and decide who's
> going to present the issue. If the issue is entirely a legal issue and a
> risk issue, then 90% of the time I would deliver the message. I'm the
> one that has the degree, and so therefore it does bring me a certain
> amount of credibility, despite my gender. But that's the key phrase,
> "despite my gender." Often times when it's an issue that's going to
> take a significant change in behavior, we will choose a male to deliv-
> er the message.

This reveals the tension between a world that is not "gender neutral" and
a workplace that aspires to be. Although these anecdotes make clear that
sometimes skeptical clients or bullying opposing counsel require that
women utilize male backing, and that women believe this is the right thing
to do for the client or case, the pivotal question is whether this dynamic low-
ers a woman's status in the eyes of her colleagues, who may hesitate to refer
cases to her, advance her to partner, or work with her on important matters.
Marcia, quoted above, says the options are more limited when she deals
with the customer/client:

> There are a couple of [men on the committee], they would take great
> pleasure in berating or humiliating me or any other woman executive
> on an issue if they didn't want it. Because they are the [customer],
> you can't fight back in the way you would in a courtroom, or the way
> you would in a leadership meeting, because you're worried that the
> men will harbor that grudge and take the business away from the
> organization. It's the politics where you let them slide.

This is reminiscent of the "customer is always right" dynamic regarding sexual harassment by clients that was explored in Chapter 2. Organizations
have a harder time enforcing standards involving gender equity when it
involves a client or customer. And the doubting clients in turn can serve as
cover for presumably enlightened male colleagues. Kathleen Kauffmann, a
former jury consultant, now with Sommer Barnard Ackerson in Washington,
D.C., says:

> If you ask a man in a law firm whether he thinks women lawyers are
> as good as men lawyers, he'll say, "Of course, I've had women col-
> leagues in law school, I've had them at the firm. I know how good

they are. And they're every bit as good as male lawyers." If you ask him if he trusts clients or juries to have that same view, he says they don't. It relieves men of responsibility for their biases. The result within a firm is that women don't get as ready a referral within firms, they don't get named partner as often, because of the attitude of, "It's not me, it's the rest of the world." Men don't trust the rest of the world to have their own enlightenment, or they actually don't have enlightenment and they project it onto the rest of the world. Also with clients, they say to themselves, "If I have a really big ticket case, can I trust a woman as I trust a man?"

Ideally, male colleagues distinguish between the proven competence of a woman whose work they are familiar with versus a client's unwarranted suspicions about her abilities. Another reaction is that male colleagues sometimes conclude that when heavy lifting is required, they can't leave it to a woman.

The Dedication Factor

Fewer female practitioners than men, plus continued hazing and testing in the marketplace, affect the estimation of women's abilities. In addition, the status of women has been downgraded over the past generation because of perceived lack of commitment to their careers, usually due to conflicts between motherhood and work.[11] In the law, competence is powerfully linked to dedication. As women have tried to reconcile the supposed clash between motherhood and professionalism, their solutions—reduced hours, telecommuting, dropping out of the workforce—appear to constitute a lack of dedication to the workplace. This affects people's perceptions of women's future promise, as one man says:

> There's a perception that the woman will not produce as much either through billable hours or through relationships as the male. There's a perception that men are going to be more predestined to be workaholics than females.

---

[11] These themes are explored in depth in Chapters 7 and 8 *infra*.

A woman who participated in interviewing for her firm noticed that conclusions were drawn right away about a young woman's future:

> I think there was outright gender bias in some cases. They would say, "She's just getting married, how long before she has kids? When she comes back she won't be as productive." There was good respect for intelligence and work product for all, we were all treated alike, but there was a strong bias that when things got stressful, when life situations changed, the women won't handle it as well as a man will. Their assumption was, a man will turn to his work and a woman will turn away from her work.

Dedication wasn't an issue with the first generation of pioneer women. They were well aware of how conspicuous they were and they determined to make their mark. Their ardor for the law outstripped that of men, although this often involved personal sacrifices such as foregoing marriage and children. Over the years, however, a greater variety of women entered the profession, not just the driven path-finders of yore. After a generation's worth of experience, along with examples of female competence, everyone also has specific examples of ineffective or underperforming women, or women who left the workplace for suspect reasons. One woman sums it up as follows:

> Earlier there were relatively few women lawyers. And the fact that women could do the job at all earned credibility. Now there are more women in the workforce, and there have been more negative experiences with having women in firms, either who've gone in-house to corporate counsel, or who have had kids and asked to go part time. So I think there's this "You've got to prove that you're going to be there like the guys" thing.

In particular, workplaces (especially law firms) have had a hard time retaining women in their thirties and forties. Everyone knows of a woman who came into the workforce only to leave shortly after having a child or two. "Why should we hire women?" I heard repeatedly, after yet another litany of the female associates who came and went. "What's wrong with these younger women?" These individual experiences get generalized into broad pronouncements about women's dedication and effectiveness as lawyers, whether or not they are valid. A man in New Jersey says that women do not seem to have the same all-or-nothing dedication as men:

I'd prefer not to hire women. They haven't had the commitment to the job and the ability to do things that are unpleasant without complaining, and just dig in and put other things aside. My sense is they never had any fire in the belly about either becoming a great lawyer or doing great things or being the best you can be, or going as far as you could in the profession. It was more, "It's nice being a lawyer."

He is offended by a woman who is only partially linked to a legal job, holding herself separate, turning her dedication on and off like a light switch. A female New York partner comments:

Questions of consistency, of reliability, are still alive. Most women try to balance both family obligations and work obligations. So a woman might ask one of the people who works with her to assist her, to cover a meeting for her. Her male colleagues would say that's her responsibility. To certain people that would be read as, she had to take her kid to school or be at the important cupcake party. I have seen it again and again.

Women who remain in the workforce are aggrieved that they get painted with the same skeptical brush. "It's a shame that with women leaving, attrition somehow connotes professional marginalization of the rest of the women," complains a high-powered female partner. And indeed, that some women leave the workforce or cut back on their hours leaves a cloud of suspicion over others.

The question is not *can* they do it; women's ability to practice well has been established. It's *will* they do it. Because competence in legal practice is so closely linked with an all-out passion for the law, any deviation from that norm, even for reasons such as motherhood or work/life balance, is construed as a lack of lawyering ability.

Trouble at the Top

There is one place, however, where "Can they do it?" remains alive as a question for women: when they hit the very top. Even those top-performing women who have proven themselves repeatedly report that colleagues and clients doubt their abilities at crucial times. They often have to re-prove themselves, at a time when they believed that their worth was established once and for all. "You're only as good as what you did yesterday," grumps one female practitioner who is very prominent in the profession.

Dr. Ron Kimball, a Washington, D.C. psychologist who counsels lawyers, says of older women in practice:

> I think that the women partners I have seen, especially those who have been partners for a while, they often are saying things like, "I'm really tired of being treated this way, not having the power I ought to have, given that I'm a partner." They still feel dismissed.

Studies confirm this tendency. Management professor Judith Oakley defines "competency testing" as "a process by a which a person is required to prove herself over and over again." In one study of senior male executives, Oakley writes, "They freely admitted that women in upper level positions were subject to competency testing much more often than their male counterparts. This behavior on the part of male executives could be seen as an attempt to band together to preserve the upper ranks as a predominantly male domain by sending the message to females who attempt to infiltrate their domain that they are less than welcome and will have to fight to gain entry."[12]

While colleagues test women at the top, clients can be doubly suspicious of women's abilities, even in long-term relationships. For instance, women said it was harder for them to get the "bet your company" case. One woman in Minnesota said:

> I bet that women are rarely hired for the bet-the-company case. You know, us gals, we can be pretty good technical lawyers and nice people, but you got to go to your board of directors, mostly men, and tell them you've made the right hiring decision in a bet-the-company decision. So you better get the guy.

Another woman in her fifties, who has been unusually successful in carving out a niche area of expertise as a litigator, and has handled long, complicated trials for many years, sometimes faces doubts from clients during high-level cases:

---

[12] Judith G. Oakley, "Gender-Based Barriers to Senior Management Positions: Understanding the Scarcity of Female CEOs," J. Bus. Ethics, at 321 (Oct. 2000).

I'm short, so I don't make a strong visual impact, I look a lot younger than I am. In one case, the client said he had to get somebody else to argue the case, and that I can write the brief. I said why? He said, "The board thinks that the court won't think we're serious if we have a short woman argue our case." This is burned in my brain. I am one of the most successful women I've encountered in my career—can you imagine people saying that to you?

A woman with a flourishing practice in Louisiana reports:

Every once in a while I am astonished to find that I have some sort of hurdle to jump over. It's odd for me that one of my very favorite clients would do this. Several years ago, I was getting ready to try a case. It was so discouraging. At the pretrial meeting the general counsel acted like I had never tried a case. He lacked confidence in me.

The doubts about women can increase as they climb the ladder. Men are assumed to consolidate their power and experience, giving them the credibility to go for "stretch" experiences, but for women, bigger and bigger challenges seem like more of a risky gamble rather than a logical next step. There's an assumption that they Peter-Principle out.

Leader of the Pack

Still another aspect of the competence gap is that it's hard for people to visualize women as leaders. If the default image of a lawyer is broadly male, the default image of a lawyer as leader is profoundly male. The statistics are familiar: only 15% of partners in law firms are female. Only 5% of managing partners at law firms are women.[13] Among Fortune 500 general counsel, 12.2% are female.[14] Minority women hold fewer than 1% of equity partnerships in

---

[13] Deborah L. Rhode, "The Unfinished Agenda: Women and the Legal Profession," at 14 (American Bar Association Commission on Women in the Profession, 2001) (hereinafter, "The Unfinished Agenda").

[14] Rosemarie Clancy Benali & Sara Yoon, "Breaking Through: Women Hold the Top Legal Job at 60 Fortune 500 Companies," Corporate Counsel (May 20, 2002) (online chart at www.law.com).

law firms.[15] In the New York gender equity survey, only 64% of the women said "opportunities for involvement in office management (e.g., partner selection) are equal."[16]

An American Bar Association study comes to the following conclusion about women as leaders:

> Particularly where the number of women is small, their performance is subject to closer scrutiny and more demanding requirements, and their commitment is open to greater question. The devaluation of women and the influence of gender stereotypes is especially likely in organizations that have few women in leadership positions. Even in experimental situations where male and female performance is objectively equal, women are held to higher standards, and their competence is rated lower.[17]

Females are sometimes simply overlooked at higher levels. The classic example is the woman who brings up an idea and is ignored, only to have it taken up at some later time by a male and celebrated. As Mary Cranston of Pillsbury Winthrop says: "Any woman at my level has been invisible, has had her idea ignored and then presented by a man to enthusiasm. Most men haven't had this experience." Psychologist Ron Kimball says:

> I still hear the same complaints. Even the women who are very successful monetarily, once they reach this upper middle level, with partners above them who are virtually all male, it's not that they are hurtful to them, they just don't give them much credence.

A top female partner in a New England firm watches with dismay as a seemingly inevitable succession plan unfolds in the leadership at her firm:

> We're in the middle of transition now, in terms of our firm leadership, with the managing partner. The successor? It's a boy. And they're

---

[15] "The Unfinished Agenda," N. 13 *supra* at 8.
[16] "New York State Gender Equity Report," at 27-28 (New York State Bar Association, Committee on Women in the Law, 2002).
[17] "The Unfinished Agenda," N. 13 *supra* at 15.

already talking about who the successor to that successor will be. They're already talking about a young guy. I can just see it, nobody is even thinking of the possibility that there could be a woman there. They can see potential in this young guy. That's who they're comfortable with. I like this guy they're talking about, he's a nice guy, but you want to say, slow down.

Even women who put gender bias low on their list of concerns grumble that integrating women into high-level management is a challenge. A female partner in the Midwest says:

> Bottom line, and I am not somebody that anybody thinks of walking around being a real ardent feminist. To the contrary. But it's still difficult for women, especially in towns like Kansas City or Boise, Idaho, to really become a part of management in law firms.

There are several reasons for this. Ida Abbott, a consultant to law firms based in Oakland, California, comments:

> I'm not sure it's resistance as much as it's ignorance. If I ask you to name leaders, whom do you envision? There still aren't enough women who are visibly in positions of considerable power. So when you say, "law firm leader," or "chair of a law firm," you don't visualize Mary Cranston's face [CEO and Chair of Pillsbury Winthrop], you see some guy.

Women also are discounted for leadership because not many have a thriving practice that is self-supporting, often the ticket to gain entrance to the inner circle. A woman with a prosperous practice remarks:

> In private practice, there are not enough strong independent women who have succeeded who are not dependent on a male partner for their line of work. When I see women in my own firm acting subordinate or quiet or demure, it's because speaking out may rub the wrong partner the wrong way. He's their source of compensation or stature in their law firm.

And it's not easy for those who try to place themselves or others on high-level committees. Even if a woman generates considerable business on her

own, it doesn't guarantee her a place at the leadership table. A female partner in a large firm, who is a member of the compensation committee, says:

> There's a much more subtle exclusion when you have a woman who
> has demonstrated the capability to generate large dollars, and she
> has no role in management. How you travel up the circular staircase
> in law firm management is not defined. It's a subtle exclusion—it just
> sort of happens. You're not part of the club. It's not a macro saying
> that, "We don't want a woman."

Even if they are qualified, many women are not interested in joining the
leadership ranks. Some resist being cast as the token lone woman at the top.
Jane, a woman in the Midwest, was upset to realize that the makeup of the
proposed new executive team would be eighteen men and no women,
which she thought sent a bad signal to their ranks of female associates. She
approached another woman to be on the team: "She was reluctant. I thought
she was incredibly qualified, well-respected, she had some business. She
didn't want to be a token or the 'one gal.'" Other women say "no" to management because they are just not interested. Says one, from South Carolina:

> The management committee? Not only no but hell no! I don't want
> to be lobbied over whether we're going to open a satellite postage-
> stamp office in Florida to accommodate our biggest rainmaker. I'll
> leave that to y'all to have some semblance of a life.

But a woman who shuns power positions is perceived differently than a
man. Martha Barnett of Holland & Knight says:

> Both men and women shy away from management. Men and
> women look at the additional responsibilities, and just say, "Hey, I'd
> rather go skiing." Many would rather do client work, or have free time.
> They don't view management as all that much fun. Nobody questions
> why the man doesn't do it. This is one of those subtleties. You get a
> really top-notch lawyer who's a woman, and you say, "Would you like
> to be on the XYZ committee?" And she says, "No, I don't think I can
> do that this year." People will question her commitment to the firm.
> If a guy says that, they say, "Well, maybe next year." It's a subtle but
> real difference. That's covert, even unconscious stereotyping. "Well, of
> course she's not as dedicated to her career."

Indeed, not "going for it" looks more suspect in a woman. A female judge recalls the experience of a woman friend in a law firm:

> The firm had come to her to interview her to ask who she thought should be managing partner, and she said, "X and Y," and they said, "You're the unanimous choice of your colleagues." She said, "I want to think about it." She called her client friend, and he said, "If you were male, you wouldn't have said you'd think about it. You'd do it." He thought this was a gender issue. Any male offered the alpha male position would not think about it. And I do think that there is an element of that.

Once a woman attains membership on a powerful committee or management team, it's not assured that she will also gain credibility. A female partner in the Southeast, the first woman appointed to her major firm's executive committee, says:

> I definitely perceive more of a need to prove myself to those people around the table who don't know me personally. People who've worked with me know how capable I am, know my client relations, and fully respect me. But I now perceive a different introductory process, the question mark, the quizzical look across the table.

A New England attorney talks about a female colleague who's on the executive team:

> She experiences gender issues much more than I do. They always seem to talk down to her, she feels like her opinion isn't valued. Particularly, they seem to think she won't understand fiscal matters. When large checks need to be signed, the administrator looks around for male partners, she never thinks to go to the woman partner. No-one thinks of her as a real full-fledged board member.

Hence, a "second glass ceiling" can prevent women from assuming power, particularly in law firms, because of resistance and unfamiliarity with the image of women as leaders. The problem is compounded because there aren't many women at such a high level or qualified enough to step into such powerful positions; as a result, people sometimes conclude that when a woman rejects a leadership position, most or all women don't really want to exercise power.

On the Outside Looking In

One of the reasons it can be hard to win credibility as a leader is that it's difficult for women to form informal relationships with their male peers, part of the life blood of power and influence. This issue came up in Chapter 2, relating to sexuality, i.e., when men ally themselves with men, and women with women, to sidestep awkward sexual overtones. In this instance, the issue comes up more because women are vastly outnumbered in leadership circles, leading to isolation.

Many women said they felt self-conscious just having a chat, and excluded at times when the men were comfortable with one another. "There's always the default sport talk," a Texas practitioner sighs. "*Always*." Linda, a female general counsel agrees:

> Seventy-five percent of the time I'm the only woman in the room. I notice that whenever there's a break in a conversation, the talk immediately turns to the football games over the weekend, or whatever the sport of the season is.

A female on her firm's executive committee says it's difficult to find things to talk about:

> I have to seek out topics to get people to open up with me, question them about their work. It's not as natural as the guys, who will all seem to talk about sports or whatever. Kids would be the last things to bring up, frill issues. Unless they initiate it. I'll talk about work, I'll talk about business.

Another woman has found it hard to strike up relationships on a high-level legal board:

> For this new board, we had an orientation meeting, and the new members of the board were waiting in the hall. I promise you that I felt, here are all these men in their Sunday best because I'm standing there. If I weren't there, they would they have been casually talking about golf, have any of you represented company X, gee I'd like to get some business from them. Instead it was awkward. That was

the essence of what I felt in that hallway with the guys. The momen-
tary suspense in the air of, what are we going to chat about?

An in-house woman who is on her company's executive team on the West
Coast says:

> I'm the only woman, of ten people. Gender is a factor. If the talk
> becomes more profane or locker room-like, there's a moment where
> all of them turn and look at me and say, "Sorry." I just kind of laugh.
> The team has been together long enough, they know I'm not offend-
> ed. But it still exists. I'm a little bit on the outside.

One company held a celebration getaway prompted by the success of a
major project. The invited guests were all male, along with their wives and
girlfriends; the female general counsel was not invited, even though she had
worked on the project. She comments:

> There are a lot of gender issues represented in that story. A golfing
> thing, all of these men, most with stay-at-home wives. I'm a female
> general counsel, where would I fit in? I'm not going to go golfing and
> smoke cigars. On the other hand, it's not appropriate for me to hang
> out with the stay-at-home moms, who are going to receive all the spa
> treatments. It's awkward.

What happens when women are shut out? Linda, quoted above about the
"all sports" talk, says, "It may diminish my influence a little bit." And an in-
house woman in Wisconsin says that it has an indirect effect on decision
making:

> The CEO wants to be gender neutral. But by virtue of habit, influence
> of others, or the guy thing, they go running together, they do sports
> things together, and therefore that breeds a camaraderie that the
> women in the organization don't have with the men. Decisions aren't
> based upon gender, but they are based upon that relationship, which
> happens because of the gender. It's very indirect.

Management professor Judith Oakley concludes: "Women executives at
the top often report that their male colleagues feel uncomfortable or even
threatened by their presence. The discomfort of men directly above them is

often attributed to the failure of the man at the top to reconcile . . . traditional values about sex roles they were brought up with . . . and with their experience of working with women as peers."[18] Sports talk and other male-oriented topics might actually be exaggerated in groups dominated by men, she wrote, which "tend to affirm the group's identity in solidarity by exaggerating aspects of their culture they believe distinguishes them from the tokens."[19] Women's lack of an informal connection with men leads to diminished influence and power.

Although such thinking and behavior are more a social pattern than a direct indication of competence, they ultimately create an environment that undermines a woman's effectiveness. If women are shut out, intentionally or not, they can't get to know their male colleagues in a way that establishes them as people others can trust and respect. They can't form the alliances that are necessary to move new policies or ideas along. Women therefore remain more of an enigma, easily caricatured, rather than three-dimensional, flesh-and-blood human beings. Those on the "outside" aren't going to have the level of influence that the insiders have, and as a result they can't command the level of respect that others do. Without trust and respect, in turn, women's actual clout is reduced, bolstering perceptions that women aren't credible as leaders.

Some women who feel shut out from the male inner circle sometimes seek out female company farther down the ladder. A female general counsel enjoys close relations with many female staff members, which affects the way she is viewed from the top:

> They [the other female staff members] see me as their scout leader. They feel more open to come to me with issues, before they would go to another member of the management team. But on the other hand, because I have a closer relationship with them, I tend to be lumped together with them. I get invited to the baby showers, while the vice presidents don't get invited, because they're all men. They

---

[18] Judith G. Oakley "Gender-Based Barriers to Senior Management Positions: Understanding the Scarcity of Female CEOs," J. Bus. Ethics, at 321 (Oct. 2000).
[19] Id.

have a different opinion about my status, then. The people at a lower level don't place me in the company's ranking as high as they would because they feel like our relationship is closer, and the vice presidents tend to see me at a more diminished level because I have that closer relationship.

Women are sometimes more likely to align themselves with staff because they are the "only woman" and want companionship. They also are often seen as the "scout leader" who can right perceived wrongs for the staff. Men in the organization might conclude that the woman is managing down rather than up, sacrificing evident ambition in favor of friendship.

If women are inducted into the inner circle and feel comfortable, there's an added twist. Because a senior woman has lofty status, and because she is accepted into the male paradigm, even bringing up gender issues or a perceived lack of competency is highly charged. Many women reported that if they did so, their male colleagues got angry with them. A general counsel is wary about bringing up gender issues with her CEO, to avoid putting him on the spot:

Can I lobby the CEO? There are moments in time when I might be able to do that and get away with it. Then there are other moments when I think that may be viewed as too threatening. It's almost like you call into question their integrity. It's a hard thing to bring up. You kind of sit back and wait for the opportunity. You might drop a little hint or two.

When women are part of high management circles, and have won the trust of their male colleagues, they violate that trust when they bring up gender issues. They risk anger and causing offense when they "call into question the integrity" of their male colleagues by even suggesting that bias might be present. If a woman has been successful, the working assumption is that she doesn't have gender issues; if one arises, therefore, she can't complain about it.

All these factors—low numbers of women, more testing and scrutiny of women's actions and behaviors, a perception of less dedication, continued competency testing at the top, lack of access to inside networks, and the inability to even suggest gender bias in the context of competency—are what keep the competency gap firmly propped open at present.

Closing the Gap

So what do women—and some men—do to close the competency gap?

Many just assume they must work harder to make an impression and counteract any suspicions about competency. In one article, female litigators advise, "[W]omen lawyers should strive to be significantly better prepared than their male adversaries. Many women lack the height, weight, deep voice, grey hair and other physical attributes that convey authority and experience in our society. Moreover, the prejudice persists that women are neither smart nor forceful and therefore do not make worthwhile opponents."[20] An African-American woman in a high-level management position in a California government office says:

> Establishing credibility? There are few images that American society has of women of color in positions of authority and power and control. The way I establish credibility is that I work my butt off. That's the bottom line.

Some women work on their own, establishing their own niche practice or specialty, to ensure that they are the only ones available to do certain work within their workplace. This is in contrast to women with a more fungible area of concentration, which allows subjective perceptions about competency to sway decision making about assignments and referrals. A female intellectual property lawyer says:

> Women lawyers have to have their own power base. That's so you're not beholden to anybody. I picked this area because twenty years ago, no lawyers did this work. Now it's a hot area. Twenty years ago they gave it to the girl lawyers. It's a two-pronged thing. If you're the only game in town, the guys have to call you. They're not going to give the money away to another firm. It's autonomy, too. You don't have to worry about being beholden to anybody. I just look at it as a workplace issue: you don't always want to be begging.

---

[20] Jean MacLean Snyder & Andra Barmash Greene, eds., *The Woman Advocate,* at p. 178 (American Bar Association Section of Litigation, 1996).

Some women say they work on their own because they worry that others working with them might do a substandard job. A woman in a Virginia firm says:

> The guys that I work with find it extremely easy to enlist the assistance of younger associates. They'll come in and they've got four people working for them. I don't ever do that. I perceive that if I do that people will think that I can't do it myself. I also don't trust [others] to do my work. Guys work in teams, women work independently. I think it's a control thing—I fear that if I ever did that and somebody did something wrong, it would be hard for me to make the argument, "Well, I relied on them." It's easier for the guys to say that.

This woman sees her credibility as hanging by a thread, and is another example of how many women address the competency issue: through sheer effort and results that can't be challenged because they work on their own.

Women will also quit work environments entirely where they feel basic competency questions are in the air, and build an independent practice, devoid of suspicions that family issues taint their dedication.[21] There aren't figures available measuring how many women-led or -dominated law firms exist, but anecdotally the number is significant.[22]

Another approach is to be wary of people who are inclined to question women's competence, and not give them ammunition. A female partner in Minnesota remarks:

> I do think that there are jerks out there, who don't like working with women, who are looking for any excuse to see a woman as an inferior service provider. You try to identify them, you try to make sure that you don't give them more reason to feel that way. "She's always talking about her kids, I'm not sure she's paying attention to my cases,

---

[21] Jennifer Batchelor, "The Perfect Fit: Dissatisfied Female Attorneys Start Own Firms," The Legal Intelligencer (Sept. 16, 2002) (online article at www.law.com).

[22] The proportion of women working as solo practitioners is similar to that of men. Deborah L. Rhode, "The Unfinished Agenda: Women and the Legal Profession," at 23 (American Bar Association Commission on Women in the Profession, 2001).

she's always dashing off to the latest day care crisis." So you keep your antenna up for those people, and with them I wouldn't get completely honest about my issues. I probably wouldn't walk into a room and say I couldn't get my kids out of the house today. I'd say I had car trouble, I was in a traffic jam.

Can-Do Attitudes

Although some women lawyers use defensive methods to counteract impressions of incompetence, others are more proactive. For instance, many try to directly challenge any impressions that they have less power than men, such as when they are first meeting with a client or colleague. A female partner in a large firm is very forthright:

I project a tremendous amount of confidence in the firm. I convey verbally a real can-do attitude. Anything anybody needs, not only can we do it, but we do it better than everybody else. We're the best. I don't ever hesitate to say that. I also say I'm the best. And it's true, I'm very well known in my field. You can't find anyone better than me. Sometimes I don't say it because I don't think it will go over well, it might sound like bragging. I try to calibrate it.

Other women establish themselves as players. Even a top practitioner like Mary Cranston of Pillsbury Winthrop occasionally finds herself in situations where no-one knows who she is, and she is being ignored. She says:

I speak up in a measured way, I work in a credential or two. That's the fastest route. The reaction is that the eye contact changes, the dynamic shifts to where I am, the center of gravity shifts towards me.

Female litigators who are experienced with aggressive male adversaries in depositions give advice about how to react. Some don't advocate either a passive role or an aggressive one, but instead suggest ways to navigate a middle ground. In one article, the writers advise that a woman can respond "affirmatively, perhaps by being disdainful. She can, for example, look bored and avoid eye contact, shuffle documents, or have a cup of coffee. She can inquire whether the reporter has recorded every word, and then ask the windbag if he has finished; or she can ask whether he has instructed his witness not to answer, and if not, she can ask the witness to answer."[23]

Others react differently depending on the situation when they believe they are not being taken seriously. A female partner in Washington, D.C. has different reactions when she's asked to do menial tasks:

> Sometimes you just do it. Sometimes you finesse it. You turn to someone who's junior to you in the room and ask them to do it. Sometimes you do it but complain about it later. I complained to a senior male, who should have intervened. I get good reactions when I do this. Now I am in the situation where if something like this comes up, my [male] mentor will stand up and say, "I'll go get the coffee."

A female senior associate supervises male associates differently from females, because otherwise the men don't take her assignments seriously:

> I motivate the guys differently. I probably try to be as friendly and accessible as possible with the guys, but I make it clear that if they make a mistake, I'll be hard on them. I tell them exactly what I want. I make it their responsibility to drive the bus but I tell them where they're driving. Sometimes guys think that because I'm female that I'm easier to work for, that they can make a mistake and say, "I'm sorry," and that's it. And it's so not.

Reaching Out

The previous examples are self-help measures that women take individually to elevate their own images. Many women also make efforts to reach out and influence others through office dynamics, participation in high-level committees, and input to senior management.

Some actively lobby to get women on executive or management committees. Jane, described earlier when she approached a woman to be on the management team, had to work hard to get the other woman on the team, partly because unofficial criteria required that team members be major rainmakers:

---

[23] Snyder & Greene, eds., N. 20 *supra* at p. 180.

I talked to others on the selection committee, I talked to others to get them to contact people on the selection committee, I got others to contact the female candidate. I spent a fair bit of time on this because I thought it was important. There was some gender bias, both anti-female and a set mental model that only business getters get on the management committee. When you latch on to a criterion like business development and you have a system where men have traditionally inherited a lot of business, there's a disparate impact. It was hard to do, but I don't think it would have happened if I hadn't kept after it. It became a big thing over a two-week period. It was kind of unlike me.

Once a woman becomes a member of an important committee or group, says Martha Barnett of Holland & Knight, "There is a responsibility for [that] woman to try to add another woman, or a person of color." A male general counsel in a company that produces female consumer products instructed a recruiter to come up with a female to succeed him. He recognized that his request was "a legal issue," but he felt strongly that his company needed more diversity:

I intentionally went out and hired a woman. I can't say that for the record. I picked someone who is brilliant whom I can teach the business to, whom I hope can succeed me. I did it intentionally because this industry and the law need more successful women. Women and men have different perspectives. If you're in a homogeneous environment, you need diversity to get the benefit of the full panoply of the challenges to conventional thinking.

Once they are in positions of power, women are careful about picking their battles. They say they can't comment too frequently or directly on gender bias for fear of being marginalized and ignored. Women say that if they pursue gender issues too often or too exclusively, they seem less credible, less independent, and less trustworthy, like an ideologue occupying a designated "woman's seat." A female general counsel on the West Coast uses indirect methods to get her thoughts across to the executive team:

They will make comments about women candidates [for senior executive positions] that they would never make about men. "Did you hear her laugh?" They'll talk about her physical appearance. "She's heavy-set." "She's dressed a certain way." I sometimes will say something. If you beat on that drum constantly—"Well, I think that's a gender-biased comment"—you tend to be excluded from things. You have to walk the line in deciding what to comment on. When can I dive in to make my point without having the conversation be subverted away from whether this is a good candidate or not? I will try to find an opportunity later on to make the point. Later on, I'll say, "Did you hear his laugh?" Then they'll say, "Oh, oh." These guys are pretty sensitive to this stuff. I do feel like I don't make certain comments that I might make otherwise.

She chooses not to confront colleagues directly immediately after the inappropriate remarks are made, but instead uses humor later on to make her point. The men then experience the dynamic as did the woman.

Other women point to facts and figures to correct a gender bias. A woman on the compensation committee in her firm noted that a woman and man—both quirky personalities with eccentric dress and hair, both with big numbers—were being treated differently. The committee was suspicious of the woman's success, and set her draw low; they paid the man handsomely. The woman recalls:

The guys said, "That's a not real number [for the woman]." They said, "It's a one-off deal." I said, "No, it's not, she's had that client for ten years." They were very suspicious. I said, "You're willing to recognize that Joe is a weird guy and you're paying him. You can't do any different with the woman."

A partner in the Midwest brings up issues of gender bias if the issue is one that could cause a risk to her firm. In that case, she believes she has a duty to address it. She was concerned, for instance, about a male colleague who was making inappropriate sexual remarks. She asked another male to talk to him and resolve the problem. Similarly, a general counsel aligns her remarks with company objectives, rather than focusing on gender concerns in isolation:

Our CEO brought it in [some marketing materials that included pictures of people in the company], and I said, "Where are the women?" The pictures included all the members of the board of directors, with only one woman. And he said, "That's what I thought too." I said, "You can't put this out there and on a billboard, and expect it to reach the audience that we intend it to. I as a woman look at that and say, there's the token."

A male general counsel in New York challenges people who make gender-biased decisions or comments:

There are situations which are clearly discriminatory, and I say, "This is outrageous, it cannot continue, it will stop." But if you listen to a conversation and you hear stereotypes, you have to be a little more subtle in challenging them. I might ask questions: "Really? What made you reach that conclusion? Can you give me an example?" I would challenge the example, turn it back to make the person think.

This man gently asks a person to pick apart their assumptions, hoping to guide them to self-realization about bias.

Marcia, the in-house attorney quoted above about working with others in her company to deliver messages based on gender to a male committee, is philosophical about the approach:

It doesn't necessarily bother me. Because we're manipulating their bias and they don't even know it. Maybe the whole idea was mine. Maybe I'm the one who thought this was something we should change, and I feed it all to the [male] person who's going to be the messenger, and the messenger sells it.

Although having a man deliver a hard message to resistant males may look like a cop-out, Marcia interprets it instead as adroit maneuvering around unenlightened people.

Some women deliberately split with supposed allies at times to show independence. A female partner on the management team in the Midwest says:

I pick my issues very carefully. To keep it away from, "Oh, well, she always does that stuff." When I voted differently from my mentor, that showed credibility. It's a view of independence.

Another powerful female has a close female friend in her firm, another partner. They intentionally keep their friendship under wraps by not sitting together at meetings and not being seen lunching together:

The men would always suspect we're just doing that, there's this assumption that we're together because we're women. That we're going to support one another. We're very good friends. We have lunch, but we hope not to be seen. When we have supported each other's controversial positions, we then had more credibility.

Others are careful to set their own internal expectations carefully, and to be satisfied with limited progress. A senior woman in a Southern firm is the only woman on the management committee:

> I have little bitty goals. I think I have gotten discussions to occur that have never occurred before. I put on the agenda that I wanted to talk about diversity issues. I wanted us to reaffirm commitment on diversity. That discussion would never have happened otherwise. It was a good discussion. That's all I can ask for. I'm very respectful and deferential on a lot of institutional things. If I can get a discussion going that's never happened I'm happy. Do things get done? No. Do all things I want get done? No.

Some women try to prevent "old world" males from entering the organization in the first place, proactively reshaping the workplace culture. Rhonda, the woman discussed above who notices that young males who are interviewing seem to take her and other women less seriously, says the behavior hurts the men. "They perceive that what I'm going to say is not going to affect their chances," she says, adding pointedly, "and they're wrong." She argues against hiring them, pointing out that the male may have trouble taking instruction or feedback from a female lawyer or client. A woman in Virginia is on the watch for these men:

> Now that I have a say in hiring, I will not hire young blustery guys. I get a sixth sense, watching them speak. I see the dynamic as he's dealing with a more junior associate, like if he grills the junior associate. Some of it is tone: "How would you feel if I did this?" "Would you be willing to do this?" They're hierarchical right away rather than giving deference and courtesy, which they do when someone more senior comes into the room. Women are involved in hiring so young guys have to keep their heads up.

A woman who works in a federal government office where (like many government settings and unlike law firms) there are many females in leadership positions, talks about the benefit:

> To the extent that there are men who are somewhat Neanderthal in their views about women lawyers, which is true in either private or public settings, having women in leadership positions tends to shut them down. I can think of a few men I've worked with in government who would be a lot more annoying. I've thought, "I'm glad there's a woman director here." The fact that there were women in these positions just kept people's less good instincts more to themselves.

These efforts at change—ranging from working extra hard, having one's own practice, avoiding the "jerks," lobbying for women in leadership, taking individual defensive measures to broaden efforts to change policy, picking battles carefully—show the importance of finely nuanced, adroit approaches when challenging the competence gap.

Mind the Gap

A female partner in a large firm—with a thick book of business and multi-million-dollar cases—can't believe this issue still persists:

> My reaction to it is a kind of weariness after all these years. No matter how high you are, no matter how many millions of dollars you earn, there's still a door closed in your face. It's as simple as the discussion about golf—golf being the metaphor about what men do and women don't do in my generation.

There is no question that, compared to a generation ago, the options for women to display professional ability have increased phenomenally. Any early suspicion that women would outright fail was nipped in the bud. There were and continue to be countless examples of high-performing women. The governing double bind—that a female couldn't be a competent legal professional—has substantially unraveled. However, the survey results, trends, attitudes, and anecdotes included in this chapter contradict the expectations of those people who assumed that sheer numbers of women in the workforce would force changes in perception. Questions of women's competency and effectiveness are still in play.

So the publicly accepted rhetoric that women are completely capable of practicing law as well as men has to be qualified in three specific ways. First, there's still a basic competence gap, as evidenced by statistics as well as anecdotes about testing and scrutiny, fueled by lingering gender bias as well as a sense of "strategy" that all weaknesses should be exploited in rough-and-tumble practice. Second, although the perceived competency of women in lower levels has increased, partly because the stakes aren't as high, there remains a competence gap at the top. And third, suspicions about a lack of dedication color all women, because of family responsibilities that raise questions about commitment. Although men have gotten comfortable with women as colleagues, they haven't gotten comfortable with mothers as colleagues.[24]

As a result, the competence gap remains open. The frustration that women feel about this—expressed with great relish when they are underestimated—is palpable. Even those who have steadfastly not used "gender as an excuse" find themselves at a loss to explain certain events other than through gender bias. This issue is also complicated by the continuing finding that social awkwardness between men and women slows the acceptance of women into inner circles.

This situation seems transitory. In a way it's a backlash against the notion that all women would be great, like the pioneers who proved themselves so ably. Not all women are great, just as all men aren't great. But each time a woman is incompetent, or gets pregnant and leaves, the episode is overblown, and all women pay for it, because each individual woman still stands as a symbol for all women.

Will more numbers do the trick? One would think that with equal numbers of males and females coming into the profession, especially because they have excelled side by side throughout their lives, the skepticism would decrease over time. Perhaps it is necessary to have half men and half women in the workforce to erase the predilection towards men as the better or more authoritative attorneys, so that people don't assume a man is in charge and don't send women to fetch *lattes*.

---

[24] This is explored in detail in Chapters 7 and 8 *infra*.

This chapter stresses the importance of women on high-level committees and as leaders. They can make change, push new policies, and spotlight discrimination. It's also critical that women get the bet-the-company cases. When there's no question, all the way up the ladder, that women are capable of dealing successfully with anything handed to them, the competence gap should largely close.

One difficulty in resolving this issue is that it's very much a woman's problem. It's hard to find common ground with men, other than to convince men that the problem exists. This is why the issue is complicated by the fact that it's definitely supposed to have been resolved. The public discourse includes strong assumptions that the idea of female incompetence is a laughable leftover from the past; that a shared understanding in the legal profession of merit prevails and overwhelms concerns of gender; and that the remaining doubters are a splinter group of "troglodytes." Most people sincerely believe they are "advocates of women." This tension between the highly polished public declarations, and what actually happens in people's minds or in reality, complicates efforts to move forward.

The issue of women's competence remains unsettled. It is far more established, however, than women's legitimacy in positions of authority supervising and managing others, the subject of the following chapter.

CHAPTER 5

BEING THE BOSS:
Making Room for the Authoritative Woman

Jan, who works in a Midwestern legal department, describes her boss's laid-back attitude towards getting ahead and promoting people who work for him:

> He's not the sharpest tool in the shed, not like a super bright fellow, but he is a very dedicated hard worker. He gets along very well with people because he's non-threatening, really diligent, and he's just a very nice fellow. What's interesting is that he's less ambitious than we are. Consequently, he's not able to aggrandize us or his department because that's not the way he thinks.

Later she talks about her skeptical reaction to a more senior supervisor, a woman and also an attorney, during a company meeting with investment bankers and corporate officers:

> She actually walked away from us—we were driving her back—she walked away to hobnob and press the flesh, lots of laughing and recounting of stories. I thought, "This woman is something else, she's on a mission, she's trying to penetrate the 'in crowd,' she's very political." I've seen that whole dynamic; there was always a subset of women who were hoping to get the keys to the kingdom.

I asked her about her reaction to the woman, given her point that the male boss should be more aggressive. She says:

> You're *right*, I was just saying that he should be more aggressive. I *did* say that. If she were a guy, I might be slightly more charitable. I feel as though that's what men have done, since time immemorial; I would feel as though men need to do that.

Jan's story shows the conventional views about leadership styles. Men are expected to be aggressive, and people notice if they're not. Whereas for women it's the opposite: they are expected to be inclusive and nurturing, and they raise hackles if they are too ambitious or imperious.

It's a challenge for anyone, male or female, to craft an effective leadership style. A lawyer is confronted not just with doing his or her own work, but with supervising a secretary, paralegal, or associate, or an entire law firm, in-house department, or government staff. And there are other challenges that require leadership, such as relating effectively with opposing counsel and clients.

This issue is particularly sensitive for women. Men enter the leadership circle with an automatic advantage. Their "normal" personality and style (assuming they possess the stereotypical masculine qualities) weave smoothly into the fabric of managerial life. Women, by contrast, confront an automatic double-bind; their femininity—an expectation of nurturing, kind, supportive behavior—collides with an exercise of authority. Studies show that people do not perceive women as automatically possessing the qualities of a supervisor.[1]

How men and women choose to exercise leadership—with a masculine and directive manner, or a feminine and supportive manner—provokes different reactions from the rank and file. Inclusive, nurturing managers, more often women than men, testify that they get greater loyalty and better performances from underlings. Sometimes, though, other people take advantage of their understanding nature, or perceive them to be weak. Aggressive managers inject more urgency into the workplace and often command more respect, but women who take this tack are marginalized and even hated for "acting like men." Although men usually get a pass for hyperaggressive behavior, even they face challenges these days, such as when they supervise younger women.

What are the advantages and disadvantages to each approach, for men and for women? Is either the most effective style for motivating strong performances? If not, can stereotypes of men and women in the workplace be modified so that organizations can be as successful as possible?

---

[1] For example, there are studies in which people are asked the qualities of an ideal man, an ideal woman, and an ideal manager. Respondents list similar qualities for the ideal man and ideal manager: independent, aggressive, fearless. However, when they list the qualities of an ideal woman—nurturing, caring, supportive—there's little overlap with the traits associated with management. Mary Ann C. Case, "Disaggregating Gender from Sex and Sexual Orientation: The Effeminate Man in the Law and Feminist Jurisprudence," 105 Yale L. J., 1, 72-73 (1995). Studies show that the actual leadership styles employed by men and women don't differ much by sex. Marloes L. van Engen, Rien van der Leeden & Tineke M. Willemsen, "Gender, Context and Leadership Styles: A Field Study," 74:5 J. Occupational & Organizational Psych., 581, 583 (2001).

Nice Work

Women often feel a pressure to act more "masculine" in the legal arena—to be aggressive, decisive, hierarchical, autonomous, directive, and cool. And research suggests that managers draw their style more from the gender composition of those they lead; that is, they tend to act masculine and task-oriented in male-dominated environments and supportive and people-oriented in female-dominated environments.[2]

However, it appears that the stronger pressures are those that push women in the opposite direction, to employ a "nice" style. This can be defined as collaborative, consensus-building, down-playing of authority, egalitarian, caring, and supportive. More women than men are "nice" supervisors within the workplace.

The first and most obvious pressure on women is that they are saddled with an expectation that they are "naturally" kind and nurturing. It's hard to know whether leadership styles show the way people are ordinarily, or whether they are responding to expectations. And to be sure, when people see men acting confident and charging ahead, or women acting deferential and cooperative, they interpret this behavior as confirmation of long-held stereotypes.

In actuality, most of the women I interviewed said that at some point they had made some adjustment in their ordinary manner or personality because of gender expectations. They tended to accept the dictum that women can't be too aggressive or too passive, and created detailed methods for walking that fine line. These women assumed that they can't just be themselves, and that they must sculpt an acceptable work persona that doesn't offend entrenched norms. They are acting by "creating strategies of gender management."[3] Nancy, a female supervisor in a California government office, says:

> I think that people who are being supervised expect to be supervised
> in different ways by a woman than they do by a man. They expect

---

[2] *Id.* (van Engen et al.) at 584-585.

[3] Judith G. Oakley, "Gender-Based Barriers to Senior Management Positions: Understanding the Scarcity of Female CEOs," J. Bus. Ethics, 321 (Oct. 2000). Oakley comments that one problem with these adaptive behaviors is that women wind up "blending in" and not standing out or catching anyone's attention.

and probably require a woman to be nicer than they require a man to be. If you're not that way, then it's perceived as being mean. It's a huge problem.

Another force compelling a "nice" manner is that women assume equality among themselves, regardless of whether they are peers or supervisors.[4] The tradition of the helpful, supportive woman leads to an expectation that women won't hold themselves above one another. This is reinforced by a notion of "sisterhood" among women. Says a woman judge, "Women tend to expect other women to be sisters: 'You'll help me out, we have something in common.'" This can extend to an expectation of friendship with a supervisor. Nancy, quoted above, says "Especially with women lawyers, there are times when they feel that if you're not their friend outside of the office, then you're cold or distant."

A further impetus is that the management press has enthusiastically endorsed a female-type managerial style. In fact, business literature from the past generation urged that all managers act like women are said to act naturally.[5] Many employees favor this approach and applaud it. For men, however, being nurturing and inclusive is more a reflection of their individual personalities, or a deliberate managerial choice that they can rescind without penalty if the going gets tough. Women have less latitude to stray from the path between "not too passive, not too aggressive."

Of course, the best argument in favor of being nice in a position of authority is that female managers who are not "nice" are disliked and rejected, which will be discussed later in the chapter.

---

[4] As psychologist Virginia Valian writes about one study: "[W]omen . . . had to show that they were not seeking status at the expense of other group members . . . ." Virginia Valian, *Why So Slow? The Advancement of Women*, at p. 324 (MIT Press, 1998).

[5] Susan J. Wells, "A Female Executive Is Hard to Find," 46:6 HR Magazine, 40 (June 2001). Wells's article reports that in one survey, female managers were rated higher than their male counterparts in forty-two of fifty-two skills measured, and in another, women scored higher than men in twenty of twenty-three management areas. See also van Engen et al., N. 1 *supra* at 582: "The recent trend in management theory and management practice is one leading towards employee participation and empowerment."

Walking the Line

So if women are expected to be nurturing, how do they effectively exercise authority? Isn't this an oxymoron? As sociolinguist Deborah Tannen writes, "Wearing the mantle of authority lightly allows it to be more easily pushed off your shoulders."[6]

To maintain a middle-of-the-road approach, some keep in mind qualities they want to project. "Assertive and still graceful," is how one woman wants to be seen. "Fun to be around, yet commanding respect," another says. These women want to get the job done but still look like a familiar woman.

Others conjure up an image for inspiration. A female partner in South Carolina says, "For the most part, women are playing the roles of women, being warm and cheerful and kind." Another woman thinks of herself as a cheerleader[7]: wholesome, enthusiastic, hard-working, all-American, unthreatening, popular, feminine. But the most frequent identity that women adopt is that of a mother, drawing upon a familiar icon and acceptable mental model to soften their authority. Says Brenda, who has her own firm in the Southwest:

> I'm kind of a mom. We try and make the firm very warm, we have [staff] over to our homes, we talk to them about their problems, we celebrate their achievements and their birthdays and all that kind of stuff.

A female partner in Florida says:

> Most people see me as a pretty nice lady, supportive, working well with people. I'm like the frigging firm mom. People come to me if they're having problems, I'm like the fixer.

A practitioner with her own firm emphasizes group outings for bonding:

---

[6] Deborah Tannen, *Talking from 9 to 5: Women and Men in the Workplace: Language, Sex and Power,* at p. 185 (Morrow/Avon Books, 1994).

[7] Cynthia Fuchs Epstein, *Women in Law,* 2d ed. at p. 299 (University of Illinois Press, 1993).

> I try to make it like a family, more than a work environment. We go to lunch a lot together. We try to do things outside the workplace, we take the entire firm to New Orleans or Key West, and hang out together. We have no distinctions.

The "motherly style" includes caring about career development and positive reinforcement. Says Brenda, "We try and encourage [women] to develop their practices, we ask them what they want to do." Teresa, who practices in Texas, notes, "I recognize I can't do anything I do without them. Sometimes they're more valuable here than I am. I think they know that I recognize that. I think I try and let them know by telling them how important they are, and through pay."

Another approach is to play the unassuming head of a team, seeking broad input. Teresa, quoted above, welcomes contributions from everyone on a problem:

> I will say, okay, guys, here's what to do; if there's a better way, do it that way. Let's just get the problem solved. And sometimes they do tell me a better way. It's a team approach.

Part of the team approach includes being non-judgmental. A female partner in Miami says:

> I am a problem solver, and when people come in with a problem, I spend very little time analyzing who's responsible. I just go right to, "How do we make sure this doesn't happen again? Let's move on." Women bring a conciliatory style to managing, and that's always the way I've approached problems. I don't sit there cross-examining people.

A female partner in the Southwest is inclusive:

> I stay away from attacking personalities or people. In all my correspondence I always say "we" and not "I." If I can, I'll say it's "our" position as opposed to "my" position. This softens the authority thing and prevents it from being too personal.

Ida Abbott, a consultant to law firms in Oakland, California, says that inclusive women will sometimes get things accomplished by letting others think a solution is their idea. She says: "There are ways that women can lead through indirection or by emphasizing the team, not their own role on the team, that allows people around them to feel better about that work." A woman who led her firm as managing partner was philosophical about her "egotistical" male colleagues: "If I had to let them think it was their own idea, I did it. That's fine with me. All I cared about was getting the job done."

An in-house attorney plays the role of peacemaker when she has a run-in with a male colleague. She described an encounter the day before when she closely questioned a male peer about a pending case:

> I really grilled him very hard. If I had been a man, he wouldn't have been as offended by it, he would have understood that I was doing my job. But because I'm a woman and he doesn't expect me to grill him, because we're colleagues, because I'm a woman and he considers me to be less than him—he's the dominant and I'm the subordinate—I shouldn't attack him. I shouldn't be aggressive towards him. But I stepped out of my subservient role and I challenged his maleness. Now I have to go mend some fences, to make sure that he knows that I haven't changed the dominant/subordinate balance in order for us to have a good working relationship, which I need and he needs. I'll call him up and smooth his ruffled feathers. It's a pain in the neck. I really shouldn't have to do that. There's a lot of extra stuff that has to get done as a woman, just in order to maintain a position. This man is an equal, but in his eyes, we're not equals.

As one researcher noted about a situation involving a peer: "For male executives competing with female executives at the same level . . . the sense of discomfort may originate more from the fear of being 'one-upped' by a woman, and the resulting sense of shame some men feel when losing in competition with a woman."[8]

All the metaphors described above—cheerleader, mother, team leader, peacemaker—draw on existing stereotypes to offer a lodestar for women's behavior.

---

[8] Oakley, N. 3 *supra* at 321.

Schmoozing the Staff

The "nice" approach for women is especially important when they deal with staff. Women are expected to exhibit cordial behavior that isn't required from men. A female partner in Oregon says:

> I feel that I have to have more personal interaction than I see the guys having with their secretaries. That's expected. If the women partners don't do the interaction they're seen as more cold. If the guys do that, it's seen as neutral, unless they're out-and-out obnoxious. Female partners are more likely to get a bad rap if they don't schmooze.

A thirty-four-year-old female in New England says:

> Partly it's the way women attorneys project themselves. They may be uncomfortable in that boss position, or giving direction, they may want to be friendly with the secretary and that can make the lines a little bit blurry. I think they're sensitive to the fact that if they're demanding, they're going to be viewed as bitches much more than the male attorney.

The expectation of equality among women is a delicate balance that women bosses can easily upset. A thirty-two-year-old female trusts and estates attorney in Kentucky comments:

> I have seen hostility between secretaries and women attorneys, where the staff treats women associates poorly. The guys will flirt with the secretaries, they play the dumb man, like, "I don't know how to do the copy machine," and suck up to them. Whereas if a woman asks for help, the secretary will say, "Do it yourself." Sometimes I think it's easier for a woman to work for a man than for a woman.

A male lawyer says, "The staff will be quicker to voice their conspiracy against a young female than they are against a young male. That social bias continues."

Women generally ingratiate themselves with staff and avoid alienating them. For instance, they take an interest in their secretaries' personal lives. "I always take the time to say, 'How are you, your mom is sick, how is she?'" reports a partner, in a typical comment. "You have to let the person know that you value them." Others use motherhood to bond. "You go into the kitchen to get your cup of coffee," describes a female partner in Arizona, "and you could easily swap stories about your baby having an ear infection. If I weren't a mom, they wouldn't do that. In some ways it enhanced those relationships and gave us common areas."

Some take on menial tasks to avoid looking high-handed. One woman says:

> I don't buzz from my office and say, "Bring me the file." I can get up and get it by myself, because usually my secretary is typing something. I have to walk past the copy machine to go to her office, so I very rarely ask her to copy something unless I'm in a hurry. I never walk out to her desk and put a fax there that's already ready to go without sticking it into the fax machine, and saying, "It's in there."

A practitioner in Virginia is meticulous on this score:

> I'm very uncomfortable asking my secretary to do things that other people do. Last week I was on deadline, I hadn't had a chance to go pick up lunch. My secretary asked if I wanted her to pick up anything. I almost didn't ask, but I realized I didn't have time to pick up food. I asked her to pick me up a frozen thing. An hour later it was still sitting on my desk because I didn't have time to cook it. I reluctantly carried it up to her desk and asked her if she had time to put it in the freezer—and she said, let me just cook it for you! And I initially protested because I said, "It's not appropriate for you to cook my lunch," and she said, "You're busy and let me do it." I felt very weird but I finally let her do it. I think some of that dynamic was a gender thing in addition to a hierarchical thing.

Another approach is to encourage the appearance of equality. Linda, a powerful female partner in her fifties, says that secretaries who have known her for a long time have always referred to her by her first name, but they call all men "Mister." In fact, when Linda meets with a male subordinate, a secretary will ask, "Linda, is Mr. Smith with you?" Linda brushes it off: "It doesn't bother me. They've been in the profession for thirty years, they've been trained that way." Linda believes she gets less obeisance but more affection, less status but more support.

Great Reviews

Efforts by females to burnish their reputations as "nice" don't go unnoticed. People who were interviewed repeatedly said how much they like working for women, specifically attributing their better management techniques to their "femaleness."[9]

Moreover, many men sing the praises of their women bosses.[10] They said frequently that women were more willing to listen and give credence to their views than were men. A thirty-one-year-old male said:

> The females that I report to tend to take more time to listen to your opinion, give you a chance to speak, take that all in and give a final decision. With males it's been their way or no way. Definitely the females had a better management style. I've had a phenomenal time working for women who are attorneys. I don't know if it's gender and professionalism, but you tend to get more space, you are able to function out of the box, you get to move up the ladder a lot faster with women attorneys.

Warren, a self-described "conservative" male in Virginia, who is thirty-four, remarks that female supervisors demonstrate greater understanding:

> Like most younger people, I think that my female supervisor was more understanding. [The women are] closer to you, they're more your peers than are the name partners, who at this point are still old men. [My female boss] was great to work for, very understanding, the door's always open, she was not impatient.

A younger male in Colorado appreciated his boss's nurturing approach:

> She's the best boss I've worked for across the board. She's a good teacher, but also gives you responsibility. If you make a mistake, she

---

[9] A recent survey found that female attorneys had more supervisory duties than did men. "Gender Equity in the Legal Profession," 20 (New York State Bar Association, Committee on Women in the Law, 2002).

[10] In one study, supervisors rated men and women as equally capable as leaders, whereas peers and subordinates rated women slightly higher than men. Wells, N. 5 supra at 40.

doesn't berate, she just says this is the way I would have done it, and you take that and you learn from it. It's more of a teaching, nurturing kind of a situation. She'll give me good directions to follow—if you have questions, she'll make a decent effort to answer.

Many men said that female supervisors were more sympathetic to family issues than males. Warren, quoted above, said, "One guy said he could do the 'child care stuff' with the woman attorney [talk openly about the subject] and he would never do that with the men." A thirty-eight-year-old man in the East, who reported for some time to several senior women, said:

> There's more humane supervision by women than men. And it's not as if the women who ran this office weren't driven and successful, but when it came to personal issues, there's no comparison. Maybe I'm more comfortable discussing those things with these women than going to an old guy and saying, "Look, I've got this problem with my son."

Indeed, women themselves often say proudly that their "natural" womanly traits come in handy for managing people. A female partner in Connecticut made a typical comment:

> We females tend to be more understanding. I've observed that when I was an associate, and having to answer to male partners, it was much more of a top-down relationship, it was much more formal. We [women] tend to be much less formal, we invite comments from the associate, we are not as hierarchical.

Again, all the traits mentioned above—being nurturing, understanding, inclusive, teaching, non-judgmental—mesh perfectly with the traditional notion of a supportive, helpful woman. Moreover, these traits are in striking contrast with traits of male leaders. Employees who are happy with their female bosses criticized males as more critical, less understanding about family issues, more likely to berate and assign blame, and more directive.

Many women say that because of their supportive approach, they get a better performance from their subordinates. One woman said that because she is inclusive, associates who work with her develop their skills more and are more likely to pitch in when there's a crisis. Says another woman about her secretary, "I actually got more out of her by being a friend than otherwise. I can remember only acting like the boss one time—she had a conflict in her personal life, and I said, 'This work has to get out, you can't go home [until it's finished].'" A woman in Oregon remarks, "I have a very good relationship with my secretary and always have. My secretary considers herself to be my friend, but even though she's my friend, she works very hard. And she knows that that's her job, and our friendship doesn't make her lax."

Pitfalls of Nice

So nice looks like a pretty good approach. But what are its pitfalls? This narrow corridor, that so many women feel forced to walk and where many men out of good intentions join them, has obstacles. Chief among them is that celebrating this approach only puts women back in their traditional box, reinforcing expectations that this is the way woman should act.

A more practical disadvantage for supportive managers is that they often find that people don't do their work, or do it on a casual schedule, after they complete other assignments, reasoning that the "nice" person will understand and not give them a hard time.[11] The managers have gotten too friendly, and the secretary or associate or paralegal's performance slacks off. For women attorneys especially, friendship with underlings limits their repertoire of managerial techniques.

"I'm in my office, frantically trying to finish up a memo," one associate gripes, "and my secretary wanders in, plops down, and starts telling me about what she did over the weekend. I can't keep her out of my office." A female partner in Philadelphia says:

> When people are working for me as well as male partners, my work is more likely to get pushed aside and not prioritized. I do the work myself instead. Now how passive is that? I should affirmatively let others do things, but if someone gives me a draft of a brief, I will frequently just do it all myself, then get stuck doing the table of authorities, rather than throwing it back on their desk.

---

[11] A female CEO in one article said: "When I first came here, last year . . . I would say 'Good morning' and leave my door open and talk to my assistants. I soon realized, 'They think they can get away with stuff because I don't act like a dictator.' I realized after the first month that I had to make sure that people understood that I meant what I said." Ken Auletta, "In the Company of Women," The New Yorker, 76 (April 20, 1998).

She says this is because she has problems giving direct, critical feedback to others:

> I have female friends who don't have any problem criticizing people. Maybe it's a more prominent problem with women. It's a non-confrontational thing for me. The con to this approach is that you are doing nonsense yourself, the pro is that I avoid that uncomfortable time period of telling someone that they've screwed up. I think, "Maybe my instruction was incorrect."

Women say they find it hard to move from a friendly, informal relationship to a chillier one motivated by disappointment in a poor performance. They describe having worked hard to build up a positive relationship, a "marriage" of equals, only to feel that they have to "break up" with the subordinate person and establish a different tone. As one woman pointed out, "Personal friendships are a double-edged sword. The person in charge will go the extra mile, but if something's wrong, it's a lot harder to give negative feedback." Female supervisory style has been interpreted as weakness, a lack of importance and heft in the managerial structure. Women wind up resentfully doing work themselves that by any logic someone else should do.

Another pitfall to nice is that those who are playing a motherly role can find that it takes too much time and emotional investment. The woman above who described herself as the "frigging firm mom" goes on to add:

> I'm sick of it. It drives me crazy after a while. Over the last seven years, there have been lots of personal issues—houses burned, lots of deaths, old relatives with problems. I'm too tired to take care of people.

Backing off from this available, sympathetic role is difficult.

Yet another concern is that an inclusive style sometimes is viewed as weakness. Men in particular may think that asking for input reflects indecision, not creative leadership. Consultant Ida Abbott says:

> Sometimes women may have a hard time. They tend to have a more collaborative style, and so men looking at that style sometimes see them as indecisive, or as not firm enough. If you're the kind of woman who likes to be direct, it can be frustrating. So sometimes women are misunderstood. They're seen as not being strong enough

because they don't fit the traditional mold. They're not giving orders or making the decisions for people. They're getting decisions made, but sometimes they do it indirectly.

However, males report that they experience the same problems with a low-key approach to management as do women. A partner on the East Coast complains frequently to others about his dissatisfaction with people's performances for him—they don't meet deadlines, they do his work after that of others—but he has trouble communicating this directly to the laggards, unwilling to violate his established "nice guy" image. Jerome, a West Coast male associate, says:

> Male or female, a person who's senior who invokes a little bit of fear is likely to get a lot more work done for them, as opposed to someone who is low key or soft spoken. They're more concerned about keeping the hard ass happy. Men who are inclined to jump up and down and scream will get more work done. I'm a very senior associate. Notwithstanding that, [more junior associates] are also not as inclined to do my work before other people's, because they're making sure that people who are more hard-edged are being satisfied. Sometimes it makes me want to change my style. If I don't figure out a way to have a better motivating tool, I end up having to do all the work myself, which doesn't make me very happy. I end up feeling resentful.

All these factors—boxing women into a traditional stereotype, poor performance, misplaced priorities for time spent—cause nice managers to rethink and adapt their style. They assume that the only way to get approval from others is by being nice, but also conclude that an easygoing managerial style can result in lackluster performance, depriving the workplace and clients of efficiently completed, superior work product.

Getting Beyond Nice

Therefore, many lawyers, especially women, must determine how to get beyond nice. It's not easy. Women think their dilemma is tougher than men's, because they feel they have fewer alternative options. A mild-mannered guy, they figure, could just elect to be demanding and get away with it.

So the nurturing managers have to be more inventive. Some continue with an inclusive approach but avoid or indirectly penalize the people who won't do the work. Says one female partner: "My reaction when I have worked with people, male and female, whose work is less than satisfactory, I have a very difficult time. I will avoid that person in the future and just fix it myself."

Jerome, the senior associate quoted above as resentful about having to pick up the slack of more junior associates who don't take him seriously, gets the message of dissatisfaction across, but very indirectly:

> I've been ignored more than a time or two for no real compelling reason. I just cease trying to interact with that person. My approach is not to yell and scream and put the fear of God in them, but I seem to harbor, I won't say resentment, but I have a vindictive side to me. I'm passive/aggressive. I don't give feedback directly to junior associates, I give it to the partner, who then feeds it back.

A woman delivers critical feedback to her secretary in a measured, softened way:

> I'm not straightforward about problems when she's made a mistake. I'll do it more subtly, I'll just hand it back and say you did the wrong heading, but I try and do it in a way that's not confrontational, where she gets the point but I'm not scolding her. I'm frustrated that I can't just be more direct.

Others take more of a middle-of-the-road approach, managing their relationships more decisively to balance "nice" and getting the work done. A frequent approach is one of alternating roles and styles. For instance, with staff who are getting too cozy, some managers respond by putting bright lines around their relationship, keeping the door closed when they have to get work done, and then devoting specific times, such as first thing in the morning, to chat with their secretaries. A female partner says:

> You have to decide how friendly you are going to get. You can be friends, but there has to be a line drawn so that you don't get too close, so that you back up and keep it professional when you want to. It's hard to do. There are times when I act friendly, then I act professional. Then my secretary will act professional toward me. We turn it on and off.

Another approach is to be friendly but flash hints of steel. A Florida in-house woman says:

> I think most people here consider me to be very affable, I'm a greeter, I really interact with people, I just always have a smile on my face. But I'm very firm when I need to be. My tone changes significantly. I'm terse, that friendliness disappears. The pace of my speech is slower, it's very effective only because it really throws people off, because it's so inconsistent. So it's rare that I have to use it. I learned within a very brief period of time that I had to do something, because for women who prefer the style of being "nice," there's a perception of weakness. In preliminary conversations with lawyers, if I'm nice or accommodating and allow them an extension, people try to take advantage of that. That's when I make it clear. I'll say, "You might be perceiving my being accommodating as my being weak, but that's not the case." Once you do that—and it's just brief—you're alerting the person that they've misinterpreted.

A New York in-house female also gets cool when things get hot:

> Sometimes people say, "You obviously don't know what you're talking about," or "If you knew about numbers you wouldn't say that." I've had this issue with colleagues, and I usually call them on it. If someone has a patronizing attitude, I usually call a spade a spade. And I try without raising my voice to say, "Look, you can either choose to be patronizing and we can stop the discussion right now, or you can help me out." It also happens in negotiations, where the other side raises his voice, and you wonder if he does it because he's a man and he thinks he'll intimidate me. The more he yells or screams, the quieter I become. I'll say, "I won't stay on the phone with you if you use that tone of voice." They usually back down. They realize that you're not a fool.

Some deliberately cultivate a frostier manner. One young woman switched her approach because of a timely tip from a colleague:

> It was hard for me to assert authority at the beginning, which is funny because I don't come across as the nicest person in world. I come across as assertive, but supervising made me nervous. I was very concerned with wanting people to like me, and trying to be helpful. I

wanted to be the senior associate whom junior associates would like. That didn't go over well at all. I got no respect. I tried to be too nice. A guy I worked for said to me, "You know, you try too hard to get people to like you and you're trying to be too nice. Nobody's going to respond to you. Look at how June [pointing out another woman] responds to people. I don't want to use the word bitch, but she's a little bitchy, she's straightforward and cold." I did that and he was absolutely right. People responded to me, they actually did the work, they didn't blow me off. From then on, I would be friendly when they came into the office, but with an assignment, I was much colder than my first instinct.

She fostered what some might describe as a more masculine approach, less personal and more directive, to transmit a sense of urgency and get things done.

Others back off when they first work with a new secretary or a new associate, forewarned by experience, and start over with a more distant attitude. Some abandon office intimacy entirely after getting poor results. One man in his late thirties, who has had five secretaries in his career, previously had been open and talkative, learning about his secretaries' personal lives and generally playing a kind role. He wasn't happy with their performances. Now he says, "My present secretary, I *think* she has kids, but I'm not sure. I know very little about her, and she's been my secretary for five years." And the performance is much better, he says.

Finally, there are women who unapologetically take a straightforward approach and don't genuflect to the "nice" expectations. One woman, a family lawyer in the Southwest whose firm has many women partners, states:

We are more in the old tradition than the new wave of kinder and gentler. We are very Type A, we work a lot of hours, we expect a lot from our employees. We don't have anybody that works part time. We have ten times more people who would like to work for our firm than we have places. We have a lot more business than we've got time to handle.

A thirty-six-year-old female partner in a Midwestern big firm advises, "I would say to women—you have to be perceived as somebody who can take it, you have to have really thick skin, you have to be tough." A female judge has made peace on this point:

> I've been called a mean judge, a hard judge, by rumors and that kind of thing. It doesn't bother me. I think I am mean, and I think I should be, and I have no concerns about that. If they don't do what they're supposed to, there are consequences.

These techniques reflect everything from simple avoidance to delicate maneuvering to more straightforward styles. That so many of the approaches are finely detailed and calculated reflects the enormous challenge women face asserting authority without alienating people. They feel greater discomfort playing a variety of roles within the workplace—ranging from friend to lenient supervisor to taskmaster—when some of those roles stray too far from accepted norms. Females who are inclined to a "nice" style have had to learn, step by step, the management lessons that are more easily available to men, who have been able to absorb instruction by watching mentors and role models through the ages. It is one of many examples of women going through the difficult process of becoming comfortable with power and leadership.

For the women who elect a more masculine approach, though, a new abyss opens up.

The Scary Woman

Being nurturing and supportive in the workplace is one approach to leadership and management. The opposite method is to be aggressive, traditionally masculine, and ambitious. But there's little question that this "choice" is a much more comfortable one for men than for women.

Across the board, men and women condemn highly ambitious, determined females in the workplace, especially those who scream and bully.[12] What is it, exactly, that so offends people about striving females? In my interviews, respondents complained that aggressive females overcompensate,

---

[12] Studies show negative reactions from both women and men when women act assertively. Virginia Valian, *Why So Slow? The Advancement of Women,* at p. 129 (MIT Press, 1998). Valian writes further that a "meta-analysis of studies . . . suggests that women are at a particular disadvantage when their leadership style is perceived as masculine. . . . Having a style that is assertive to the point of appearing autocratic, rather than cooperative and participative, is especially costly for a woman." *Id.* at p. 133. At the same time, she notes, "it is also true that the more a woman is perceived as a woman the less likely it is that she will be perceived as professionally competent. . . . The qualities required of leaders and those required for femininity are at odds with each other." *Id.* at p. 136.

display free-floating, personalized anger, are inflexible and insular, and at times just scary. A female former practicing lawyer recalls that outspoken women stood out:

> Very few local female attorneys gave me any trouble, but the handful who did were worse than the men: rude, uncompromising, stupid, obstructive, and wasteful of everyone's time and money. The pendulum had swung. They were trying to prove themselves. They went much too far.

A fifty-six-year-old male partner in a small New England firm is irked by a lack of flexibility:

> The female lawyers that I find to be the most successful and professional are those who don't try to overcompensate. I have seen situations with women lawyers who absolutely come on very strong and won't be flexible. They never can get to that point. The ones who are most successful are those that can act like one of the guys. They don't have an axe to grind, don't have a chip on their shoulders, they don't feel that they need to overcompensate. There's a lawyer in town who's good, but she overcompensates, she's got a mouth like a truck driver. Sometimes I want to say that it's not necessary for every word out of your mouth to be a curse. This is going too far.

Many say female partners in law firms are overly intense and angry. A female senior associate in a New York City firm says:

> Female partners, they are too strident. They just err on the side of being bitches from hell. That's their idea of manifesting power. I think that these women are thinking, "I should lead with my fist pounding on my desk."

Jim, a West Coast attorney, says:

> I think that I find some of the intense women I know tend to kind of personalize their anger more. That's why they're feared more. The anger seems to be directed not at the situation, but at the person.

And some said these women were insular, working intensively alone and being self-promoting, rather than promoting others as well. An in-house female lawyer in New Jersey described a more senior colleague:

> Everyone, male and female, does not like to report to her. They think that she's very aggressive, extremely ambitious. She works every single night, eats dinner in her office every single night, is rude and sort of blunt with the client and with the other attorneys, particularly ones who work for her. The ones who work for her, she never gives them credit.

Others complained that older women actively worked against more junior women, seemingly because they were threatened. A woman in the Southwest reports:

> What ultimately killed me at [my old firm] were two older female attorneys. I'm not even sure I understand all of that. They really disliked me. Neither one got married, neither had children. And I suspect that they went through so much personal pain, and I don't look like a lawyer, so they just resented me and everything about me.

People aren't just offended by this behavior—they're frightened. Jim, the West Coast attorney, says:

> As between an aggressive woman versus an aggressive man, I think that the woman is more feared. One woman here was happy to learn that associates were afraid of her, she used to tell me that. She wanted power. It could be that it's such a contrast with the stereotypical woman. I guess I do feel like there's more of a willingness to go back in the face of the angry man than the angry woman. People avoid the conflict with the angry woman. It's too unpleasant, too scary.

Lynn, a former practicing lawyer, is impatient with bullying women who reinforce what she considers to be a discredited management style:

> When I do meet women who try to bring down the hammer, it makes me crazy, whereas if I meet a man who does that, I think that I don't really respect him but I will probably still work with him, because in some ways I think to myself, "That's just especially a man of a particular age, that's how a man asserts authority." I'm less tolerant of a

woman doing that, they should know better than that. That is what
women have said they chafe under, they want to have freedom.
When I see women trying to emulate that style, it drives me nuts.

Lynn's words suggest that women's aggressive behavior is illegitimate, that
they should "know better," that they are automatically cast as reformers who
should want to change things rather than simply adopt the worst of men's
habits. The reaction is, "Who does she think she is?" Determined ambition
and power-seeking behavior contrast starkly with fixed stereotypes of the
caring, eager-to-please female. And women in particular are put off by
super-ambitious women, in part because women assume they are all equals,
as discussed early in the chapter. So when a woman acts overauthoritative,
other women see her as imperious, making an illegitimate grab for power
with a brazen and defiant challenge to established norms.

Another theory is that women react negatively to outspoken females due to
envy. They may wish they had the courage—or felt they had permission—to
say what they think, rather than having to defer or soften their responses. A
psychologist in Washington, D.C., Dr. Ron Kimball, comments, "They may see
a personality that they would have liked to express, and are angry about it."

At this early stage in the open expression of female authority, there are still
relatively few models for hierarchical women except mothers and teachers.
Take the remark of a college-age female basketball player, talking about her
preference for a male coach: "You might respect more what's coming out of
a man's mouth about basketball. . . . The only woman yelling at me is my
mom. . . . That's the way I'd like to keep it."[13] (That the image of "mother"
here is so unflattering—the nagging shrew—should be contrasted with a discussion in Chapter 8, which deals with the contradiction between the
stereotype of soft, nurturing images of motherhood, on the one hand, and
professionalism, on the other.)

The Unloved Woman

Very ambitious women usually succeed handsomely in their careers. Like
their male counterparts, they work very hard, bring in business, are

---

[13] Jere Longman, "Debating the Male Coach's Role," The New York Times, at D5 (Mar. 29,
2002).

supremely dedicated, and otherwise fulfill the requirements for success. However, because their behavior is perceived so negatively, they pay for it dearly in other ways that men don't. An entire infrastructure marginalizes and demonizes those women, to make sense of what is still considered unusual, almost bizarre behavior.

Most significantly, people just don't like them. As sociolinguist Deborah Tannen writes: "[W]omen in positions of authority face a special challenge. Our expectations for how a person in authority should behave are at odds with our expectations for how a woman should behave. If a woman talks in ways expected of women, she is more likely to be liked than respected. If she talks in ways expected of men, she is more likely to be respected than liked."[14]

This personal rejection takes many forms. A woman with a hard-hitting personality is universally labeled a "bitch," a hostile slap of a word. (There is no one epithet for hostile men, and a common term such as "bastard" has some positive connotations of the warrior who fights for his clients.) Colleagues trade snide assumptions about the supposed reasons for female aggressive behavior ("She doesn't have a sex life," or "She has no husband or children"). As one man observes:

> Something I found interesting—and other women have said this—if you're a woman and you make it, then you must be a really unhappy person, your kids hate you, you're lonely. I was talking to a woman [associate] the other day, and she said, "There's not one woman partner whose life I'd like to have." I think there's nothing really different about their lives, but these women are perceived as unhappy. Men wouldn't be considered as unhappy.

Some women said that, because of negative encounters they have had with other women, they prefer working with male lawyers. A female associate who works in real estate in Chicago comments:

---

[14] Deborah Tannen, *Talking from 9 to 5: Women and Men in the Workplace: Language, Sex and Power,* at p. 202 (Morrow/Avon Books, 1994).

> I have to tell you, I like dealing with men a lot of times more than with women. I'll deal with other women lawyers, and for some reason I find they have a chip on their shoulder—as in, be rude. Rude to get what they want. "This is my position and I'm sticking with it," as opposed to a lot of guys who are just easier to deal with. I have no problem dealing with men.

These are ways to make sense of an aberrant person, one who doesn't fit neatly into accepted stereotypes. If she can be explained away, she can be taken less seriously, especially if she is critical of a colleague's performance. Dr. Ellen Ostrow, a D.C.-based psychologist and coach to attorneys, talks about the difference between reactions to ambitious men versus aggressive women:

> On an emotional level, people respond with equal aversion. But I think that the ways in which people cope with it differs, if it comes from a man or a woman. It's easier for men to make themselves feel better by being globally pejorative about the woman than about the man. There are ways in which women are written off, which usually have to do with, "She hasn't gotten laid recently," a lot of very demeaning ways of thinking about the person. If [a woman] treats you [in an aggressive manner], a typical coping method is to reduce the power of the message. It seems more difficult to do that with powerful men than with powerful women.

The result is that people can more easily rationalize away the anger and aggression of a woman than that of a man. Jeannine, a female partner in a Michigan firm, recounts a story about a young male who tried to take advantage of "the bitch rationale" to divert attention from his poor performance:

> A male associate hired last year was supposed to be my backup. He came in somewhat arrogant, and didn't want to listen, and didn't want to incorporate stuff, he just thought he should be able to do what I do the first day out. I began to supervise him and mentor him and found that he wasn't up to par, that his research skills were not tracking, and I wasn't happy with his work. I think he tried the bitch rationale, where he would say, "Jeannine's just hard to get along with, she doesn't tell me what she needs." That worked until others started giving him work.

> He thought it was all my fault, but other [supervising lawyers] had the
> same issue. He just would not accept it. He's leaving now.

Because of their visceral dislike for women who are intense and pushy, people devise ways to obviate their importance or merit.

This controversy over aggressive women versus aggressive men uncovers another genderation gap. The first generation of women who entered the law shared the characteristics of trailblazers everywhere: they were quirky, ambitious, thick-skinned mavericks, different sorts of people. A male in a Southwestern firm says:

> When I started practicing, the big rap was all women lawyers are a
> bunch of bitches. Men made no qualms about it. And I've got to say
> there was a little bit to it. Maybe it was because only the aggressive
> women were coming in. It seems to be different now. There are definitely still people like that.

Indeed, some younger men see a limited number of "types" among the older women in their firms. Says Jim, the West Coast partner:

> I do think when I look at older women in law firms, I mostly feel sad
> for them in some ways. Because I feel like there are two types that
> have succeeded. One is sort of super hyper-aggressive, very male but
> more so, real intensely aggressive, kind of a nasty personality, that is
> feared in law firms. There's a lot of those. Or there's the perennially
> moderate, wishy-washy, milquetoasty kind of woman, who may do
> well because she doesn't offend anyone. She may be very bright, but
> she's not going to rock any boat in any way ever. These women either
> had to fly under the radar and be the nice daughter, or be this kind
> of feared intense type that nobody wants to offend, and therefore
> they succeeded for those reasons.

Regardless of how many "types" there are among older women attorneys, there's little question that the range of styles has expanded along with the sheer numbers of women. Currently, with 50% of many law school classes being female, it is no longer a novelty for women to become lawyers. Jim goes on:

When I look at my own generation of women lawyers, which is younger, I see a much broader range of personalities, [which is] completely acceptable at this stage. The first ones were warriors or they were brilliant political strategists.

It turns out it's hard for a woman to "act like a man." It appears angry and scary, provoking intense dislike and social rejection, as well as hostile rationalizing about the reasons for such behavior. Such conduct strays too far from stereotypically female actions.

Evolving Styles

When aggressive women respond to negative reactions they receive at work, some of their management styles evolve as a result of the women's own observations, coaching, or even therapy. Some talked about how their style changed, such as the following female partner on the East Coast:

I have evolved in my criticism style. I used to criticize more directly, which was less productive. When I was just starting out I would say, "You really did that the wrong way and I'm not happy about it." And now I try to engage in much more constructive criticism designed to encourage people to want to do a better job next time. Now I would say, "Let's think about an alternative way of doing that the next time, and do you think that's a good idea, too?" [The more direct approach] wasn't working as well. I didn't want to be viewed as the enemy. I want them to want to win my approval but not fear screwing up.

Others say they want to be tough but believe they need to soften up at times. A New Jersey woman, who is six feet tall with a firm voice and handshake, has grappled with feedback that she's overly direct and intimidating:

I don't perceive myself as intimidating. I'm sincerely a little quizzical. I just don't understand. But sometimes the world works better with indirection. I realize there's a lot I have to learn about how to do things in an indirect manner.

She contrasts herself with another aggressive woman who has been well-received, perhaps in part because the latter has a softer, high-pitched voice. "Sometimes the manner of presentation of women makes people more comfortable. People feel less threatened."

139

Another woman claims, "I don't act like a woman in the workplace, like a typical woman. I don't take crap from people. I have a hard time kissing ass." For instance, a male client sent her an abusive letter, demanding something immediately. She wrote him back a curt note rejecting his demand but suggesting some alternatives. "I do not take any shit from him, so he treats me with respect," she says. But even this no-nonsense woman observes, "I think being a more typical kind of acquiescent, subservient woman works better with some men."

Some people described ambitious women who made themselves welcome by showcasing other traits. A West Coast male lawyer worked with a driven woman in another firm:

> Her personality type is a masterful people person; you turn her loose
> at a cocktail party and she'll romance a room. She's got great humor,
> does really well with juries. She has very successful, finely honed abil-
> ities to work people and it's impressive.

A woman who now works in-house described a woman at her former law firm who is an "extremely ambitious and driven partner." But, she says, "People like her because she's nice looking, a sharp dresser, she's funny. These are compensating characteristics for the fact that she's kind of like a barracuda. She's not like a mean person." A D.C. recruiter, when asked to describe aggressive women who were well-liked, said:

> They are all to a person very feminine, in the classic characterization.
> They have been able to blend traditional female qualities of listening,
> a demonstration of care about their clients, about their colleagues, a
> sense of approachability, a sense of willingness to mentor others, but
> they have a firmness that comes across. They know their stuff cold,
> but they're not harsh in the delivery. They can be the tough taskmas-
> ter and the bet-the-company kind of litigator, be in your face, but it's
> not for sport.

Many lawyers act as change agents or coaches to help others shape more successful work personas. A West Coast male partner talks about counseling a young, go-getter female in the firm:

> Probably my closest friend in this firm is a very aggressive woman. I
> have coached her on not becoming [like another woman in the firm

who is considered hostile]. Having some humor is really very helpful if you are an intense, aggressive person. I would say, "When having strong feelings about things, including failings, try not to seem to be angry at people personally. Try to control the venting of personalized, directed, focused anger." I think people react badly to that from any-one, and I guess my own maybe sexist view is that it's more com-mon that when it comes from women, it is received very negatively by people. Don't be utterly disparaging of the person's abilities. Try not to act too much in the heat of the moment.

His advice is to be realistic about how angry women are perceived and to tone down anger so that it is more acceptable in the workplace.

For those with more serious issues, problems with workplace style can prompt them to take courses to mold their behavior or to undertake therapy. There are conferences and courses specifically intended to help aggressive women modulate their behaviors.[15] Therapists and psychologists urge adopt-ing techniques that can better manage anger or hostility. Dr. Ron Kimball counsels aggressive people to state their reactions in less hostile, overtly angry ways. For instance, saying, "You're always doing this to me. I really hate it. It makes me so angry," is alienating. Instead, Kimball advises, "Be more thoughtful, like, 'I was thinking about the way you said that to me yes-terday, and I was uncomfortable with it. Is there a way we can talk about it so we communicate better so you get what you want and I'm more com-fortable?' It's playing around with style."

Part of the problem with some people, notes psychologist/coach Dr. Ellen Ostrow, is that they are trying on a new aggressive style in reaction to being too passive in the past, and they sometimes overdo it. They sound "unmod-ulated because they're anxious," Ostrow declares:

---

[15] Many consultants and training programs assume that the most helpful approach is to conform to society's expectations and help women work within traditional stereotypes. Neela Banerjee, "Some 'Bullies' Seek Ways to Soften Up," The New York Times, at C1 (Aug. 10, 2001). One study reports: "Current approaches designed to help women move up the hierar-chy usually focus on helping women to find ways to adapt and blend in rather than speak out and find their own voice." Judith G. Oakley, "Gender-Based Barriers to Senior Management Positions: Understanding the Scarcity of Female CEOs," J. Bus. Ethics, at 321 (Oct. 2000).

> They're focused on getting it out and not on the audience. So there's no finesse. [The woman] also is struggling within this system herself, so I'm sure that affects her behavior, there's been a self-conscious-ness throughout her career, that the equivalent male has not had to deal with. You probably see less of her warm side, because it's not congruent with being successful. [You can] deliver the exact same message with a different facial expression and a different voice and a whole different manner.

She points out that an "assertive" style can be acceptable, but that too much aggressiveness is what alienates people. She relates, "I work with women on forming alliances with men as a way to address this. When you have that kind of a support base you have a lot more maneuverability. You have some-body in the locker room who can say, 'No, she's not a bitch.'" If there is a variety of data available in the workplace about a particular woman, posi-tive information can counteract negative forces.

Although an aggressive woman may be successful, she may be informal-ly rejected, sometimes leading to attempts to recast her personality and approach.

The Ambitious Man

The equivalent male, however, doesn't confront the same opposition. Driven men, even "screamers," get far more latitude for their behavior. Colleagues offer excuses and compensatory reasons for their striving, bully-ing, or obnoxiousness ("He has a bad temper but can be very charismatic," "He brings in a ton of business."). As a fifty-one-year-old male partner in the South notes:

> An aggressive man is never going to be viewed as bitchy. He may be viewed as obnoxious and egocentric and egotistical, but none of those carry quite the connotation of being labeled bitchy. It just isn't the same. And there are some pretty obnoxious guys out there.

For instance, within the same workplace, people frequently approve take-charge behavior in a man while criticizing a high-flying female. John, who has left the practice of law, said of his former big firm in D.C.:

> What's approved behavior brings up two different questions. One question is whether a person is approved for advancement and making partner, and the other question is social approval. There were women who did well but were just despised. And I think I would say that the same personality in a man was not nearly as despised. There were many more male partners who were just complete jerks, and people kind of laughed it off a little bit.

Contrasting two aggressive lawyers in his firm, one male and one female, a New York lawyer observes:

> He does more of the male-speak, it's not emotional. He fits in with the guys: "Aw, that's bullshit, that's a bunch of crap, fuck this," that type of stuff. I think it's a personality issue. They like the guy and they didn't like the woman. Even though in many ways in terms of skill, ability, and what they were doing they were very similar. I'm sympathetic to her but I can also understand that if you're working with her she can be a pain in the ass. The guy is not perceived as a pain in the ass. He's a good, hard-working lawyer who will defend a client vigorously.

Working with these ultrapowerful men can be a quick ladder to success. One in-house woman described a man who "people didn't like to work for, but he was one of the people where if he liked you, your career was made." She summed up, "You wanted to work for him but you didn't want to work for him." These men, in her view, are viewed as "tough but really nice," meaning they are tough on the people who work for them but willing to share credit and promote them so that they advance.

Although colleagues don't like aggressive behavior in males (indeed, may abhor it), that behavior is merely a stretch from "normal" male behavior, and so it is deemed excusable or understandable. As Jan and Toni, quoted earlier in the chapter, put it, they deferred to men's bad behavior because men have "always done it" and "need to do that," and "that's how a man asserts authority." It suggests that the men almost can't help themselves and therefore can't be blamed or held accountable for their behavior.

There are also many examples of hierarchical males for other men to model themselves after. A male partner in a New York firm says:

It may be that there's an easier stereotype for men to fall into. There's a longer history. Probably somewhere in the back of my mind, in how I comport myself at work, I probably have an image of watching my father [who is a lawyer] at work, or watching television shows, or movies, and having a better sense that culturally it's a better defined role to play.

But it's not as if men have a totally free ride on the management train, now that there are so many women around. As Chapter 3 on sexuality explored, an entire universe of open behavior based on off-color jokes and assumptions about female availability in the workplace has radically shrunk due to sexual harassment laws.

And men have some other supervisory issues. One woman talks about the male supervising partner at a litigation department where she formerly worked:

It was like one of those battered women syndrome things. He was a big shot who took a liking to me. He talked me up to everyone and said how wonderful I was and how smart I was. Then he would call me on a Friday and say he needed a memo on Sunday morning—who needs anything on a Sunday morning?—and I'd kill myself all weekend. After the fact he would rave about me and say how wonderful I was. He would abuse you in the beginning but he was very good at giving positive feedback after the fact. It was like an ego stroking and of course you would like it. And you would give up your weekend for him.

A young woman in the Southwest has a similar story:

The main partner, this is going to sound weird, but he and I had a "battered wife" syndrome. He would make me feel like the most brilliant lawyer on the face of the earth. I'd get notes from him, "This is fantastic work, I'm so proud of you." The very next day he would call me into his office and would make me feel as small as a mouse. My self-esteem would plummet so far. That, in combination with the other factors, made me leave. When I told him I was leaving he literally begged me to stay. I said, "You don't like me, I wouldn't do what you wanted," and he said, "That's why I like you." And that's part of the battered wife syndrome. He was literally almost in tears. He said,

"I thought we had a relationship, a trust between us, you have come so far and I spent so much time training you and teaching you." It was like I was breaking up with someone. It was bizarre.

Even though abusive bosses are hardly news, men who are abusive towards females can be perceived more like abusive husbands, with echoes of dependency, the cycle of abuse and making up, and hostile sexual overtones.

Less egregious but considered "borderline," are men who maintain control over females in a way that seems unnecessary. A woman in New England told about a partner who did "belittling" things to a female associate, such as calling her into meetings where she had no real function:

She would just be there, and it was infuriating to her. He would be having a conference call for two hours and she never would be called upon to do anything. "I can make you sit here," seemed to be his angle. It wasn't textbook harassment, but another form of abusive behavior.

A female in New York says:

This partner used to sit me down, forced me to sit down and stay seated until he was finished with me. He would take a phone call and make me sit there. There's another woman in the firm; he does the same thing. He belittles us. We're mature women. It was borderline abusive.

A female partner in New England says that men don't understand that their style can be too "rough and tumble" with females:

They don't recognize the reaction that they're getting on the other end. They just have no clue that they're really intimidating. They get people very upset, very angry. They don't work through those issues well. Their style is curt, abrupt, with tough interactions. They don't realize that people shut down on them, then they don't get the best performance. Women sometimes are crushed. The men have no idea, they're accustomed to yelling. They figure that people get over it. I've had no yelling women colleagues. The guys are bullying, they think it's an effective management style. It's really not. We've had to work harder with several of the male attorneys to help them understand these things.

Her firm had success in dealing with one of the bullies, a male in his mid-thirties:

> He came out of a big firm, and I suspect that was the environment he grew up in. He had a strong sense of pecking order, and if someone was below him, he would yell at them. I would find people with their doors closed, mostly women, in tears. He had no idea of the havoc he was wreaking, because that was how he had been treated. So we had a lot of meetings with him. We said, "We are not going to let you yell at anybody. We are not going to let you try to intimidate." It took about a year. His reaction initially was surprise. He didn't realize that he had left in his wake this emotional havoc. Finally he recognized that it was not acceptable.

She tried doing some fixing on the other end as well, reasoning with offended women about their reactions:

> I would find out someone was in tears, I would go in and tell them, "You're taking it far more personally than it was offered. You've got to understand the personality of this guy. Men like that get upset, they blow up, and generally afterwards they may feel bad but they won't say anything. You've just got to do the same thing. It doesn't mean you have to like it."

Another issue is how older males supervise young females. One approach is to adopt a father-daughter interaction, which fits a familiar template over a new relationship and tends to limit rumors (as explored in Chapter 3 on sexuality).

This relationship is considered harmless or even beneficial for women, allowing them a safe relationship with an older, experienced male lawyer without sexual overtones. However, it has some disadvantages. "They call someone a girl," says a senior litigation associate, "and say something about a nice dress, give you a big kiss to congratulate you for being pregnant." Said another woman: "They were always asking, 'How's your love life?' or 'Who are you dating? We've got to get you married off.'" A senior associate remarks, "I find that as a thirty-something woman, I am much more forgiving of the statements of older guys. I don't bristle at their remarks, whereas if it were a peer, I'd think, are you kidding me?" Many young women are willing to put up with some of this awkwardness in order to get good assignments and the other benefits of working with powerful partners.

Others say this syndrome is unfair to both male and female lawyers. For instance, they noted that a paternalistic attitude towards women (which assumes that women are weaker and need to be protected) can be coupled with a harsher attitude towards male lawyers (who presumably don't need such cosseting). In one firm, said a female associate, "A few partners treated male associates horribly, but had that father-daughter relationship with the women. They almost treated women better than men."

Sometimes bad treatment of the males is not rejection but actually makes them part of the "club." A woman who worked in a government office says about her supervisor:

> He treated the women better. Maybe he was a gentleman, he was much more reluctant to bawl out or abuse a female staff member, but the men complained about being abused and belittled and treated badly. Mostly he liked what I did. One or two times I could tell he wasn't completely satisfied, but he would point out something in a subtle way. Whereas a guy in my office would say, "He blasted me." The flip side is, you're not quite one of the guys. You'd never get in all the way and be buddy-buddy. I was glad I wasn't being abused, but you also think he wasn't being as straight with you as with a guy on his staff.

Some men want to work with women more than with men. A fourth-year associate talked about a male partner who openly proclaimed, "I prefer to work with women." Her analysis: "He's a very egomaniacal person, and may feel threatened by another man. Women are not as threatening; maybe they're softer and he likes that." The result, according to the associate, was that "he was rotten to the men. He was beaten down as an associate and had a hazing attitude towards the males." A male associate told a similar story about one department in a Midwestern firm:

> The lead partner is a man, and he's one of the most powerful partners in the firm. He's very, very demanding of his associates. He has gone through three or four male associates and discarded them immediately and has continued with his two female associates. I questioned one of the people who were sent to another department, and this one who did not succeed suggested it was because the male

partner felt threatened by men but not women, in terms of taking away clients and things like that. The man gets one or two shots to screw up and the women get more.

Another frequent syndrome was with white males who prefer to supervise black females rather than black males. An African-American female who is in-house in Florida says:

I've observed it outside of my personal workplace. I've seen it in courtrooms, hearings and so forth. I can only tell you that is a common perception. And for some reason I hear a lot of African-American male lawyers say that they find white men are very intimidated by them, there's almost this very aggressive stance that's taken in interacting with them.

A black male observes:

White male partners give black females better work assignments, they will be more willing to take them under their wings, in a protective capacity—to feel that they're doing something good, an honorable chore, like they should get some medal for doing this thing. At least include me on some of these things. White male partners are more comfortable with black female associates than males, because of ignorance and believing a stereotype of fear. In my experience, it all comes down to power. And power on a number of levels: money, intelligence, perceived intelligence. The bottom line is almost the caveman mentality as to who can beat up whom.

It should be emphasized that, despite this perception, black women and other minority women fare worse than their male counterparts in the workplace. As Professor David Wilkins of Harvard Law School found in a 2000 survey he conducted of black Harvard Law School graduates, the black women were significantly less likely to be equity partners in law firms or general counsels in corporations than their male counterparts, and they earn substantially less money, even controlling for age and employment setting.[16]

---

[16] Professor Wilkins's survey revealed that, among 1980s Harvard Law School black graduates in private practice, 74% of men are equity partners compared to 48% of women.

Indeed, women of color have the lowest law firm retention rate of any group.[17]

Although men have a larger toolbox to select from in their leadership and management styles, and their "normal" personality and attributes more easily align with traditional leadership traits, they still face challenges because of the greater presence of women in the workplace.

Re-Drawing the Borders

The options for leadership styles have expanded for males but remain restricted for females. Because of management trends and other social dynamics, there's more freedom for men to act compassionate, inclusive, and "feminine" than there used to be. The "organization man," featuring top-down, strictly hierarchical behavior, is not as common as he used to be. However popular the more inclusive management style might be, though, males still retain permission to revert to hierarchical behavior.

But management options for women are limited to the channel between too aggressive and too passive. And the nice approach is not bad—it's a perfectly acceptable mode of engagement. What's difficult is the assumption that a woman will act a particular way because she's a woman, and that there aren't similar expectations for men. A woman has fewer tricks up her sleeve when things go wrong with the nice approach. It's a trap: the management literature says it's good, you get lots of positive reinforcement, then you're stuck once again in the same ideological rut.

As a result, the double bind for women—trying to balance "nice," on the one hand, and "authoritative," on the other—has loosened only a little. Women (and the fewer men who adopt this approach) definitely experience success as nice managers, but have far more trouble when their approach

---

Similarly, of black graduates in corporate law departments, 67% of men have attained the rank of general counsel as compared to only 13% of women. Finally, black male graduates from the 1980s who are in private practice earn an average income of $324,190, compared to $184,683 for women. David B. Wilkins & Elizabeth Chambliss, "Harvard Law School Report on the State of Black Alumni 1869-2000," at 39-42 (Harvard Law School Program on the Legal Profession, 2002).

[17] Deborah L. Rhode, *The Unfinished Agenda: Women and the Legal Profession,* at p. 16 (American Bar Association Commission on Women in the Profession, 2001).

hits a roadblock such as trying to motivate an underperformer or deliver criticism. And the image that comes to mind when people think "leader" or "manager," as explored in Chapter 4, remains more male than female. Hence, whereas people applaud a feminine approach to management, they still see the male as the default leader and masculinity as the default management method.

Thus, the workplace has preferred styles based on gender and punishes those who deviate from them. Many people—most women and some men—tweak their personalities to better conform to gender expectations rather than just being themselves. How will this play out in the future? Should there be a broader range of permissible behavior for both males and females? Will people get used to hierarchical behavior in women and come to accept it as they do with men?

The answer starts with some historical perspective. Statistics obtained by the National Association for Law Placement ("NALP") as of December 3, 2001 show that women attorneys hold 15.8% of partnerships, whereas forty years ago there were very few female partners who were exercising authority and supervising people. Similarly, 10% of senior managers in Fortune 500 companies are currently women.[18] In sheer numbers, people are far more familiar with the female supervisor than a generation ago. Today there is greater respect for women who exercise power and act in a hierarchical manner. A female boss originally was a source of curiosity and extreme hostility, and now may still be conspicuous but is hardly unusual.

This shift in perception demonstrates change in action, the boundaries of gender stereotypes inching outward to include more elastic notions of what men and women are permitted to do. The techniques for managing gender that we described above had to do with navigating within accepted borders, but there are ways to shift the borders. Indeed, research has shown that negative gender stereotypes start to dissolve as people in positions of power become known as personalities.[19] Rather than being cardboard cutouts, they

---

[18] Debra E. Meyerson & Joyce K. Fletcher, "A Modest Manifesto for Shattering the Glass Ceiling," Harvard Bus. Rev., at 127 (Jan./Feb. 2000).

[19] Judith G. Oakley, "Gender-Based Barriers to Senior Management Positions: Understanding the Scarcity of Female CEOs," J. Bus. Ethics, at 321(Oct. 2000).

are flesh-and-blood people with strong points and weak points. That we as a society have stretched the boundaries already suggests that we can expand them even more.

Exercising authority and retaining informal acceptance are a challenge. The logical next issue, instilling and developing the confidence necessary to get ahead, is the subject of the next chapter.

CHAPTER 6

Getting Ahead:
Are "Confident Insiders" Born or Made?

———————— ⊬ ————————

———————— ⊬ ————————

Leo, a thirty-seven-year-old partner, is worried about a young male associate he works with:

> I think he has a lot of potential and did very well in law school. But he's so deferential, and so obsequious in his very strong desire to please. At some point I need to talk to him about it. You're allowed to have your own strong opinions—the immediate reaction when I point out something to him is fear. I think of myself as a nice, non-punitive kind of manager. So I don't think it's me. In a way it's good there's a strong desire to succeed—I like that there's a real investment there, but the sort of fearful and deferential reaction, you do need to be assertive. You do need to be able to go toe-to-toe with someone. It raises a question in my mind about how effective he's going to be if he's so nervous and deferential. There's some importance in pushing back and being assertive and being really aggressive.

When asked if he would have the same concerns about a similar woman, he replied:

> I might be more concerned about her, simply because people are going to expect that from a woman. I'm more inclined to think that the guy is going to grow out of it. I'm less inclined to think that it's an innate characteristic.

Leo's remarks sum up another stereotypical view of men and women: men are assumed to be confident whereas women are traditionally viewed as deferential and retiring. Therefore, women's behavior that lacks assurance seems "natural" and "innate," and perhaps is less condemned or even welcomed because it conforms. However, if people think a woman's demeanor is hardwired, they're not going to work too hard to change it, in contrast to a male whose timidity may look like a glitch in the software that's easily re-coded.

Getting ahead in legal workplaces demands confidence: asking for what you want, seizing opportunities, barreling forward. Some people do indeed lack this trait and can't cultivate it. The definition of "confidence," however, is limited. Some people—more women than men, in fact—are self-assured but don't project that quality in a standard way because of stylistic variations in behavior that don't fit neatly into the usual male behavioral model, and because of societal factors that limit their ability to be "insiders." Although some people assume that a person who doesn't display confidence immediately is a lost cause, others believe that self-assurance is a trait that can be developed and will grow. This chapter asks whether "confident insiders" are born that way or can be taught.

Naturally Confident

It is widely believed that a traditional, masculine profile of confidence is a baseline requirement for success in the legal profession. Such confidence is defined as assertively stating views, convincing clients to acquiesce to one's advice, speaking up and asking for assignments and better pay, aggressively pursuing business, staying cool under pressure, swiftly making decisions, and speaking authoritatively. "This is a confidence business," one woman states. "You do have to play a good game of poker." A female associate in Boston makes a typical observation:

> I think you really have to convey a certain level of self-assurance. Certain female associates have trouble with it, and it's less with guys. I can think of more examples of women who are more shy, more self-doubting. That works fine when you're a junior person. But as a senior person it really doesn't work at all. The way you gain someone's confidence is by being confident about the advice you're giving.

Another woman agrees: "I think that confidence is extraordinarily important in a lawyer being successful. Perception is reality. If you get someone who can't make a decision, or who waffles around, it won't work." There's little argument that confidence is critical when discharging one's official duties: advising a client, arguing to a judge or jury, or negotiating a settlement.

Within the workplace and among colleagues, however, it appears that confidence is a requirement more in law firms and less in in-house departments, government jobs, and public interest organizations. Indeed, in a study conducted by Catalyst, men and women agreed overwhelmingly that the chief requirement for advancement in law firm settings was "taking initiative."[1] By contrast, in-house women were more likely to cite "developing

---

[1] *Women in Law: Making the Case,* at p. 36 (Catalyst, 2001).

a style with which managers are comfortable" as the top advancement strategy, rather than "taking initiative." And in-house men said that "being a team player" was the chief strategy, although they rated "taking initiative" highly as well.[2] A woman who is now a partner in a Western law firm, but who formerly worked for many years at the Department of Justice, says:

> One thing that's really critical in private practice is to be supremely confident, even if you don't feel that way. Letting clients know that you know what you're doing, so that they feel comfortable with that. I think I've developed it some. At DOJ I would be more open about expressing concerns, saying, "I don't know." I could talk to colleagues. I certainly would not do that with clients here.

Business pressures in law firms exacerbate this difference. Recruiters point out that law firm environments are challenging for women and minorities because of their tremendous pressure on revenue generation. The stakes are high, which affects how assignments are doled out and also affects decisions on whether to give people room to make mistakes and take risks. There are also burdensome time pressures where people feel that they simply don't have time to "experiment" on people whom they don't automatically trust.

Marginalized Men

Many women whom I interviewed said that confidence was not a problem for them, that they had assertive personalities and had no trouble asking for what they wanted. However, a significant proportion of women say that although "naturally" confident young men enter the workforce expecting good assignments and demanding them, women are more likely to hang back, timid and unsure. (This is borne out by a study that compared eighty-five women and 255 men at the director or vice president level, and found that the only competency on which women managers scored lower than men was self-esteem.[3]) A New Jersey career counselor for lawyers, Phyllis Lieberman, notes this phenomenon:

---

[2] *Id.* at p. 52.
[3] Susan J. Wells, "A Female Executive Is Hard to Find," 46:6 HR Magazine, at 40 *et seq.* (June 2001).

One of the things I've heard from people is that women would come in, starting their work life in some of the firms, and they would be so nervous about how they were doing, whether they were doing things properly. A lot of the men came in, and they just went on about their business. They just didn't seem to be as uptight. Men just seemed to be, "Well I'm here, I'm doing my work." It wasn't clear if they were just whistling in the dark, but the outward persona was that they were more comfortable and confident.

That confidence is a *sine qua non* in the legal workplace is reflected in the treatment of men who are quiet, deferential, and circumspect. Just as women who lack bravado are less likely to move ahead, so too are diffident males. A West Coast male partner says:

We have a guy who made partner finally a couple of years ago. A very smart guy, very good writer, a litigator. And he is incredibly reserved, shy and retiring. His style is to sort of look at the ground when he's talking to you. He certainly doesn't come across forcefully in any way. The guy has tremendous value. If you want a good brief written, there's nobody who's going to do a better job than this guy. He made partner finally. It took a while because people talked about this person who would hide from social situations. I didn't think it was fair or true, but that was a difficulty for him. The male [who acts this way] maybe is offending norms more than a [similar] female.

The same syndrome existed in another firm, according to a male associate in Washington, D.C.:

Quiet men, men who have a collaborative, low-key style, that's very disfavored. I'm thinking of particular people who are not really ostracized, but are dismissed in a firm. They are looked at as not fitting in. They get relegated to regulatory work, tax stuff, transactional, something that's okay for someone with that kind of personality.

A female partner in the Midwest took a male associate with her to a meeting:

There's a guy who was an associate at my last firm, very, very bright. Very, very quiet. His writing was great, and he was funny. He was so understated and so quiet that it just didn't build confidence. I took him out to a plant to interview a co-worker of a plaintiff in a case. I said to him, "Feel free to jump in, to participate." He didn't. He just kind of sat there. This guy that we were interviewing at one point turns to [the associate] and says, "What are you doing here? Are you some kind of paralegal?" The HR person for the client was there too. I said to her before she said anything to me, "I'm going to use a different associate on this case."

An East Coast recruiter says that quiet men are denigrated:

Quiet, reserved men are perceived as lightweights. They're marginalized except in a certain type of practice. Like in an appellate brief drafting sort of brain trust capacity, they're fine, or in certain esoteric areas of regulatory law, ERISA, tax, intellectual property/patent. Those are seen as slightly softer practice areas, and regulatory work tends to be more predictable in hours. These people are viewed less as gladiators than in other practice areas. It's expected that that personality type is quiet, more cerebral, not the person who hustles for the business.

Although it's clear that both males and females must have overt confidence to advance swiftly, there is a split of opinion as to whether reserved men suffer more rejection than women who lack self-assurance. Some say that this behavior is a major departure from masculine norms and, as a result, colleagues may treat meeker men more severely than reserved women. Conversely, co-workers may tend to rehabilitate a modest man more readily than his female counterpart. A female partner says about such men:

They are slightly less of a disaster than women. There is a model of a company man who's quiet, but effective. People will say, "He's not chatty, but did you read that brief he wrote?" Whereas with the similar woman, they won't even make the effort to say, "Did you read that brief?" Unless someone takes up her cause.

In this way colleagues provide "cover" for a quiet male in much the same way that they balance good news with bad news for hard-charging men, as described in Chapter 5. Nonetheless, the status of reserved men is generally suspect as compared with their more garrulous colleagues.

Social Darwinism

Initial impressions about confidence matter greatly because judgments are made quickly about perceived ability, especially in law firms. The informal machine quickly swings into gear to decide who's good and who's not, on the assumption that ability is inbred. One woman observes:

> I do think that there's a certain amount of feeling among lawyers, that you've either got it or you don't. And if you have to be told [how to do things], then it ain't going to work out.

Another factor that encourages the snap-judgment model is that many people dislike giving negative feedback. "Individual project managers need to sit the person down, and say, 'This thing you did for me, it was awful, here are the reasons why,'" says a female partner in New York. "A lot of people don't want to have that conversation. It's time-consuming and unpleasant." As a result, lawyers with deficiencies don't always get specific feedback about how they can improve, and as a result they fall further behind.

For those people who don't project poise and conviction right away, a bad experience at the outset can spell doom. The same female partner in New York observes:

> The male model here is that associates who don't perform immediately are put on an ice floe and sent to die. It's social Darwinism at its worst. I've seen it happen more than a dozen times. One misstep, one bad word, and the firm won't touch you.

An experienced legal recruiter agrees:

> What happens with those early assignments sets your reputation. Suppose you have the unfortunate luck to be assigned to work for the jerk, the most demanding attorney, the person who can never be pleased. You're new, you don't know what you're doing, and he thinks your work is a mess, and the word goes out. So other people don't pick you up. You can be broken or favored early on. If there's no system that allows you exposure, you can be broken early. Most firms operate by survival of the fittest. That rewards the lucky and the aggressive, but those who are less confident, like women and minorities, often fail. They haven't developed those skills. If they're browbeaten early, their

confidence goes down. The point of view in the firms is survival of the fittest: you've got to be strong; if you're weak we won't help you along.

This swift sorting-out scheme is exacerbated by the fact that women must prove themselves based on actual results, whereas men can advance based more on perceived potential.[4] Therefore, people in power may think that a person who initially appears to lack confidence is lacking the raw material that a good lawyer requires. As an African-American woman notes, "If you're not sensitive to that dynamic, you may think a person is insecure because he or she is not talented." Partners, managers, and others in charge may overlook alternative explanations such as an anxious desire to please or uncertainty about how to succeed.

My Apologies

Because confidence is so critical, and because impressions about confidence morph quickly into predictions about future potential, how workplace leaders decide who is confident and who is not is vital. These leaders frequently draw conclusions based on surface behaviors, such as how people communicate, make decisions, and react to criticism.

For instance, women's speech patterns often include facilitators and rituals such as elaborate deference, apologies, and self-deprecation. A male intellectual property lawyer in New York believes these habits project weakness:

> I have noticed, and I view it honestly as a flaw, that some women will, instead of just stating a position, first apologize for having to state it. Like in taking a negotiating position with an adversary. I hope if I've learned anything it's just to say what you need to say and don't apologize for it. Because an apology comes across as an admission of weakness. You should be confronting something head on instead of backing into it.

---

[4] Studies involving minorities also show that minorities must demonstrate solid results before being advanced, and that strong mentoring is critical to success. See David A. Thomas, "The Truth About Mentoring Minorities: Race Matters," Harvard Bus. Rev., at 98 (April 2001).

Other gambits meant to be humorous or to build relationships can boomerang. Marie, an in-house woman, recalls the beginning of work with a team of people on a protracted case:

> We all agreed it was a complicated project, and I made a self-depre-cating joke [that her usual work responsibilities weren't so complex], and said, "Why am I in this situation?" And from that point on, one other guy just kind of put me down in subtle ways and some not so subtle. He didn't trust anything that came out of my mouth; he got it into his head that I'm just this girlie lawyer. I'm convinced that if I hadn't started out by making a cute little remark, he wouldn't have done that. That's sexist, I think.

Another ambiguous communication pattern is that more women than men avoid asking for or demanding things they want, be it assignments, compensation, alternative schedules, or business from a client. A female associate says:

> It seems like the men are definitely more vocal about what they want, and the expectations that they have, especially in the beginning. They go around saying, "I want to do exclusively M&A." I've never heard a woman say that.

A male partner says a female colleague bided her time before asking for more money:

> A woman partner who was here for years had been very polite about compensation. She finally said this is ridiculous and started making noise and acting up, and wound up getting paid more in the end. Was that situation gender-related, was it because of personality dif-ferences, or was it something about compensation, that men are more likely to pound the table and get this and that and women are more likely to go along with things? Men are more aggressive on compensation.

A woman says men are more likely to employ brinksmanship: "Men will go in and demand more money or threaten to take their book of business and leave. Women don't do that." An in-house woman says this is partly out of fear: "Women don't negotiate as hard as men when it comes to salary. If they are not the main supporter and not dependent on the job, then they don't push too hard, for fear they may lose their job."[5]

Many women reported that they or a female colleague are the logical attorneys within their firms to handle particular cases, but frequently the cases are funneled to men instead. Often the women don't speak up about it. A female partner in the South recalls:

> We had a securities case come to the firm, I'm the most seasoned in securities litigation, but the call went to the corporate partner, and he sent it to another partner. I was livid. I called two women partners. I should have gone down to see the partner and asked him why he did that. I have not grabbed the bull by the horns as much as I should have. I don't usually go down the hall to the powerbroker.

Not speaking up, for whatever reason, has consequences. That is, women are less likely to get the plum assignments, fat salaries, and high-profile clients, which instead go to their more vocal colleagues.

Forceful Views

Yet another dynamic that can make a woman appear less than assured is a restrained style of speaking, resulting in less-than-forceful statements. A male partner in the East says:

> Women litigators, at least the ones that I know, have a harder time projecting strength than men litigators. We have a female partner

---

[5] All surveys on the subject reflect that a significant proportion of women believe that men in similar positions are paid more than women are and, in fact, women receive far less full-time pay than men, although that is partly because they are less senior and younger. In a 2002 New York State Bar Association survey of 363 women and 289 men, 94% of the men believed that women and men are compensated the same, but only 71% of the women agreed. "Gender Equity in the Legal Profession," at 27 (New York State Bar Association, Committee on Women in the Law, 2002). In an ABA survey, 51% of both men and women said that high salaries were equally available to both men and women. Hope Viner Samborn, "Higher Hurdles for Women," ABA J., at 33 (Sept. 2000).

The other major reasons for gender pay disparities are that women don't originate business and pursue business development as much as men, which is explored in this chapter and in Chapter 7 *infra,* and because of continuing stereotypes of the male as breadwinner, described in Chapter 9 *infra.*

who is a terrific lawyer but she is quiet and reserved. She has a harder time persuading clients to do what she wants them to do. She speaks in a smaller voice. She winds up getting in fights with clients, who tend to take her advice less seriously than the same advice given by someone projecting strength, conviction and forcefulness. She says, "Settle" and they say "No way," or [she says] "Don't sue" and they say they're going to. She's been fired a couple of times where she's been right. We say, "Damn it," and then we say, "That wouldn't have happened with us." The consensus might be that the client was an asshole. Is there an undercurrent of, "I could have done it better?" I've thought it myself.

A female partner in her late thirties who heads a thriving department is frustrated by women who don't state their opinions vigorously:

In my reviews of women who work with me, I know that I definitely have had to consistently encourage them to be more aggressive. With the women who have worked with me more than the men, there's much more of a tendency to convey less of a sense of absolutism in giving advice, in their tone of voice, in the loudness of their voice when they're talking to a client. When I say this to these women, I get a timid, "Okay, I'll try." One of them is definitely doing a better job, but it's taken a couple of years. She speaks very quietly. When she's on a speakerphone people can't hear her. I'm always having to say, "Speak louder!" Men really project their voices. Whether they know what they're saying or not it sounds convincing because it's louder. I haven't had any men who are that way [acting timid]. Even the man who's a junior associate, he's a little more tentative than the other men, but he's still conveys a real sense of assurance most of the time.

The same lawyer had to fire a female who wasn't giving her clients sufficient reassurance:

The woman who was let go, part of it was, the clients didn't feel comfortable that she was really guiding them because she was very tentative in her advice. She was very feminine, which is good, but she didn't convey a sense of strength and authority. Several clients asked me to have her taken off their accounts.

164

As the above comments suggest, women sometimes don't project as much assuredness for purely physical reasons. For many people, such as a female judge on a state supreme court, a high voice is simply less convincing than a deep, commanding voice:

> There is nothing more sonorous in a courtroom matter than a boom-ing low voice. I see it in oral argument: a high voice comes across as shrill. That's still my own stereotype. It's probably psychologically more calming to hear a lower voice.

Another woman says: "I have an alto voice, a second alto, a very low voice. I have a friend with a Minnie Mouse voice, and she swears that clients listen to me more."

Some believe that lawyers who make decisions in a non-traditional way are equivocating. At a meeting, a female head of department asked for everyone's thoughts on an issue. A man afterwards said disdainfully, "See? She doesn't know what to do so she's asking everyone else." A woman in a not-for-profit notes that the collaborative style set by her female CEO can make decision making slower. She contrasts this with a newly hired male:

> When we have to make difficult personnel decisions, he's not so con-cerned about it. If the answer is clear, and the performance is not what we need it to be, he says, "What's the problem?" I find myself all entangled about whether I've been clear, whether I've set expec-tations properly, do I share some of the responsibility? I'll drag my feet. I'll try and give somebody as much of the benefit of the doubt, as much of an opportunity to get back where they need to be. To drag it out essentially. I don't know that it's a good thing. I think it's not sometimes. Maybe some of it is my concern about my role in their failure.

Another distinction regarding authority or forcefulness of each gender is the differing ways people react to criticism and negative feedback. The clas-sic observation is that males play up the good news and dismiss the bad, whereas women take criticism to heart while discounting praise. A female general counsel on the West Coast sees this pattern with her staff:

> Men think they do nothing wrong. They're entitled to be successful. I work with a great staff, but the men feel entitled to rewards for showing

up. Women are more critical about their performance. They are more likely to say, "I should have done this," a continual self-assessment that is more critical.

As studies of evaluations of women in the law conclude, women's intense reactions to negative feedback can result in a perception that they are too "emotional" to field criticism effectively, causing others to avoid delivering tips for self-development.[6] A related observation is that women can take losses hard, says a woman in the Southwest:

> Women have a hard time, because they can lose in the courtroom. I know women who quit after they lost a case, because they put their heart and soul in a case and lost. And what would happen to these women in the courtroom, they would take it personally and they never learned to understand that it's not a personal reflection of them at the end of the case.

All of these stylistic traits—apologetic or self-deprecating rituals, failure to ask for assignments or cases, stating views diffidently, and speaking softly, along with inclusive decision making and taking losses and criticism too hard—can fuel a perception that a person doesn't have enough conviction about his or her abilities. And indeed, one explanation for all the foregoing behaviors is a lack of confidence.

Alternative Explanations

But there are many alternative explanations. Some are positive. For instance, people can be apologetic and self-deprecating in order to build consensus, project empathy, and forge meaningful relationships that facilitate their work. As sociolinguist Deborah Tannen, who has written extensively in this area, suggests, "For many women, and a fair number of men, saying 'I'm sorry' isn't literally an apology; it is a ritual way of restoring balance to a conversation." It's an "expression of understanding—and caring."[7]

---

[6] Jeanne Q. Svikhart & Abbie Willard, *Fair Measure: Toward Effective Attorney Evaluations*, at p. 8 (American Bar Association, Commission on Women in the Profession, 1997).

[7] Deborah Tannen, *Talking from 9 to 5: Women and Men in the Workplace: Language, Sex and Power*, at pp. 45-46 (Morrow/Avon Books, 1994).

In addition, individuals might react passionately to negative feedback or a major setback because of great dedication and devotion to their jobs. They may insist on ultra-high standards and be gravely disappointed if they fail to achieve them. Their reaction, rather than a loss of confidence, can just as likely be a redoubled effort to improve their work and accept suggestions for better performance. Those who resist criticism may actually be less likely to improve because they are not as open to feedback. A legal recruiter points out that men who always look like they are sure of themselves can actually be disadvantaged:

> Men feel they always have to look like they know what they're doing when they don't. It's harder for them to ask questions, to admit a mistake. That's its own box. They run around and ask each other, which may or may not be helpful. They pretty much hide from the higher-ups any weaknesses of any kind.

Similarly, some people don't give advice forcefully because they are not convinced that the answer is crystal clear, and out of a sense of integrity believe they should say so. They might argue that an individual who states views strongly even in the face of uncertainty, or with insufficient knowledge, is not doing the best thing for the client (as in the above anecdote, where the males are applauded because, "Whether they know what they're saying or not, it sounds convincing").

Further, being collaborative and asking for different views can be the polar opposite of weakness. Rather, this behavior can indicate that a person is open to different viewpoints and willing to make up his or her mind based on more data. People with an inclusive approach to decision making might fault those who act autonomously for not gathering enough information beyond their own narrow viewpoints to make an informed decision.

Other explanations for reserved behaviors are due to the constraints of female stereotypes. The overriding reason that women don't state their views forthrightly or demand high pay and desirable assignments is because they believe they will be marginalized for violating expectations of compliant behavior (as explored in detail in Chapter 5 in connection with leadership styles). Tannen points out that, "Since many women use ritual apologies, it is possible that women are expected to, so those who do not use them may be seen as somehow hard-edged."[8] And although this behavior reinforces an impression of timidity, the greater fear is that too much ambition will backfire. As one woman explained in a typical comment, "The squeaky wheel gets the grease. This disadvantages people who are not as comfortable tooting their own horn, or who think that if they do so they'll be punished." For instance, some people fault women for taking criticism too hard, but women respond that if they fight back or dispute negative observations, they may be seen as too angry.[9] A male's similar actions would be interpreted as standing up for himself. Similarly, although a presumed criterion for getting ahead is sufficient "toughness" to play the game, women who seem too hard-hitting may be disliked and rejected.[10]

Women themselves heap considerable scorn on their get-ahead sisters. A female partner says that female colleagues who avidly promote themselves fall into one of two groups—the "super bitchy" crowd versus the "super marketers who are better liked":

> The ones who are super pushy are very clear in their communications to everyone: "I'm going to make partner." It's impolite to say, "I'm the smartest person in the room." I've met plenty of guys who do that and it's forgiven. The women who are more acceptable, they have a gift of making everybody in the room feel good, they are no threat. That takes ambassadorial talent. They promote themselves to benefit the collective. So that's not unattractive. [They project an attitude that suggests:] "I'm helping you guys make more money. Happy? And I don't want to take the money away from you, I want to share it with you."

Just as with leadership styles, accordingly, if females flaunt too much ambition, people don't like them, but if they demonstrate too little ambition, their colleagues think they don't have the goods. The only way to garner both respect and acceptance is to possess "ambassadorial" talent and to be unthreatening—a tall order.

---

8 *Id.* at 50.
9 Svikhart & Willard, N. 6 *supra* at 9.
10 *Id.* at 10-11.

If a person in power uses a "sink or swim" model, and relies upon surface observations to determine whether people have what it takes, these stylistic differences can spell doom. When a first impression suggests that a person doesn't have the natural attributes necessary to succeed and that it will be hard—or too much trouble—to instill them, that person is more likely to be written off.

Not "One of the Guys"

Stylistic, behavioral characteristics aren't the only signals of a person's predilection for confidence. There are also more substantive distinctions that suggest a lack of drive or less engagement in the workplace. Specifically, women don't pursue opportunities for advancement as assiduously as males, such as facilitating political connections, seeking out high-profile assignments, and going after new business.

Women tend to spend less time cultivating informal relationships than men, a key to becoming an "insider" taken under the wing of powerful higher-ups. In her book on mentoring, consultant Ida Abbott wrote: "Many women shy away from issues of power and politics. . . . [T]hey do not pay enough attention to forging ties with influential power brokers who might serve as mentors. They do not appreciate the commanding role of politics in the organizations where they work, so they do not engage in the kind of networking and mentoring relationships necessary to get ahead."[11] She believes that women can't always recognize a helpful informal relationship. In an interview, she says:

> The political aspects of relationships are things that women don't clue into very much. An associate told me about her mentor, about what a great guy he is. He spends lots of time with her, he will say, "Are you sure you understand?" He's solicitous and helpful. She then told me, "He's not like that to Joe," another associate. She said she and Joe were meeting with the mentor, and the partner started dissing Joe about things, he was being sarcastic. It was like two guys in the

---

[11] Ida O. Abbott, *The Lawyer's Guide to Mentoring,* at p. 54 (National Association for Law Placement, 2000).

169

locker room punching each other in the arm and snapping towels. I thought to myself, "When the partner has to take an associate to a major assignment, which one is he more likely to go with?" It's easier to take Joe. Look at their relationship. It's real comfortable. If he takes her, he's got to maintain a distance, a politeness that he doesn't have to worry about with Joe. Politically, that's something that she missed. It's a very subtle distinction. But it's the kind of thing that can make a very big difference the next time that an assignment has to be made, or there's travel involved. While women are great at a lot of interpersonal things, politically they may not be aware of how to maneuver in the workplace. Having those informal relationships is critically important and a lot of women don't forge them.

Informal networking lays the groundwork, over time, for more formal arrangements: mentoring, higher profile case assignments, referring cases and clients, passing on files when partners retire, and championing people for partner. A male associate in his thirties recalls interviewing for his present firm:

I find golfing to be critical. When I started here, a main question in interviews was, "So, do you play golf?" Every one of them asked me that. I could tell that with golf stories and which courses you've played, the doors just kind of opened on their own. I had a feeling that if I didn't play golf, they'd be like, "Oh, now what are we going to talk about?" If you can tag along with one of the partners who's got a golfing date with big clients, especially if you're a good golfer, it's an advantage.

Thus, when women pay less attention to networking they indicate less awareness about the effective pathway to success.

Another point is that women may also appear to "self-select" on assignments, preferring work that is out of the limelight. A male litigator in D.C. quoted above says:

Women may hone their skills towards research and writing and client contact and not towards trials and depositions and travel and all that stuff. It's hard to separate the two. If you self-select out, then you're not going to get the training. If people perceive that you don't care much about that, then they'll just give you the research.

A female associate in Kentucky comments on this point:

> Work assignments, it's sort of hard to figure out for yourself how much your gender plays a part, and how much it is your personality, which very well could be tied into your gender. For me, I do a lot of research, analysis and writing. I worked for the courts so I basically researched and I wrote and I like to do it. One friend who worked on the court with me, she thinks that women are told, "Oh, you're so smart, you can do these research things," but you don't get court time, face time, which can affect how you're viewed for advancement. Like to make partner you need trial experience. I wonder sometimes, because I don't want to do that trial stuff. I'm happy to do these things.

A related idea is that women sometimes avoid high-profile roles. Says one female partner:

> On the risk issue, women just don't get it. They don't get that the world is a pretty forgiving place, and it might be worth going up when the bases are loaded. Women are not the risk takers that men are.

A young male practitioner heard an older male partner claim that his female colleague failed to step up to the plate in a case:

> A male partner probably was more candid than he should have been. He said that this particular woman partner didn't have enough confidence in her abilities to step forward when she needed to. She's in her mid-fifties. I think everyone perceives this particular woman as being extremely intelligent. That's why I was surprised that this partner made this comment. It was oral argument before the state supreme court, and she was definitely expected to make the argument, but she declined to do it and deferred to a man partner. There may have been a specific reason, but the other guy said she was not willing to step up. It seems like she would want to seize it.

A woman now on a state supreme court, formerly in the state attorney general's office, says women are inclined to fold under pressure:

> A problem with some women is they're afraid to go to trial, they back down, they plead out or settle it. They cave in a little too early. I've

heard of it. I can't say I never shrank from going to trial, but you've got to learn to say "ready trial" and go to trial if you need to.

Yet another challenge is effective business development. Getting ahead, especially in the law firm context, is firmly linked to the ability to get business and cultivate new clients, and women are far less aggressive than men at business development. Women say that men are more comfortable pursuing business and "asking for the order."[12] A young female associate says:

> In some ways, I think it might be a little bit harder for women to be out there, and to force themselves to make the final pitch and actually ask for business. That can also be difficult for men. From my experience, it's more likely to be men than women who are better at it.

Without exposure from assignments or trials or deals that get attention and respect, and without a book of business to one's credit, a woman finds it's more difficult to advance. Women don't try to grab the brass ring as enthusiastically as males partly because of a lack of nerve or confidence.

Left Out

But again, there are other reasons for behavior that seem to block advancement. Women assert that in some cases the decks are stacked against them. Therefore, they don't have an internal failing or a lack of desire; the cause is external. For instance, many women do not believe they can build the strong bonds that men can with partners and supervisors, claiming they are consciously or unconsciously left out of the "insider" circle. In the Catalyst survey, when women lawyers in firms reported obstacles to advancement, 52% cited "exclusion from informal networks within the organization" and 53% identified "lack of mentoring opportunities."[13]

---

[12] Fifty-five percent of women in the Catalyst study said that "lack of client development" was a major obstacle to advancement in law firms. See *Women in Law: Making the Case,* at p. 37 (Catalyst, 2001) (hereinafter, "Catalyst Report").

[13] *Id.* at 18.

This results in the informal patterns noted in previous chapters: men banding with men, women with women. In Chapter 2, the focus was on segregating by sex because of awkwardness due to sexually ambiguous situations. In Chapter 4, relating to competence, the difficulty with informal relationships was ascribed to the fact that women are isolated at the top and can't form such bonds as easily. In this chapter the problem is that social relationships begin in a seemingly innocent fashion, with men gravitating to other men due to commonality of interests and greater comfort level. Most people agree that this doesn't occur because of malice, as this female partner in Maine concurs:

> I don't think that the men socializing with men is a mean thing, like they don't want to bring women along, at least here at my firm. Nobody consciously is saying, "I'm going to sabotage these women."

Indeed, men are sometimes surprised when women point out that their "social" time might cut off quasi-mentoring opportunities for those left out. A female partner in a Western firm says:

> You see with the younger, athletic guy associates, they get invited to the golfing outings. I brought that up, "Hey, you guys have to be mentoring the women, and you've got to find ways to do things with them socially." I think people were surprised. They hadn't thought about it as a gender issue. They just thought, well, Joe Blow was a golfer and I golf. They didn't think about their other primary associate, Jane Doe.

A woman pushes her lawyer husband to include female associates when he golfs, to little effect:

> He is wonderful, but when he is going to slip away Friday at 4 p.m. to play eighteen holes, he's calling four male associates on his team. I ask him if he's asked Susie, who likes to play golf. It's a gray area of what's fair, but also a real side of mentoring. I think men over fifty don't recognize it, don't buy it and don't care.

This exclusion can turn off some women and cause resentment, according to a male partner whose daughter is an associate at a law firm:

I was talking with my daughter. She had a conversation with a [female] summer law student whom the firm really wants. But she's having some difficulties because she sees the male law students being asked out to lunch with the guys in the firm, and that's not happening with her. She's observing this and is bothered by this. Part of the assumption is that the guys are going out to lunch to talk about the baseball games, and they may assume that the females aren't interested in those topics.

A woman, now a partner, remembers that as an associate she didn't feel comfortable going along on some of the all-male social get-togethers, and says it wasn't fair:

I thought this is not a real good thing that the two guys who started working there at the same time I did will have a relaxed atmosphere. When you're with someone in a social setting, you get to know them. It's a comfort level. The partner may say, "Hey, I've got this case coming along you ought to work on." The guys get the ability to start working some of those relationships.

The connection between the more relaxed relationships and the issue of confidence is that women, if left out, have less opportunity to get to know powerful people and overcome possible misinterpretations of their behaviors. Those in charge then have less data on which to build beliefs that women have what it takes, and in turn don't give them assignments, referrals, and promotions. This can make the difference between being frozen out or advancing. Dr. Fraeda Klein, a San Francisco consultant who works with law firms on issues of bias, diversity, and harassment, says:

The difference between an open-ended, end-of-the-day, casual drink or dinner leaves much more room for exploring who these two individuals are and how they can overlap, how they can connect. Everyone recognizes that there's some essential ingredient called chemistry. Chemistry can't be cultivated in a forty-five-minute breakfast meeting when the partner is alternating between looking at his Blackberry, taking cell phone calls, and looking at his watch.

Indeed, these informal patterns multiply with greater and greater consequences, as a legal recruiter comments:

That's where that comfort thing comes in, with ideas about who's tough, who can handle it. For example, a female senior litigator told me that the key as you moved up the ladder was that you would get the cases that would put you in touch with clients that would give you that visibility. She was finding it hard to get those, because by the time you're a senior associate, mentors have developed, and the plum assignments go to the favored ones, who tend to be more like the ones who are giving the assignments.

These dynamics carry on into partnership. A female partner in her fifties says one of the reasons higher-level women aren't compensated as well as male colleagues is that senior partners don't bequeath major files to women when they retire. A woman who is a partner in trusts and estates in the Midwest remarks:

In litigation and corporate, the files are more likely to go to the males. They don't have a problem with a female working on it, but when deciding who's going to get the file when a senior partner retires, it goes to a male 95% of the time. Female colleagues have actually left our firm because a client that they had worked with and nurtured, when someone retired, the client got assigned to another male rather than them.

Nor do men routinely refer cases to women. Another female partner, in the Midwest, says, "Passing cases on, I would say here it definitely goes more to men." A woman gets sidestepped even if she is the logical person to get a case, as this female partner in the Midwest says:

We have a woman who's head of [one of the regional offices], and now she's head of a big group. She's been president of the local bar association, and tried tons of cases. She's got the goods. The calls for the work in her area go to a guy who has less experience. She should have been getting the phone calls. The junior guy is a great golfer.

A male partner in Alabama is candid on this point:

If I have a conflict, if a case comes to me and we have a conflict, I would refer it to someone who is very competent, but I'm probably going to send it to a friend of mine. I'm much more likely to send it

to another man than to a woman, primarily because for whatever reason most of my closer friends are men. I think a lot of women's closer friends are women as opposed to men. If that came up with one
of our female partners, they would refer to females that they are
friends with.

The importance of these links is evident when male-dominated workplaces
are contrasted with those featuring more women, especially more women in
leadership. One woman works in a federal government office where half the
supervisors are female. She says, "I feel more comfortable with them. I am
more likely to be friends with them, and I have better informal relationships
with them." And indeed, women refer cases to other women. For instance, a
female general counsel is careful to look out for qualified women to act as
outside counsel:

> I will say that where I can, everything else being equal, I will hire a
> woman as outside counsel. There's a certain affinity of understand-
> ing. I have no problem hiring a man attorney as outside counsel, but
> when you are going to work with someone, there's got to be a cer-
> tain kind of chemistry. It's not as if I have a checklist. Perhaps that
> gives some credence to the old boys' network, or at least an expla-
> nation. They were the same way. I certainly don't hire only women
> outside counsel. And I will never say to a partner, "I only want women
> working on transactions." But as I retain counsel, I look at, do they
> have a lot of women on staff, do they have women attorneys, and
> when I talk to them, I want to feel comfortable. There's a natural ten-
> dency that you will relate more easily to another woman.

Women's seeming reluctance to pursue informal relationships, which may
resemble a lack of drive and ambition or confidence, in fact is driven by
rather different forces, with lasting results throughout their careers.

Backroom Work

Many women comment that although there is some self-selection regarding assignments, there also are stereotypes that relegate woman to backroom
work rather than high-profile opportunities, especially in litigation. A D.C.
male litigator says:

The observation in litigation is that there is an initial push that the women on the case are not given the same assignments that men on cases would be given. The initial inclination is that the women don't do the heavy lifting. The women are steered more towards the organizational tasks, preliminary research tasks, as opposed to really getting in there and doing the court appearances. There's a perception that the women play more of a backroom role in a lot of litigation than a front office role.

Many agreed that men are more readily awarded the assignments that require more personality and aggression.[14] Said one woman:

Male partners look at females and think, "Sure we'll introduce them to the clients, sure they can arrange the schedule, but oh, to go fight it out with the other side, let's send the guy."

A senior female associate in a major New York firm says this is a step backwards:

Women aren't given the same opportunities. They play a research role and background role, they're not going to court, their names are not on the briefs. That's permitted to happen here. It's so nineteen fifties.

A woman in Maine remarked that sometimes women are overlooked:

I wonder sometimes if women attorneys are kind of invisible in terms of when there's work to be allocated; sometimes they just don't think to give the work to a woman, particularly if it's a commercial matter.

This is a chicken-and-egg scenario. There are women who prefer behind-the-scenes work, and those who prefer the more visible assignments. Supervisors with a conscious or unconscious bias see women who are

---

[14] One survey showed that only 59% of women said that high-level responsibilities are available equally for men and women. Hope Viner Samborn, "Higher Hurdles for Women," ABA J., at 33 (Sept. 2000).

happy to do research as confirming stereotypes, and assume that other women prefer to do similar work.

Finally, there are some functional reasons completely apart from lack of drive or confidence why women don't pursue business as avidly as men. One stumbling block is that women have far less freedom to network and get business because of family responsibilities.[15] Another is that issues of social propriety complicate the socializing women can do in order to cultivate new clients or deepen existing bonds. As described in Chapter 2 on sexuality, many women don't feel comfortable socializing with male clients.

As with stylistic variations, women can appear poorly motivated and unsure of themselves because of a failure to "go for it." However, there are forces at work other than a lack of confidence that help explain a woman's apparent lesser ambition.

Overconfidence?

Although male-style confidence is the default mode, there are limits to its utility. With the increasing presence of female general counsel, what some might call confidence others might view as arrogance or condescension.

For instance, in some cases men have to modify their style in courting business with female general counsel and other female clients. The usual assumptions about relating to a prospective male client can backfire when dealing with a woman, according to Mary Stewart Mitchell in an article about the effect of body language between the sexes. She uses an example of a male rainmaker trying to impress a female general counsel, but instead alienating the woman by using expansive gestures and intimidating stances (such as putting his hands behind his head in a "power spread" or leaning back jauntily in his chair). Although the man means to send a confident message, the woman may believe the man is just trying to one-up her professionally.[16]

Moreover, a certain level of condescension can backfire. A female partner and a female colleague called a female general counsel to pitch for business:

---

[15] One study found that 74% of women listed "commitment to personal and family responsibilities" as a top barrier to advancement. See Catalyst Report, N. 12 *supra* at p. 37.

[16] Mary Stewart Mitchell, "When Actions Speak Louder Than Words Between the Sexes," Law Practice Management (July/Aug. 2000).

We're doing the usual spiel. She stops us and she says, "You know it's so nice to be talking to two women, and the best part of it is, no one's asking me what year I graduated and where I went to law school!" We just burst out laughing. Here's a general counsel, interviewing all these law firms, and the men attorneys dared to ask the general that. We got the job.

A sixty-year-old male partner in Florida is frustrated that his firm seems behind the times:

We should have more women in our firm. It's even bad for business. The corporate world is no longer an old boys' network, it's an old girls' network, and if the women perceive there's an unfriendly place, I think they're probably likely to punish you for it. Women general counsel, that absolutely makes a difference. There are corporate clients who don't use us because they think the firm is not friendly to women. I've made this argument to my partners, at an executive committee meeting, and I've said there's an old girls' network. But I don't think it fell on particularly receptive ears.

The very presence of women in the workplace in greater numbers may impose some limits on traditional confidence, especially when it metamorphoses into arrogance or condescension.

Individual Resolve

Against this backdrop, what are the solutions for lawyers, men or women, who don't feel confident at the outset, or whose self-assurance is less apparent than that of others?

Some people learn to project confidence on their own with techniques to manage or change behaviors. One forty-one-year-old man in New Jersey talks about his shyness:

I'm not a real aggressive litigator. You're supposed to be aggressive. I'm not comfortable in the tense deposition situations. I think that at times I've probably not served my client as well as I should have, I've backed off a little. For me, it's a personality issue. You let your emotions, your personality affect how far you're willing to go, how much you've done. I've walked away from a deposition thinking I shouldn't have backed off there. My technique has been to learn to prepare better, that really helps. To go back to your script. I've also discovered over the years that I should be much more aggressive about the mechanics of it. If I'm in a situation that's untenable, if I'm losing my position, I take a ten-minute break. Which I wouldn't have done when I was younger and sort of inexperienced.

A woman, now sixty-three, got some timely tips from male practitioners about her communication style when she was younger:

Two guys in my very early career said two things that taught me about style. One of them called me up one day, and asked something, and I said, "I'm afraid I don't know." He said, "What do you mean, 'I'm afraid?'" I realized that I was softening what I said. I stopped using that. I realized I must have done that growing up to hide the fact that I was intelligent. The second time, another guy out of the blue said to me, "You know, you're thirty years old, and you still sound like a lit-tle girl. You have a high-pitched voice, a whispery voice." He was right, it was like Jackie O. That's all he said, he never said another word. And I thought about it. I practiced dropping my voice to a very author-itative level. I thought, "If he thinks I'm a little girl, what impression am I making with others?"

When she was first in practice, Rose, a thirty-year-old woman in Texas, charged way ahead in an effort to mask her uncertainties:

I wound up trying to overcompensate for a long time. I would try to act real tough, overly aggressive. I would walk into a deposition and I would put my hand out first, I would shake the hand of the other per-son, just kind of aggressive, like a Napoleon syndrome. During a dep-osition, I would always be the first to lay down all these rules, I would steamroll, making sure that I was the one in charge.

Rose relaxed after a while:

That style evolved. What happened is, I began to gain a lot more con-fidence in my own abilities. And when that happened I relaxed. If people want to make assumptions I don't mind because I feel more confident about what's going to happen in the end. Any assumptions they may have had usually are shattered within the initial meeting.

Now I allow people to assume that I'm even younger than I am and dumb as a doornail. They tend to underestimate me.

A woman in Boston learned to strike out boldly and ask for business:

> I learned to ask for business from the guy who manages our firm. You're never going to get it unless you ask for it. I internalized that message about seven years ago. It just made so much sense for me. I ask for it. That's why I have more business than everybody else.

There are few practitioners who don't benefit over time from learning, growing, observing others, handling a case successfully, and being recognized and rewarded. Even those who begin practice with less certainty can transform reticence into resolve by convincing themselves to change, gradually crafting a persona that suits their personality but is tailored to the profession.

New Ways of Thinking

Other people re-examine and change assumptions that prevent them from progressing. For instance, many people avoid demanding or even politely asking for things because they believe their actions would be too confrontational, or might jeopardize their careers if they rock the boat. Several interviewees resolved this worry by using their lawyerly skills to marshal facts, figures, and arguments to "prove" their cases. Instead of feeling like they were making a brazen grab for power, they consciously presented a logical argument to attain their goals. A female general counsel in an East Coast company prepared carefully before asking for a raise:

> I had to learn how to play the game. When I started, no question I was paid less than my male colleagues. At the time I was married and they felt I didn't need as much of an income. [She is now divorced.] I had to ask for everything I've got today. Here in corporate America everything is negotiated. As a woman in that regard, I was less assertive about my worth. I found out what my colleagues were making, then I was put on the management committee with no accompanying raise, and I thought, "This is not right." I asked for a meeting with the CEO, and pleaded my case. I said it's not fair. I had to learn to put my numbers together, I had to justify my existence every year. I had killed myself, put together several deals. They could not refute the record. I've had to ask. I did it in a firm but rational way. You can't

scream and say just because I'm a woman I should get more money. You present your case with the facts. I must say they've come through.

A woman in an East Coast firm presented a closely reasoned memo to the executive team in support of her bid for partnership:

> To be considered for partnership, you have to show that you produce $1 million of business or manage it. Since I was doing my own thing, nobody was promoting me, nobody was thinking about me. I had to think about myself and promote myself. I submitted a five-page, single-spaced memo about everything that I had done and why I deserved to become a partner. It really bowled people over. There was no way they could not make me a partner. I bided my time and waited until I had a solid case. My memo was so long, I had covered every possible reason, it was just so airtight.

Assembling their "cases" based on solid "evidence" allowed these women to transform a seemingly nervy request into a detached description of the logical reward for their work that was appropriate and well-deserved.

Indeed, some women hesitate because they feel that they don't *deserve* the fruits of their labor. A female partner in a Southern firm who had a difficult pregnancy was advised by her doctor to stay in bed for nearly four months. She called a senior partner to explain that she would be out for the duration of the pregnancy and told him she thought it appropriate to cut her partnership income accordingly. He refused to do that, stating, "If one of the guys had a heart attack, would you expect him to come to you and offer to cut his draw?" The woman partner said no, whereupon he said, "So why would we do that to you?" This conversation had a profound impact on the woman, who says:

> My greatest lesson of sisterhood was learned from that male partner. To this day I can't understand why I was compelled to make that offer to him. Part of it, I believe, was that I am a woman. One of the lessons is to think about what you're asking for. Don't ask for something as a favor when it's something that you're entitled to. That's real important. I see a lot of women asking, "Can I go part time?" There's a lot of "part time" across the board, male and female. If you're professional in getting your work done, who cares if you leave at 3 p.m.

on occasion? I might offend some women who have asked for things, and I don't mean to, but some of us have a tendency to ask permission when we're entitled as professionals to exercise an option. As long as you think first about whether you're living up to your part of the commitment, being professionals and getting the job done, you may be entitled to some flexibility. Ultimately, you may end up saying, I have to ask, it's not a given. But you owe it to yourself and other women to go through that analysis first. You're shortchanging yourself if you don't. A lot of young women are afraid to do anything other than ask permission. I admire those women who aren't.

Self-promotion is more positively viewed as a mechanism for supplying valuable information to key people. Dr. Ellen Ostrow, a Washington, D.C. psychologist/coach who works with lawyers, says:

> You have to promote yourself in any kind of a work setting, because most of the actors' acts are not visible, so if you want people to know what you're doing, somebody has to supply that information. Women are socialized not to do that. They have a lot of internal obstacles to overcome, and if they overcome them often they're punished, and they get very discouraged.

A woman who recently made partner in New York talked about how she kept people informed of her activities:

> If you're not working for people who are popular at the firm, or have interesting work, then you have to go on your own little personal PR campaign. A project that I was on at one time pulled me out of the office a lot, but it was a high-profile project. I gave people memos that reminded them exactly what I was up to and how complex it was. When you work off-site people lose track. So the best way to let people know was to give them a status report: here's what I'm achieving.

Rather than choosing between staying silent or making a fractious demand for a raise or assignment, each of these women envisioned her issue as a neutral business transaction, where she need only air the facts so that others could understand and sign on.

Another mental adjustment to help women in self-promotion is putting risk and failure in a larger, less personal context. A female trial attorney in New

Mexico says that there are ways to help women who take losses too hard so that their confidence falters: "What sports teaches you is that no matter how good you are, no matter how hard you work, on some days you lose. I played with the boys' tennis team in high school, and some days you just lose. And it's not personal to you." Another litigator echoes this thought: "Maybe the fact that I ran track helped, and I learned how to take losing in stride. This helped me, because I lost one big case one time." The New Mexico trial lawyer thinks there's a "genderation gap" in this: "Our generation was never taught how to fight. And we weren't taught it because we weren't allowed to play sports. The thing that will change all that, the reason that women will be more successful in the future, is that women are now allowed to play sports in school." These women don't see losing as a personal affront, but instead take it in stride as something that just happens now and again. They separate it from their core personas and view it dispassionately.

Lawyers can also re-think their approach to dealing with clients when their advice is less than definitive, rather than uttering doubts in a painfully honest way that rattles clients. Instead of feeling "dishonest" because they are not expressing their doubts, lawyers can work toward maintaining the confidence of the client. "You can express to a client that you're not sure what to do in a way that makes the client think that you're in charge," a female partner in Kansas City recommends. She goes on:

> In my world, because the law is not black and white and because judges decide all over the place, I will often say, "The law is inconsistent on this point. So all we can do is come up with a strategy. I can't guarantee that you won't get sued. We can come up with a strategy so you know what the risks are, and you can make an informed decision. I will try to make this as defensible as possible. Let's talk about the options here that you have." I'm not saying, "I don't know! I don't know what a court's going to do. Boy, that's hard! This is really a tough question."

In sum, carefully contemplating difficult workplace dynamics, and re-thinking them—mounting a case rather than demanding things, feeling deserving rather than unworthy, thinking of self-promotion as supplying useful information instead of unattractive bragging, putting loss into perspective, and formulating a role that's comfortable for one's client—can illuminate new concepts and attitudes that help lawyers navigate the workplace.

Helping Out

As people rise in the ranks, some become change agents, willing to hold out a hand to help those who don't brandish the automatic badge of confidence that ensures advancement, shaping an identity that's more aligned with traditional models. A female senior associate in Boston says that it helps if a senior person pushes a junior person to the next level:

> It sometimes helps to have a senior attorney tell the person, "You can do this, just do it." I've encouraged people to speak up, and reminded them that they know what they're doing, not to be shy. Sometimes people just need permission. There was a point where I had been here three years, and a woman senior associate said, "You're senior enough to just take them on." She almost gave me permission to transition from a junior associate who deferred to a senior attorney to taking the next step. This was a really important conversation for my career.

Because of their differing reactions to criticism and feedback, says one New York female associate, men and women must be managed differently:

> Women need more positive reinforcement, whereas males snap on the swagger right away. They don't suffer too much when they don't get positive feedback. I've watched women just crumple like plastic over heat in the first six months because they're uncomfortable with "no news is good news."

Many people told stories about seemingly "hopeless" people who bloomed into superstars, usually because someone took an interest in their development and coached them on how to improve, whereupon they took the initiative and ratcheted up their performance. A female partner in the Midwest worked extensively with a female associate who had been dismissed as potential litigator material. The partner instructed the younger woman on techniques for effective advocacy, for instance, distinguishing between a position statement for an agency that was an even-handed document, and a brief for the court, which was pure argument in favor of the client. Because of guidance like this, after a few years the woman became a "superstar" and "surprised people."

185

Similarly, a young woman in New York arrived from a Southern law school believing that she wasn't up to New York standards, that she "knew nothing," and that she was going to "get crushed," and complaining to a more senior female that she wasn't going to be able to do the work. The senior associate reassured her that she would be fine, and gave her training and tips:

> I gave her advice on how to process feedback, and on how to get feedback because some guys are skimpy on giving feedback. I gave her advice on projects to stay away from. As she got more experienced, you could see her confidence coming and developing. She began to believe in what people told her. Now she's the star in the mid-level associate range. She's definitely perceived as trustworthy and successful. She speaks with confidence. It could have gone the other way. If I were a betting woman, it was 50/50.

Sometimes men seek out women to mentor, reasoning that they need more specific guidance than do men and aren't as likely to fall into natural mentoring patterns with more senior people. One male partner in Washington, D.C. reports:

> My inclination is not to *not* mentor white male associates, but I don't wind up doing that. I've mentored about three or four female associates. I do that in the litigation area in particular, in order to have successful women litigators, which is good for the profession, good for professional development. There's probably a little extra effort that needs to be made, because there are so few women litigators.

A senior female partner in the South has worked closely with younger women so that they present themselves well for internal marketing during office retreats and meetings where they do presentations. She makes them rehearse their presentations and tells them:

> "This is marketing within the firm. If a man wings it, nobody will care, but you're supposed to be a litigator and you're an attractive female, so if you don't do a dazzling job, they'll think, 'Oh, what kind of litigator are you?'"

Some try to replicate mentoring experiences that helped them earlier in their careers. An African-American woman in government says that black female judges and lawyers mentored her when she started out:

> They would take me to lunch, talk to me about cases, put my experiences in the context of their experiences, so I would know some of the experiences were universal and not a function of what I did.

She now mentors many people herself, because she finds that sympathetic mentoring can help people deconstruct their fears and conquer them:

> There is an Asian woman I mentor. We were talking about how she's grown in the last twelve months. I had checked in with the judges. Both she and the judges said that since I've been working with her, her confidence level has grown tremendously, and her talent has blossomed. I could see and identify in her that [at first] she was feeling insecure about her professional talent. I encouraged her to get training, I talked to her. There were a couple of cases where I would say, "Why didn't you object?" We would deconstruct it. [The mentee would reply]: "Because it wouldn't have been sustained." "How do you know?" It's a matter of pushing people because you know they're talented. You know they have the ability.

Another approach is to demystify seemingly insurmountable challenges. A female partner in Florida directly takes on the notion that "naturally" shy or retiring people can't learn to develop business and market themselves. Even the most deferential person can learn, she maintains determinedly: "It can be learned. At retreats I'll say [to women], 'Get over not talking about yourself; this is not something that men have a problem with.'" She asks women to come up with a three-minute description of themselves, before the mirror if necessary, so that they have a prepared speech in the event they spend time with a potential client, so that they feel comfortable. And if they are given a chance to pitch for business, she emphasizes, they *must* ask:

> You make this big effort, you contact the client, let's go to lunch, and you have this long talk, and you get up from the table and you never say, "You know, this is what I do, I'm sure you have some work in this area." You have to commit at the beginning of this lunch to asking. It can be in a completely unobtrusive, mellow way. You are a lawyer,

187

you are looking for business. They have to remember why you're there.

Beyond mentoring, others try to reshape the culture by managing differently and promoting people who otherwise might be overlooked. A female senior associate in New York tries to solve the problem of dealing with males who are impatient for more high-profile work, supervising them differently than females:

> A lot of the work is detail-oriented stuff, they come to it thinking it's a blow-off assignment. It's not sexy work. I explain that it is very important. I have to do a little front-loading on the education. Once they do that that seems to motivate them. If they can see where the piece fits in they don't feel so dronish.

A female partner, also in New York, noticed how men shepherded along other males, and tries to do the same for women:

> There's an adoption [model] among males that you don't have among females. There has to be a vibe, there has to be talk at the campfire. "George did a good job on that memo," and then that morphs into extravagant compliments. So there's this hype that develops among the guys, a swagger that rises from a murmur to a din so that they can't be ignored. I'd try to mimic this sort of hyping of a certain woman. I try to build a buzz for a woman. Like, "You've got to put her on your next project." I had a young female associate come to the firm, in the top of her class, she was clearly well-qualified. I'm telling you for the first six months no-one would give her work. She was very attractive, people were intimidated, they didn't know where to fit her in. It was oafishness. I gave her projects, and was very impressed. Every time she pleased me I would make sure that the partner knew about it. Now other people give her work.

Some women talked about how men and women can learn from one another's reactions and approaches to workplace dynamics. A woman who is general counsel on the West Coast says men and women can swap ideas about their approaches to feedback:

> The good thing [for the women] is that they improve more continually; the bad thing is it's perceived as weakness by male colleagues.

I think you can acknowledge a weakness and say, here's my plan to address it, and it leaves you much stronger at the end. For males, their ambition is a good thing. Being persuaded you're right can give a certain force to the personality that can be effective if it isn't ego without substance. Men tend to be perceived as looking for opportunities to move ahead.

One woman points out that the "social Darwinism" model of snap judgments, determining promise early on and interpreting any early misstep or apparent lack of confidence as a fatal error, should be thrown out:

When a person's work is bad, I give them a chance to remediate. If the firm invests in these bodies, you've got to train them. You can't expect people to learn to be good lawyers out of the air. You have to give them a chance to fall down and get up.

A legal recruiter agrees: "It's an unfortunate attitude. A lot of talent, it's there, it just needs to be nurtured. Once people have confidence, they will astound you with what they can do." An employment lawyer in Kansas City advises her corporate clients to develop seemingly unpromising performers, and says it's equally applicable in legal workplaces:

There are people who are superstars, but there aren't enough of them to fill every job. That's what I tell managers all the time. If you tell people what it is that they're doing that's not meeting their expectations, on the one hand, you're building a record if you want to fire them, but you never know, it might actually work! Wouldn't that be better for you? It's less expensive than turnover.

These change agents have determined that, rather than ignoring people who don't seem to fit right in, they'll show them some of the tricks of the trade. They "hype" a woman, pick apart another person's fears, force people to stand up and present themselves, seek out those who might not otherwise have a mentor, and insist that behaviors can change. They weave a safety net under people who might otherwise plummet. These actions and their results refute the idea that only "naturally" confident people will succeed.

Learning to Love Difference

Leo's concern in the opening anecdote of this chapter about the "deferential and obsequious" young man, and Leo's bigger worry about a similar woman, shows that this issue is inextricably connected to several basic assumptions.

First, people who assume that other people are either born confident or not are more likely to concentrate their mentoring efforts on those who fit in from day one. Moreover, some people who assume, further, that men have more natural potential for confidence than women may concentrate their efforts on coaching an obsequious male, but not a nervous female. In the alternative, however, some people assume that anyone who appears to lack assurance can benefit from feedback and guidance. These views divide people.

But another remaining assumption—that "male confidence" is the best model for the legal workplace—is widely shared. This seems to have as much to do with clients as anything else—organizations react to what their clients want and groom people accordingly, rather than asking what's the best approach in the first instance. Yet there are definite pitfalls to the male model. It tends to crowd out collaboration, diversity of input, and sharing of accountability. It leaves less room for people to vocalize uncertainty on issues that are not clear-cut. It encourages people who don't know what they're talking about to boldly offer advice, and makes it harder to say, "I don't know." The story within this chapter about the men who, "whether they know what they're saying or not," still "sound convincing," would not be reassuring to a client. Do clients want advice from someone who has no more to offer than a cocksure attitude?

Many workplaces don't measure skills that women may be more likely, at present, to bring to the office, and that are desirable for any good lawyer. Other firms or in-house departments within corporations that feature highly developed human resource systems are more likely to measure and rate "female" characteristics such as teamwork, collaboration, communication skills, focusing on a business objective, innovation, creativity, and getting along with the client. When more skills are measured, the likelihood of a broader mix of styles and approaches increases. If only one model is available, not only are people with different personalities automatically left out, but the workplace also loses by excluding diverse influences, attitudes, skills, and viewpoints. A variety of voices and abilities strengthens a workplace.

Sometimes it's hard to celebrate a breadth of styles. Every workplace has a unique personality and culture, the result of the founders' initial imprint, the practice areas, the rituals and legends that build up over the years, social patterns, the blending of personalities and effect of teamwork, and things as basic as décor, how people dress, talk, and interact, whether the office is quiet and hushed or noisy and chaotic. But as time goes on, the concept of "who fits in" can become oppressive, and people who resist the corporate culture may be rejected. The workplace is then deprived of the fresh air and new ideas of people who don't think and act exactly like others. Therefore, evaluating each new person as a complex of characteristics, and seeking to reinforce strengths and minimize weaknesses, or transform a presumed weakness into a positive, is vital to developing each person according to his or her identity, rather than accepting pre-conceived ideas, especially those built around gender expectations. Differences that are perceived as opportunities, rather than threats, will strengthen a workplace.

At present, the get-ahead success formula hasn't altered much with respect to expectations related to gender. Males and females are required to display masculine-style confidence, and women have the added burden of not acting too ambitious or confident lest they alienate people. The double bind—that women can't be either too indecisive or too driven—remains in place. And there's little question that the "insider" part of the "confident insider" get-ahead formula has more to do with cultural realities and social patterns than with inbred talents for cultivating political connections and going after high-profile assignments and business. The assumption that confidence overlaps more comfortably with male qualities, combined with informal networks where powerful men draw younger males into their orbits more readily than women, means that at present a welter of forces weigh significantly in favor of the advancement of men over women.

How can this change in the future? More and more women within the workplace, gaining in seniority and available to mentor, are bound to have an effect, especially as they recognize people who are much like they were when they entered practice. Managers might have more empathy and be more willing to assume that the likelihood for transformation exists. Like the African-American woman quoted above in this chapter who mentored others as she was mentored earlier, positive patterns should multiply as more women achieve higher positions. Moreover, since males and females are both downgraded for a less-than-positive façade, there is already some over-lap and thus understanding between the sexes that this is a personality and cultural issue rather than a sex-based difference.

The next chapter examines the importance of the definition of a "real lawyer" and the effect that definition has on work/life balance issues.

CHAPTER 7

Real Lawyers Don't Work Part Time

The Case for Flexibility
(Career) Death by Part Time
The Disappearing Lawyer
A Lack of Equity
Hostility to Change
"They Aren't Committed"
"I'm Not Respected"
"I Feel Guilty"
Redefining Commitment

A woman who has practiced for sixteen years in various states now works full time in a Southwestern firm. She worked part time in some of her previous jobs to spend time raising her four children.

While she was working part time she was given less responsibility than she could handle. For instance, she would do all the work for a summary judgment motion, but wouldn't get to argue the motion. It was not that she couldn't do the work, but rather that she wasn't considered "up to snuff" as a part-timer.

She said the message was clear: *"We're the real lawyers and you're not."*

As was related in Chapter 1, all the people who were interviewed for this book were asked to identify the main gender issues in the workplace today. By far the most frequent answer was work/life balance, usually expressed as a problem for women with children. Respondents said the clash between work responsibilities and motherhood was enormous, and the supposed solutions—flexible work schedules, reduced hours, telecommuting, job shares, etc.—rarely worked out. "Life stinks for all these lawyers, but it becomes nearly impossible to really function competitively once you've had a kid if you're a woman," pronounces a New York recruiter, in a typical remark. Indeed, because women spearheaded the drive for alternative schedules, and are far more likely to use them than men, the issue of work/life imbalance appears to be a towering gender issue. And there's no question that the tenacious stereotypes of motherhood and fatherhood impact lawyers when they become parents, which will be discussed in the next chapter.

This chapter explores more fundamental reasons for this conflict, unrelated to gender. Males and females alike are discouraged from flouting accepted work norms. The "real lawyers" staunchly resist changes to the proven success formula, charging that alternative schedules are inequitable and that part-timers lack commitment. These tensions make the part-timers feel resentful for the lack of respect they get from their colleagues, but also guilty about "slacking off" on the job.

The Case for Flexibility

Alternative work schedules should be booming in the legal trade.

Here's why: There's high turnover and broad dissatisfaction in legal workplaces due to work/life conflicts. Further, societal trends reinforce the push for flexibility and clients are receptive to alternative schedules. Moreover, sophisticated technology supports flexible work, alternative schedules can reduce costs and increase productivity, and the success of some part-time arrangements show that they can work well.

First, turnover in law firms is sky-high. After eight years, 77% of associates leave firms overall, with a slightly lower percentage leaving smaller firms (61% in firms with fifty or fewer attorneys).[1] Consequently, law firms lose huge sums in high turnover (anywhere from $100,000 to $500,000 per attorney)[2] as a penalty, in part because they have been very slow to adapt their policies in response to balance issues.

And many people leave expressly because of work/life conflicts. The vast unhappiness of lawyers, as compared to people in other professions, is widely documented, and frequently work/life dissatisfaction is the culprit. One article begins, "Satisfaction and success in the legal profession—an oxymoron, you might say."[3] And at a college reunion I attended recently an announcement boomed over the P.A. system that "the unhappiest of our classmates are lawyers."

A woman in the Midwest says:

> The practice of law affects men as much as women, and I think lawyers have a tremendously high level of dissatisfaction with their job. You don't get any sort of, "Hey, you did a great job," from your quote/unquote boss, because there's no such person in a law firm, and you don't get anything like that from your client, except on huge occasions. The day-to-day interaction is stressful and not that humanizing. I think that the job is dissatisfying for a lot of people.

A recruiter jibes:

---

[1] The survey covered 10,300 associates in 154 law firms who were hired from 1988 to 1996. See "Keeping the Keepers" (National Association for Law Placement ("NALP"), 1997).

[2] Joan Williams & Cynthia Thomas Calvert, "Balanced Hours: Effective Part-Time Policies for Washington Law Firms," *The Project for Attorney Retention, Final Report,* 2d ed., at p. 10 (Aug. 2001) (hereinafter, "PAR Report").

[3] Marcia Pennington Shannon, "Charting a Course for Satisfaction and Success in the Legal Profession," Law Practice Management (Mar. 2000).

It's not as if they're sitting there discovering the cure for cancer at midnight. They're at the printers proofreading. It's crazy. I think that's the fundamental problem, at its best there's not much gratification.

This is in part because the crush of hours has intensified in the last twenty years. In 1963 the ABA recommended 1300 hours a year as an appropriate billable hour level for full-time lawyers.[4] That would be less than many people in *part-time* positions would be expected to bill these days. Even practitioners in small, rural firms are often expected to bill 1800 or 2000 hours a year. In addition, corporate in-house jobs, seen as a haven from law firms, have become more demanding due to lean staffing. In one survey, 66% of women in-house counsel reported only a slightly lower level of difficulty with work/life balance than their law firm sisters (71%).[5]

Thus, lawyers are crying out for more time to enjoy life. A survey of associates showed that many were willing to accept smaller salaries—even smaller bonuses—if they could work fewer hours.[6] The push for flexibility isn't just a parent's issue, as it is usually framed; many lawyers want more time to do something other than work. This leads directly to choices for more balanced and predictable work environments. A 2001 survey of lawyers found that one in two women, and one in five men, want reduced schedules. It also revealed that two-thirds of women and half of men who shifted to an in-house employer did so because of work/life issues.[7] A 2000 study by the Women's Bar Association of Massachusetts indicated that over 90% of respondents who worked part time said that the availability of a reduced-hours schedule affected their decision to join their firm or remain there.[8] All

---

[4] *Lawyer's Handbook,* at p. 287 (American Bar Association, 1962).

[5] *Women in Law: Making the Case,* at p. 20 (Catalyst, 2001) (hereinafter, "Catalyst Report").

[6] Laura Pearlman, "Whistle a Happy Tune," American Lawyer (Sept. 28, 2001).

[7] Catalyst Report, N. 5 *supra* at 57

[8] "More Than Part-Time: The Effect of Reduced-Hours Arrangements on the Retention, Recruitment and Success of Women Attorneys in Law Firms," at 36 (Employment Issues Committee, Women's Bar Association of Massachusetts, 2000) (hereinafter, "WBA Report"). The study concluded: "Most women who work part time and leave their firm do not leave the profession. They leave to work in smaller firms, inhouse positions, or for the government." In the survey, of 67% of respondents who had been working part time and who left because of

these factors show that the law firm environment in particular is ripe for a lifestyle overhaul.

Another factor is changing societal trends. There are increasing ranks of men who don't want to repeat the patterns of their fathers, and prefer to have more involvement with their families. Their wives have trained for careers and want professional along with personal satisfaction. Many in the younger generations want a life and time to enjoy it, totally apart from child care, and they are unwilling to join the all-work, all-the-time example set by their elders.

A third point favoring alternative work arrangements is that clients are changing their attitudes. Many care less and less about the status (full-time or part-time) of their lawyers, so long as their work gets done. In a 2001 survey, only 17% of attorneys reported that clients were uncomfortable with nontraditional work arrangements.[9] In addition, there are increasing numbers of family-minded general counsel in family-friendly corporations who are unimpressed with sweatshop law firms and avoid them when awarding work. As a legal recruiter points out, "As long as the person says I'm available, why should the client care if it's from a soccer game?"

Fourth, technology makes working at home and keeping connected much easier than in the past. The total cost for outfitting a home office is minimal as part of overhead, and the connectedness provided is huge. Legal work in particular, often solitary in nature, lends itself well to off-site venues.

Another issue pertains to the legal business model. Some maintain that, especially in law firms, "you just can't be a part-time lawyer" because of the reliance on a billable-hour structure. But studies of reduced-hour arrangements show that where there's a will, there's a way, even in supposedly untouchable areas. The Project for Attorney Retention in Washington, which conducted a rigorous study of reduced-hour work schedules, profiled individuals who were working part time both in litigation and mergers and acquisitions. The report stated: "What seems to determine the environments that are 'good for part-timers' is not the practice area, but the attitude of the

---

their firm's part-time policies, 30% went to small firms or solo practice, 15% to in-house positions, 7% became contract attorneys, 4% took government jobs, and 11% didn't reveal their next step. *Id.* at 42.

[9] Catalyst Report, N. 5 *supra* at p. 73.

supervisor."[10] In addition, more and more clients are requesting alternative billing arrangements such as flat fees,[11] which obviate some of the business model objections. Indeed, a recent report from the American Bar Association notes that the heavy reliance on billable hours exacts a major cost in terms of lifestyle and productivity, and labels the process a "villain."[12]

Also, financial objections are only half thought out. Firms rarely add up all the costs of high turnover, including recruitment costs, training costs, dealing with dissatisfied clients who must get to know yet another new attorney, decreased productivity, lost billings, lost institutional knowledge base, and so forth. Intangible costs—such as low morale due to an unstable environment and high stress—also increase in high-attrition firms.[13] Firms' bottom line may in fact be suffering because of poorly developed reduced-hours arrangements that could retain talented lawyers.[14] Says Mary B. Cranston, chair and CEO of Pillsbury, Winthrop in San Francisco:

> One thing I still run into is the many managing partners of law firms who think part time is uneconomic. I just kind of roll my eyes. I certainly try to get them more educated. The truth is that when doing an analysis of part time, most firms only look at the short-term incremental cost. They don't look at the full cost of what losing talented women, midstream in their careers, amounts to in terms of replacement, training costs and everything else. I think that part time is the only way that you can give women a life of quality in the child rearing years. . . . It's totally clear to me that if you want to have very . . . qualified, talented women with you for life, you've got to have some

---

[10] PAR Report, N. 2 *supra* at 47.

[11] An American Bar Association study in 2002 showed that 55% of respondent firms had used flat fees some time in the past year. Kate Coscarelli, "Legal Bills Are Even Upsetting to Lawyers," The Star-Ledger, at p. 1 (Aug. 9, 2002).

[12] *Id.*

[13] Corporations that have systematically measured the costs of attrition report substantial savings with the use of flexibility programs. For instance, Aetna saved $41 million. PAR Report, N. 2 *supra* at 11. Deloitte & Touche saved $13 million in 1997. Douglas M. McCracken, "Winning the Talent War for Women: Sometimes It Takes a Revolution," Harvard Bus. Rev., at 159 (Nov./Dec. 2000).

[14] The PAR Report does a close analysis of overhead expenses versus revenues with respect to part-time workers. N. 2 *supra* at 42-43.

kind of balance for those years. There are other reasons for going part time, too. There are men who want to go part time as well. Law firms that really get this, I think, are going to have more longevity and more loyalty for career paths. As I watch law firms still arguing about whether it makes economic sense, I kind of just chortle because I think we're going to clean up.[15]

Indeed, many non-traditional work arrangements are a win-win. I talked with employers who raved about being able to hang on to talented attorneys who worked part time. And many part-timers say their schedule is the most important aspect of their work life.[16] A New York City associate with children who works part time complained at length about many aspects of her job, but conceded:

I have been able to work part time. That's been very important to me. It overrides other considerations, because it's something I wouldn't be able to get elsewhere. There are plenty of things I'm extremely angry about it, but realistically I get to work four days a week.

A part-time real estate lawyer, mother of two, exults:

It's unique, I'm a lawyer who has control over my life. They treat me extremely well, because they need mid-level people who can do everything without much supervision.

And another woman, working reduced hours in a government job, says:

In government, you work X number of hours and that's it. It's task-oriented. The best part is that these days are flying by because it's way more fulfilling work [than her previous firm job]. I love my job. For a woman who wants to be with her children more, this is so ideal.

---

[15] "Reflections on a Glass Ceiling: How Women Are Faring in the Profession, Part 2," The Recorder (Mar. 18, 2002) (online roundtable discussion at www.law.com).

[16] Over 90% of the respondents to one study who worked part time said that the availability of a reduced-hours schedule affected their decision to join a firm or stay there. WBA Report, N. 8 *supra* at 36.

With this array of forces lined up, one would think that flexible schedules would be flourishing. The economics make sense, the arrangements are popular when they work, they help with attorney retention, clients are on board, and technology makes them far more feasible than in the past.

(Career) Death by Part Time

But that's not the case. Hardly anyone does it.

A report written in 2000 about part-time attorneys reveals that 94.5% of the offices responding allowed part-time schedules.[17] However, the number of attorneys reported to be working on a part-time basis was 3.2%, as compared with 2.9% in 1999. Similarly, the Women's Bar Association of Massachusetts report showed that 4.5% of all associates responding and 1.5% of partners had reduced-hour arrangements in 1999.[18] Usage rates at Washington, D.C. firms also were low.[19]

It doesn't seem better in workplaces other than law firms. Although exact figures for the numbers of people working flexible schedules in corporate departments and other venues were not available, the in-house and government lawyers I interviewed said that part-time schedules were rarely used, either in their offices or in others they knew about.[20] The Catalyst survey of lawyers revealed that although 22% of law firm women believed that flexible schedules wouldn't affect their advancement, only 9% of in-house women believed the same.[21] Moreover, about equal percentages of men (71%) and women (70%) who work in-house felt that alternative work arrangements would adversely affect their advancement.[22]

---

[17] National Association for Law Placement ("NALP"), 2000-2001 *National Directory of Legal Employers* (2000).

[18] "More Than Part-Time: The Effect of Reduced-Hours Arrangements on the Retention, Recruitment and Success of Women Attorneys in Law Firms," at 12 (Employment Issues Committee, Women's Bar Association of Massachusetts, 2000) (hereinafter, "WBA Report"), quoting Massachusetts Bar Association, "Part-Time Schedules for Attorneys Available, But Used Infrequently in Law Firms," Lawyers J., at 13 (Sept. 1999).

[19] Joan Williams & Cynthia Thomas Calvert, "The Project for Attorney Retention, Interim Report," at 3 (Mar. 2001) (hereinafter, "PAR Interim Report").

[20] In-house women interviewed for the Catalyst Report also reported that flexible work arrangements were not available to them. Catalyst Report, N. 5 *supra* at p. 56.

[21] *Id.* at p. 20.

[22] *Id.* at p. 56.

This is partly because the management structure governing part-time arrangements frequently is weak. Policies which employers say are widely available are often unwritten and unclear.[23] For instance, 90% of the respondents to the Massachusetts bar survey reported their firms had relevant policies, but of that number, only 42% had written policies. Fifty-four percent had unwritten policies or offered part-time arrangements on a case-by-case basis.[24] Vague, unofficial policies develop in unpredictable ways, often driven by individual personalities and situations rather than consistent guidelines. For example, a female associate in a large firm was telecommuting one day a week while reporting to a young, workaholic male partner. A colleague says:

> He would say she monopolizes the phone on the day she's telecommuting, she monopolizes the secretary, he can't reach her, and that she's inaccessible. He constantly complained to a partner, and at the end of that year, it was decided that there would be no more telecommuting allowed.

As noted above, the Project for Attorney Retention report concluded that success for alternative arrangements depended "on the attitude of the supervisor."[25] This emphasizes the *ad hoc* nature of governing policies, dependent more on luck (stumbling on an amenable boss) than anything else.

A female partner in New England, although comfortable herself with part-timers, notes that being flexible requires that others change their habits, which they may not be prepared to do:

> There are attorneys that frankly don't appreciate the part-time employee, because it puts more of a burden on everyone else in the office. They're accustomed to having those attorneys available to them when they need them. A lot of senior partners aren't used to planning ahead.

---

[23] PAR Interim Report, N. 19 *supra* at p. 3.

[24] WBA Report, N. 18 *supra* at 9.

[25] Joan Williams & Cynthia Thomas Calvert, "Balanced Hours: Effective Part-Time Policies for Washington Law Firms," *The Project for Attorney Retention, Final Report,* 2d ed., at p. 47 (Aug. 2001) (hereinafter, "PAR Report").

Even the rhetoric about reduced hours arrangements suggests they are doomed from the start. Firms "accommodate" people, who are given "special deals," and part-timers are expected to be (and often describe themselves as) "grateful" for their firm's "supportiveness." These phrases—the language of dependency, of firms doing favors—suggest the resentment that simmers beneath the surface. Magnanimity and gratitude result in an imbalance of power, an unlikely foundation for a long-term, successful working relationship.

The Disappearing Lawyer

These circumstances have a major impact on lawyers who are pursuing alternative schedules. Not only are part-time schedules rarely utilized, but in the law, it's a truism that working part time is a "death sentence." Typical is this blunt remark of a female permanent associate in an East Coast firm: "When you ask for part time you pull yourself out of the race." A male associate in a big Midwestern firm concurs: "Part-timers? They all leave. Part time is not something that was really looked at terribly favorably around here."[26] Indeed, attrition can be higher with people in reduced-hours situations than for those lawyers who work conventional schedules. The Massachusetts bar study found that attrition for full-time men was 9%, for full-time women was 12%, and for reduced-hours women was 20%.[27]

Attorneys who work reduced hours complain that as soon as they cut back on their hours they are instantly viewed as less visible, important, and worthy than others. They complain that they get proportionately less pay; have their agreements on hours routinely violated; are automatically given

---

[26] From the WBA Report, N. 24 *supra:* "Over one-third of Respondents reported that they believed that, as a result of law firm cultural factors, reduced-hours schedules are detrimental to one's career." *Id.* at 2. Part-time respondents who left their firms said that they left for three reasons: "(1) lack of institutional support from law firms for reduced-hours arrangements, (2) deterioration of professional relationships within the firm, and (3) adverse career consequences." *Id.* at 38. Similar results were revealed in another survey, conducted by the American Bar Association, showing that 46.1% of women respondents in 2001 said it was "very likely" that a leave of absence or part-time status would affect their advancement, and 35% said it was "somewhat likely." Terry Carter, "Paths Need Paving: Women and the Law," ABA J., at 35 (Sept. 2000).

[27] WBA Report, *id.* at 60.

"second-best" assignments; and are less likely to make partner.[28] Part-time respondents to the Women's Bar Association of Massachusetts Report said partners refused to work with them because they were part-time, and the partners "tested" their availability by giving them outsized assignments. Over time, their relations with colleagues deteriorated.[29] The quality of assignments apparently is no better in government or in-house jobs, either, and the opportunities for advancement just as minimal (since there are only two or three positions available).[30]

I heard many stories of people who were marginalized after going part time. A woman in New Jersey, now in-house, recalls of her days in a firm:

> Once I had a child, I was part time, I was on a different track, I couldn't make partner as a part timer. I was out to pasture doing grunt work. The quality of work I was getting decreased, and the quantity of work decreased, whereas before I was literally a star in that department.

Another woman with a thriving practice in New England took several months off to be with her children. When she came back, a colleague says,

> She was in constant conflict with the managing partner, fighting and struggling. She was sort of like a leper. She was cautioned strenuously not to do it, because when she got back she would have no clients. And, lo and behold, when she got back she didn't have any clients. It just never worked out.

Some workplaces systematically drop part-timers' perks. A woman in a corporation had her office moved to a dark corner because, as a colleague pointed out, "She's only part time." Another woman in the office commented, "That sort of stung."

---

[28] This is documented in exhaustive detail in both the WBA Report, *id.*, and the PAR Report, N. 25 *supra,* as well as in Cynthia Fuchs Epstein, Carroll Seron, Bonnie Oglensky, & Robert Sauté, *The Part-Time Paradox: Time Norms, Professional Life, Family and Gender* (Routledge, 1999).

[29] WBA Report, *id.* at 21.

[30] Epstein et al., N. 28 *supra,* at pp. 64, 73.

The dominant scenario is the slow, steady winding down of a career. The narrative goes, "I worked for a few years, had my first child, then went part time, had my second child, and then it got to be too much. So I left." The image one comes away with, after hearing countless similar stories, is of a disappearing lawyer. The face-time decreases, status shrinks, work fizzles out, and eventually the person dries up and blows away altogether. It seems like an inexorable roll downhill and out of the workplace, no matter how exalted the lawyer's status before going part time.

A Lack of Equity

Why don't these arrangements work out? The single biggest obstacle has to do with perceptions of equity. People working traditional schedules believe that the way alternative schedules operate isn't fair and takes advantage of others.

A male partner in a small Southwestern firm described the fallout from a reduced-hours arrangement involving a woman who had constantly changed her working hours:

> We were always bending over backwards, and it kind of beat up people pretty bad. I don't think that we'll be that flexible again. This brought up bad feelings from other people in the firm. They felt that the perfect woman was being pampered. They felt that she was kind of dictating what was going on, and felt that they themselves could never have done that. We have some people who are just loyal troopers, who salute smartly and charge up the hill any time we ask them to do anything. Those kind of people felt, "This is unfair, I'm totally committed and don't ever ask for anything, whereas anything she wants she gets."

A sixty-year-old male partner in South Carolina describes his mixed reaction to temporary maternity leaves:

> The lady lawyers we have are great. They're smart, capable and hard working. But they are trying to juggle an awful lot in their lives. They want to have a family, they want to have a career. They want to have six weeks off to have their babies and they get it. And that's great and that's fine. But in thirty-three years of practicing law I've never had six weeks off. I never will. Do I resent them? No. Is it an issue? Yes.

Because the guys here can work till 7 or 8 o'clock at night if they
need to without batting an eye.

Some full-timers say people on flexible schedules overlook the differences
between their situations versus those of the "real lawyers," as a female partner in Missouri points out:

I think there are some women who are unfair. They work shorter
hours, they have different schedules, but then with compensation,
they tend to forget that and complain that someone else who's been
working here ten years and sixty hours a week gets more money.
There are women who look only to the quality of the work and not
the quantity of the work. Well, yeah, but you're only here from 8 to
7, four days a week. There are women who tend to forget some of
the facts.

A female partner in the South says sometimes part-timers get too focused on
perceived inequities and forget the big picture:

We have two women who are now senior associates. Each had a
baby and negotiated her individual deal, but they're not working out,
and I'm waiting for them to leave. There was this huge issue as to
what got counted as credited hours, like business development, or
what have you. One woman recorded her time improperly. We were
frustrated that the young woman hadn't shown gumption. There are
some costs of doing business. The young woman wanted to nickel
and dime it and have everything on the clock.

In these accounts, the "loyal troopers" are practicing the conventional way,
working hard and missing personal time with family and friends. It seems
obvious to them that those who work harder should be favored, get the better assignments, more money, and more respect. Instead, with the use of
alternative arrangements, the criteria for success seem murky, and those who
grind away year after year start to feel unfairly used. They believe the long-
established "contract" between a firm and a lawyer is starting to erode. They
watch part-timers exit at 5 p.m. on the dot while they're left to sweat far into
the night without any "excuse" for leaving.

"I'd like a day off once a week to go golfing," comments a full-time lawyer
sardonically. "Why can't I do that?" The stark contrast between the frantic

rush for hours by full-time lawyers, and the more controlled schedules of part-timers only increases the resentment of the full-timers.

Hostility to Change

Beneath the concerns about equity is a deeply held belief about what it means to be a "real lawyer," for both men and women.

The first wave of female lawyers and their male peers had traditional assumptions about work schedules and the formula for success in the legal profession. Indeed, the sheer accumulation of hours has symbolic as well as substantive importance.[31] Those who have fulfilled this real-lawyer norm are firmly wedded to it and suspicious of those who don't complete the usual time commitment. And the time commitment is well understood: a recent gender equity survey found that 87% of both male and female lawyers agreed that "expectations to work late hours/weekends applies equally to female and male lawyers."[32] In effect, real lawyers think people who work alternative schedules are brazenly presuming that a new success formula exists, one that lacks sincere devotion.

Indeed, some of the most heated opposition comes from female lawyers who have risen through the ranks the time-honored way, blazing trails, only to see younger women taking for granted the paths cleared for them and demanding new ones.[33] A sixty-one-year-old male partner in a large Midwestern firm notes:

> The most difficult people that we have in our partnership when it comes to evaluating younger women are older women. They are harsh judges. They say, "I put up with it, why shouldn't they? I didn't get any breaks."

A female associate with children, now working reduced hours, says the attitude towards her status varies among the older female lawyers. "Certainly there are some who are hostile to it, who think that it's a cop out," she says.

---

[31] *Id.* at pp. 17-25.

[32] "Gender Equity in the Legal Profession," at 27 (New York State Bar Association, Committee on Women in the Law, 2002).

[33] Epstein et al., N. 28 *supra* at p. 66.

"They almost feel betrayed by it, they overly personalize it. Others are very understanding and completely willing to work with you." She had a total break with one older woman after she, the associate, had a child:

> The first year I was here, I worked with one female partner. She's got tons of clients, she's a great mentor and great teacher. We had a great working relationship. When I told her that I was expecting a baby, everything changed. The relationship completely disintegrated, and when I went part time she refused to work with me. I went in reviews from I was a "godsend" to being told that I wasn't taking responsibilities seriously. Once I had to leave at noon because my son had an asthma attack and had been taken to the doctor, and this partner screamed at me. I screamed back at her that when push came to shove my son came first. That was the end of our relationship.

Many women are skeptical about flexible work arrangements. A forty-one-year-old Midwestern female partner with a round-the-clock practice says tartly:

> Law firms are not touchy-feely places. We're not here to make people feel good. We're here to practice law, and frankly people in law firms are kind of aggressive. It makes it kind of hard for somebody who wants to just dabble. You can't dabble in the law.

This intolerance can be seen even with smaller adjustments, such as the female partner who occasionally works from home for a day:

> There is one guy that I have a running battle with, he gives me such a hard time every time I work from home. This colleague always gives me a hard time because he just assumes I'm not doing anything and I'm very resentful of that. Is it sexist or is he just thinking that everyone will take advantage of this? He teases me, "What'd you do yesterday, go to the movies?" I always get very indignant, and ask my secretary to tell him how many documents I've faxed in. I'm not sure if it's a sexist thing, or if he thinks only women would ask for that.

The persistence of the traditional model, however, frustrates the younger generation. A thirty-five-year-old woman left a pressure-cooker government job, where the management refused to consider flexible arrangements. She is now home with her children, and vents:

To me there's nothing sacred about the unit of forty hours five days a week. That's like the standard unit and anything less than that is sub par. I don't understand that. Who ordained from on high that legal work must be done Monday through Friday between the hours of 9 and 5? And any other schedule is sub par? Why is it that if somebody chooses to work four days a week, and is compensated in a fair way, that is different?

Part-time lawyering inspires the typical reaction to change: hostility and resistance. It challenges the basic choices traditional workers have made, suggesting that what they did was wrong and misguided, that they neglected their families while pursuing their careers. They worked hard, attained professional respect, supported their families handsomely, and don't like the suggestion that their approach was flawed.

"They Aren't Committed"

Another objection to flexible schedules is the perception that part-time lawyers lack "commitment" to the profession. One study revealed that 70% of partner respondents who work reduced hours said their colleagues believe they lack commitment.[34] Commitment requires an utter devotion to work, a single-minded purpose that excludes other pursuits. Cynthia Fuchs Epstein writes that this emphasis on commitment echoes the historical notion of law as a "calling," not just a job.[35] The language of commitment sours any work done under a reduced-hours schedule. It suggests that even superb work by a part-timer is suspect because it's not performed with enough overall loyalty and dedication.

A former managing partner of a large Midwestern firm confirms, "It can taint someone forever. It's stupid, in my opinion." In his firm, a number of years ago a man took a leave of absence to accompany his wife when she took a consulting assignment overseas for several months. When the man returned to his job, the partner notes:

---

[34] "More Than Part-Time: The Effect of Reduced-Hours Arrangements on the Retention, Recruitment and Success of Women Attorneys in Law Firms," at 21 (Employment Issues Committee, Women's Bar Association of Massachusetts, 2000).

[35] Epstein et al., N. 28 *supra* at p. 116.

He totally carved himself out of the practice. His male peers were very critical of him. "He wasn't showing the kind of dedication he needed, he obviously had his priorities all wrong. He put his family ahead of his law firm!" I'm not sure that guy has totally recovered in terms of firm stature.

A divorced woman, considering whether to accept a more demanding job in the spring of 2002, debates out loud whether to ask for an afternoon a week to be with her two young children. "You don't want to go into a job saying, 'I don't want to work hard here,'" she frets. "You're even afraid to ask." One man took two months off from work for paternity leave. His colleague remembers:

> This was a guy who had the benefit of coming from a wealthy family and had no intention of staying with the firm, so he didn't care about the consequences. But he knew he was going to take abuse for it. People treated him totally differently when he came back. He started getting fewer quality assignments, he was not on high-profile matters anymore. He was sort of bumped from the top of the A-list of young attorneys to somewhere in the middle or below.

Martha Ann Sisson, a legal recruiter in Washington, D.C., says there are rituals to getting ahead, including pulling all-nighters, making work a priority to the exclusion of everything else, and other displays of exertion. She calls them a form of hazing required for entrance into the club.

Louise, who has a job-share position in a corporate legal department, thinks that people don't like the idea that she "compartmentalizes" her job, leaving on Wednesday night and apparently not thinking about her job until returning on Friday. Her colleagues, she says, prefer the idea that a lawyer is obsessing about the company's legal problems all the time:

> I definitely feel as though people, whether they say it or not, scoff at the fact that we [she and her job-share partner] just sort of trot off, unburdened. There's a lot of lip service to acting burdened. They are saying you don't have the fire in the belly, you don't have the well-developed sense of accountability that you have when 100% of the effect of what you do is what you get.

She reports that her time may indeed be compartmentalized, but not at the expense of quality, saying:

> I have got a really big sense of pride, probably half the reason I work is to get a sense of pride. I think that maybe I don't have urgency [because she's not the primary breadwinner in her family], but I have pride in the time allotted, and maybe that's the caveat. I throw myself into what I do, but it's always with the sense of "in the time allotted."

"In the time allotted" can look like a lack of commitment to others. A man noticed that a former female colleague with children seemed to have things she would do and wouldn't do; for instance, she didn't spend time developing her practice, going out with clients, and working long hours. "There's always sort of a rigid boundary around what she would do," he observes.

A woman reveals that she has deliberately set up a boundary, by crafting her practice to avoid travel so that she can be more available for her family:

> One reason that I work for a regional firm is so I do not have to travel. It's not unintentional that I don't have to travel. I do a lot of work for [a local government agency], which is reduced rate work, a pain, but I jump on it because there's no travel. I'm careful about the cases that I take. It's definitely awkward. It's been a problem in refusing cases. I had a trial recently in a city two hours away, and I had to refuse going the night before. I'm seen as less dedicated. And in a way you are.

People on reduced-hour schedules may look like they lack momentum and are running in place, challenging the constant drive for more money and more status. Says Louise: "It's not like we're hankering to take over our boss's job, so maybe that makes people suspicious, when you're not looking for the next rung. The idea of success is to move on."

Many commented that what can look like a lack of commitment is in fact hyper-efficiency. A successful female partner with children tells a story about her regimented schedule:

> Two other women partners and I happened just by coincidence to meet in the cafeteria. We were all getting our lunch on the line, and we all ended up walking from the cash register to the elevator banks to our desks, to go back and keep working. We went past a table of

male partners, who every day just have this leisurely lunch together, sitting around the table and shooting the breeze and networking. It was just a stark contrast—all of the women have kids, none of us have time to sit down and have lunch. It's very unusual to see women just taking an hour and sitting in the cafeteria. It's very symbolic of the whole thing. We just have to work so much harder and leaner, with no time for anything, just the most important things.

Another woman sums up:

Working mothers are perceived as unavailable. I'm putting myself in the partners' shoes. They clearly see a woman who's not heart and soul there. A lot of the women were actually working more efficiently and diligently, they wanted to get the work done so they could get out and go home, not sitting around schmoozing and having coffee with the guys. You kind of literally get off the train for a while, and if you're not going to be in that groupie, schmoozie thing of being there late, having dinner late, that's almost part of the deal—it's uncomfortable for both sides.

The fear, says a male partner, is that the part-time trend is the thin end of the wedge. "You suddenly make a statement that this level of effort is acceptable," as he puts it. This could open the floodgates, where everyone will want reduced hours, and the firm's financial edge is dulled. Commitment, say skeptics, will be diluted, so it's important to keep the traditional rules, rewarding those who work full-time schedules.

The rhetoric of commitment, like that for part-time work, is not benign. Repeatedly, part-timers say they are "not taken seriously," as if they are being patronized, allowed to practice law as sort of a hobby. Their jobs are treated like a joke, not weighty and sober and deserving of respect. Many part-timers speak of themselves (and are viewed) as "not pulling their weight," as "slackers," as if they are betraying their colleagues by cheating. "Part time is a pretty good racket," says a full-time woman sarcastically. A woman worked three days a week for a year after her child was born, until the partners demanded she go back to full-time status or leave. "They thought I was getting away with something," she said in frustration. Management often engages in brinksmanship, saying, "It's our way or the highway." So despite a proportionately lower salary for part-timers, the vocabulary describing them suggests laziness, neglect, and betrayal of co-workers.

Interestingly, even people on flexible schedules can find their own feelings conflicted when they imagine themselves as a client. Louise, the lawyer in a job-share, says:

> Let's say my spouse and I were in a fierce custody battle over our kids. Would I hire a job-share divorce lawyer to get custody of my kids? No way! It would stick in my craw that on a Wednesday the same person who has the power to help me keep my kids would be at a matinee with a group of her friends.

When asked if this was inconsistent, given her own job-share situation, she responded, "Maybe it's more about form than substance. Maybe it's people convincing other people that they really care about your problem."

"I'm Not Respected"

The "real lawyers" resist change and doubt the commitment of their part-time colleagues. Another obstacle comes from people who go part time. It's harder than people anticipate to deal with a lower status as a trade-off for the benefit of fewer hours. What galls many experienced part-time lawyers is that they experience a lack of respect from colleagues. A male lawyer in New York talked about a female colleague who began working part time after many successful years as an associate:

> She has been hugely sensitive to people less senior than her rising above, while she remained the world's oldest associate. She's tired of sitting across tables from people, also from Harvard, with a different status. She winced every time we addressed her as an associate. There's a pecking order in all of this, the way you introduce people. Her concerns about status made it more difficult for her to accept working for younger partners.

A woman, now in a corporation, reflects on her feelings when she was a part-time associate at her former law firm:

> It made me feel terrible. I hated going to my job. I felt like I had a high-paying dead-end job. How could I complain? I was earning good money. But in my heart I was feeling like I was being so mistreated, and it's so unfair, and I should sue these bastards. And I really seriously started taking notes, keeping a journal about whether I could

bring a lawsuit against them, because I felt like it ruined my career. It plays a horrible game on you. But when you work, and it's so much a part of your life, you give them a lot of power over how you feel.

Her solution was to get involved during non-work hours with her children and volunteer work: "I just built my life as if I was a cashier, went to work, did what I had to do, left it behind. Then I had this whole other life, things to feed my soul."

A female senior associate with a large New York City firm, who works part time and has children, complains of her firm:

Their attitude is that "we want to penalize you because we're afraid that if we don't, everybody will want to do it this way." I figure I've held up my end of my bargain and I should get levels of respect. When someone has a title over you who has less experience, it's dehumanizing, it's disheartening. You're not allowed to buck the system. You're snookered. I think, "Gee, I really didn't think that I'd hit a glass ceiling."

A legal recruiter in Boston says that part-timers' expectations often aren't unrealistic, but that workplaces need to be more sensitive about respecting them:

Those working part time all recognize that they're not going to get the most important deal, or the thing that would require the most time or effort. They're willing to make that tradeoff. But they feel once they're doing that they are perceived as inferior. That's the mistake. If you send the message that someone is not valued, they leave. It's a vicious circle.

A female partner in a New England firm is trying to get a female partner who works reduced hours placed on the compensation committee. She has tried everything to talk her male colleagues into it, without success. She fumes:

If she doesn't start working full time they won't do it. Because the other partners won't respect her. You can't be a part-time partner on the management committee or the compensation committee because of respect. I have said to them, "Look, she's a good person and she'll do the work." I've gotten nowhere. They all say, "She's not around. We've got to have her around." There are still guys here that believe that if you're not full time you're not a real lawyer.

Being a good lawyer part of the time is not enough. Full-time allegiance is part of what adds up to respect in the law. And a lack of respect is extremely hard for proud, well-educated, accomplished people to endure.

"I Feel Guilty"

Even as they resent feeling disrespected, however, many lawyers who work part time also feel guilty. As one female partner explained it, "It's a series of competing guilts. You're either feeling guilty because you're spending too much time at work or guilty because you're not spending enough time at work." A female partner in a New England firm says:

> I've never seen it be a really happy situation, because there's always that tension there. But I don't sense that there's this enormous sense of satisfaction; quite truthfully, the reverse is the case. They feel they're inadequate, women are hard on themselves, they put high standards on themselves, so the sense is they're not doing their best in either environment. That's a guilt burden that women impose on themselves.

Colleagues may assume that someone considering working reduced hours will feel guilty. A young male associate at a Midwestern firm described a female colleague who announced she was leaving:

> The associate said she was going to another firm, and working reduced hours—and [our firm] said fine, we'll match that, she's a very valuable associate. So they should want to try to keep her at all costs. But at the same time, she knew that it wasn't going to work. Her family situation is not working for her now. I don't think it would have worked. At the end of the day, it's four o'clock and she's leaving, and the deal's still going on? And she's a very conscientious person, a great lawyer. Is she going to leave? Is she going to feel guilty? Yes. There's no doubt that that would be a burden on her, that she's not keeping up her end of the bargain even though really she is. Nobody believes she'll actually be able to leave when she's supposed to.

Guilt as a routine ingredient of a work arrangement is a recipe for failure. As with a perceived lack of commitment, guilt results in feelings of shame and inadequacy, even from those doing excellent work.

Redefining Commitment

Altering the full-time work formula hits a raw nerve. Today there's a stand-off—a turf war—between full-timers and part-timers, with little mutual empathy or common ground. The wide psychological gulf between them, brimming with mistrust and hostility, limits their efforts to work together effectively.

The "real lawyer" is still the ideal, and "part-time" an unacceptable variation. Fundamental concepts like commitment and respect are tied directly to the simple rituals of dedication: coming to the office each day and working as much as it takes, day after day and year after year. Adherents to the never-ending legal mission don't work "in the time allotted," they don't "nickel and dime" on credited hours, they don't put "boundaries" around what they will and won't do. They are "loyal troopers" who race up the hill when asked without question. Part-timers, by contrast, are considered outlaws who are breaking the rules. As a result, both males and females find that options for alternative work arrangements are slow to emerge, even though trends run strongly in favor of flexibility.

Therefore, the real lawyer conundrum is less about gender and more about all lawyers in a broad sense, mirroring the high expectations for everyone in workaholic America. Full-time females are at least as resentful of reduced hours, if not more so, than their male counterparts, and men fare just as badly, if not more so, in loss of esteem and respect when they throttle back than do women. Some might argue that because the "real lawyer" issue arose out of women's desires for reduced schedules, the opposition is gender-biased. That factor probably increases the resistance, but the qualities championed throughout American culture—limitless ambition, hard work as a core value, dedication to the job as an all-or-nothing proposition, one's value in dollars trumping all other measures—suggest that gender is only one of many factors influencing the real lawyer debate.

There is a genuine confusion about how flexibility can work, for both sides. But there can't be a real commitment to strengthening systems until the basic validity of a lawyer working different hours is accepted. So long as lawyers believe that full time is "the standard unit, and anything less than that is sub par," there's little motivation or zeal for revamping policies and procedures and enforcing systems rigorously.

Setting a new goal can start to change the "real lawyer" expectation. Commitment can be redefined, from "Real lawyers are totally devoted to work at all times" to "Real lawyers can work different schedules when they do excellent work and make a profit or otherwise fulfill the mission of the workplace." Redefining commitment can reduce guilt if part-timers are not seen as slackers and traitors, and more as hard-working creators of alternative versions of success, whose goal is a well-rounded life.

However, the real lawyer stereotype is not the only one getting in the way of reduced-hour schedules and a balanced approach to work and life. Even tougher to shake are the deeply held stereotypes of motherhood and fatherhood, the subject of the next chapter.

CHAPTER 8

The Kid Thing:
Redefining Success at Home and at Work

What's a modern-day judge to do when her twenty-month-old daughter is sick?

Cradle her against Mom's black robes while arraigning criminals on the bench, of course. Recalls Judge Elizabeth Earle, who presides in a municipal court in Texas:

> We had a courtroom full of people, and there was an amazing sense of calmness. They were all smiling. All kids bring out the best in people, I really believe in that. Children have this freeness and innocence that make people happy. Since then, people who were re-arrested will come in and say, "How's your daughter?"

Now there's a scene that few might have anticipated when women first started trickling into law schools.

But although Judge Earle's story is a happy episode, most accounts of combining work and parenthood, especially from mothers, are far more ambivalent. In the forty years that men and women have been learning how to work together within legal workplaces, probably no part of the experiment has been harder than sorting out their roles as lawyers-cum-parents. It was perhaps the most radical challenge to the entrenched stereotypes of motherhood and fatherhood.

In the last chapter we saw that basic attitudes about dedication to the profession stand in the way of a lawyer of either gender adopting alternative schedules or deviating from accepted work norms for any reason. But once parenthood enters into the equation, questions arise that definitely implicate gender issues, such as: Once a female lawyer becomes a mother, how can she be viewed as a competent lawyer and a good mother at the same time? And can a father who wants to be more involved with his children continue to win respect in the marketplace?

Answering these questions reveals a cultural collision between traditional stereotypes and newer ways of thinking, because of false expectations and unrealized assumptions. The first wave of working women dismissed childcare as a concern, only to realize belatedly that raising kids was a tricky business that didn't take care of itself. Younger women, confident that the world is sexism-free and that they can do anything they want, confront the unglamorous reality of trying to "have it all." The older generation of men, who never worried about the 6:00 p.m. race to the day care center, are surprised that their way of fatherhood (providing for their families) is now seen as lacking. Finally, younger men want to satisfy "active father" ideals but fear censure at work if they spend too much time being actual dads.

It's little wonder that many people feel the work/family issue is intractable, almost impossible to solve. The solution many reluctantly embrace is an inexorable slide back into familiar patterns: dad at work, mom at home. Many people said to me words to this effect: "I just don't know what you can do about this." Examining the issue can suggest routes out of this seeming morass.

Learning About Parenting

When women first entered the workforce in great numbers, nobody thought a lot about what would happen to the kids.

Jane, a female partner in a small Southwestern firm, is now in her forties with three children. She thinks back to when she graduated from law school in the 1970s and promptly had a baby:

> I came out of law school with very little awareness of parenting. I didn't have siblings or close friends with young children. My theory was, it was going to be a piece of cake and we would do it all.

A generation down the track, the "piece of cake" hypothesis hasn't worked out. In a 1983 ABA survey, 81% of women lawyers said that it was realistic for women to combine the roles of lawyer with those of wife and mother. By 2000, only 64.5% agreed.[1] In retrospect, as law professor Joan Williams writes in her book about work/life issues, *Unbending Gender*, feminists ignored the problems of integrating women into the workforce, a drawback that became apparent early on.[2] She concludes that many people feel that having both parents working full time is inconsistent with the level of parental attention that children need.[3]

---

[1] Terry Carter, "Paths Need Paving: Women and the Law," ABA J., at 35 (Sept. 2000).

[2] Joan Williams, *Unbending Gender: Why Work and Family Conflict, and What to Do About It,* at pp. 44-45 (Oxford University Press, 2000).

[3] *Id.* at pp. 51-53.

And that seems to be the verdict from most lawyers, as evidenced in my interviews and as reflected in statistics. They would prefer a spouse or partner at home taking care of children, as does Melinda, a big-firm partner with three children:

> My husband is the primary caregiver and has been since the children were born. Although I dearly love my children, I found on maternity leave it was stressful to never feel like I was accomplishing anything. I knew they were in good care and I could go to the office. I never thought that part time would be right for me because I get wrapped up in things and can't walk away. If my husband had been full time, I don't think I would have worked full time. It's too hard to give the care to the kids that I think they deserve.

A male partner in a big East Coast firm, who has three children and a wife who is the chief caregiver, talks about the emotional advantages such an arrangement affords him:

> Part of the way I maintain some sanity, there's sort of a division of neuroses in a family. I am the one who worries about money, my wife's freed up not to worry about money. The fact that I can, with a somewhat clear head, do what I've got to do, and ignore that my daughter is upset about something, and put it out of my mind and focus on other things—I don't think you have that luxury if you're being the principal caretaker and one of the principal breadwinners.

Having a "clear head" and keeping "sane," untouched by "neuroses" about the home front, resonate strongly in a world of dual-career couples who feel tugged in all directions, unhinged and unable to focus. Many attorneys believe that having a family conflicts directly with work success. In a 2001 survey of lawyers by Catalyst, a New York not-for-profit research and advisory organization, 74% of the female respondents said that commitment to personal and family responsibilities was the biggest barrier to female advancement.[4] Further, 56% of the women said that having kids is a hindrance to women's career.[5]

---

[4] *Women in Law: Making the Case,* at p. 37 (Catalyst, 2001).

Indeed, because of the harried experiences many have had trying to be heavily involved both at home and at work, they urge others to do things differently. A female partner with four children in a Midwest firm reflects:

> Managing life? I'm not very good at it. I almost never cook dinner anymore. I buy carryout or Boston Market or whatever. I used to really make a full course meal every night. I just can't do it anymore, I'm tired. I would recommend to people: don't work full time, work part time. Or come home when school lets out. My kids, when they turned into that preadolescent phase, were basically unsupervised from the end of school until I got home. That was not good. They suffered because of it. If I knew now what I knew then, I would have done it differently.

A female federal judge—who went to law school when her children were young and has worked full time ever since—reflects that the path she took in dealing with her own children may not have been a good one:

> I was not happy staying at home. I just was miserable. What was I thinking about? I left my kids when they were two and four. I must have had a hole in my head. I don't know what I was in such a hurry about. I worry about kids who are not in the care of their parents on a regular basis. I worry about the day care thing, even though I took advantage of it.

And a forty-seven-year-old female lawyer who left the workforce is convinced that dual career couples are doomed: "Someone has to be a reminder that there's something important about the family unit."

Back to the 1950s

This growing consensus has resulted in an exodus from law firms, as reported in the previous chapter, often for reasons of work/life balance. The 2001 Catalyst survey of lawyers revealed that 45% of women and 34% of men cited work/life balance as one of the top reasons they selected their

---

[5] *Id.* at p. 38.

current employer. Moreover, a 1997 National Association for Law Placement ("NALP") study of associates in numerous law firms showed that the attrition rate for women each year was 3 to 7 percentage points higher than for their male counterparts, and was most evident in the sixth through eighth years.[6] A report by the Women's Bar Association of Massachusetts found that the attrition rate for women from law firms, for the time period from 1995 through 1997, was 70% higher than for men.[7]

Many practitioners find that corporations and government are more amenable than law firms to being flexible and understanding about lifestyle and parenting issues. Dr. Fraeda Klein of Klein Associates in San Francisco, who consults for professional services firms on issues of diversity, harassment, and bias, notes: "People find across the board that corporations are much more flexible for parenting." (However, interviews with people in government, corporate, and public interest organizations did not reflect significantly greater flexibility in terms of scheduling; those organizations did, however, seem to accord more respect to people who had alternative work arrangements than did law firms.)

Although there was once a perception that women in law would attain roughly equal numbers with men in seniority when there were enough women in the pipeline, that has not occurred, especially in law firms where the majority of men and women practice.[8] Most legal workplaces feature a majority of males in more advanced positions. NALP figures from December 3, 2001 show that although nearly 50% of summer associates are women, that number shrinks to 42% of associates overall, and is reduced sharply in the upper ranks to 15.8% of partners (barely up from 12.27% in 1993). Fortune 500 general counsel are 12.2% female,[9] which is impressive

---

[6] "Keeping the Keepers" (National Association for Law Placement ("NALP"), 1997), was a study of 10,300 associates in 154 law firms who were hired between 1988 and 1996.

[7] "More Than Part-Time: The Effect of Reduced-Hours Arrangements on the Retention, Recruitment and Success of Women Attorneys in Law Firms," at 16 (Employment Issues Committee, Women's Bar Association of Massachusetts, 2000) (hereinafter, "WBA Report").

[8] The most current statistics are from a 1995 report. Clara N. Carson, *The Lawyer Statistical Report: The U.S. Legal Profession in 1995* (The American Bar Foundation, 1999).

[9] Rosemary Clancy Benali & Sara Yoon, "Breaking Through: Women Hold the Top Legal Job at 60 Fortune 500 Companies," Corporate Counsel (May 20, 2002) (online chart at www.law.com).

compared to women's leadership in law firms, but also proportionately below women's numbers in the profession overall.

As a result, a thirty-five-year-old female associate in a small Pennsylvania law firm looks around her and finds, to her surprise, that at a relatively young age she is becoming a rare species:

> What does seem to be happening is a lot of the women start out with these great career aspirations, and then they all start fading off right around this age, thirty-five. They have children, a family, and they're fortunate enough to have a husband who makes enough, so they stay home. It's weird. It's almost like we're reverting back to the fifties [where women say], "Okay, this is my priority, I'm going to raise my children, I don't have to work."

A New York City legal recruiter is cynical about the viability of a law firm career for women:

> The traditional model hasn't changed. There are hardly any women who hang on long enough to make partner. I don't blame them. It's a lousy life in any event. The men who do hang in have wives at home. And many of the wives started out as professionals, but they all bail out.

This leaking pipeline results in a predictable reaction. Women leaving the workforce to be with their children affirm long-held stereotypes that the proper place for women is in the home. Although you might admire them and affirm the validity of traditional mothering, the reasoning goes, you should be careful about hiring women for that very reason. As one female partner concludes ruefully: "It makes people wary about hiring women." A male partner in Massachusetts recounted his firm's history with female lawyers who had left, one by one, and laments: "It's a shame. You feel a little bit burned by it but what are you going to do?"

There are few figures to differentiate between those who leave their careers voluntarily and those who leave because they are frustrated by attempts to negotiate alternative schedules to help balance their personal lives. One study found that almost 40% of all full-time and part-time attorneys surveyed who left their firms between 1996 and 1998 said "their firm's policies or approach toward reduced-hours arrangements affected their decision to leave."[10] The words of one participant in a study of part-time lawyers are telling: "To the extent that women . . . leave altogether, it's probably more because they're thoroughly disgruntled and demoralized than it is that they lose their will to work."[11] A legal recruiter says, "Part of the reason so many women who are married and have kids bail out is because they have husbands who are not around, so there's no choice; somebody's got to be at home. If everybody was working reasonable hours, then they could do it. I know many women who bailed out with huge misgivings and very unhappily." This "back to the fifties" look of the workforce has resulted in "a system that produces overwork for men and underemployment for women," which is "not efficient," in Joan Williams's view.[12]

Some women (and a few men) leave work for full-time parenting without so much as a backward glance. A woman who formerly worked at the Justice Department, and is now home with her young children, says: "If you had said I was going to stop working for a while, I'd have said, what, are you crazy? But I'm very happy. Life takes turns." Another woman has stayed home periodically, and says: "Some people say they would hate staying home with their kids, but I loved it. I found it extremely fulfilling." A male partner in a small firm, aged forty-four, mused on how work/life arrangements have worked out for lawyers:

> I think people, including women, underestimated the gravitational force of having kids, and the kind of commitment it would require. A lot of women who thought they would never slow down find themselves voluntarily removing themselves from either a firm that is really rigorous or from a partnership track. That has a lot to do with the winnowing out of women, especially in the big firms.

Some women who continue to work full time after they have children are ambivalent as time goes on. An in-house attorney who formerly worked in a law firm says:

---

[10] WBA Report, N. 7 *supra* at 2.

[11] Cynthia Fuchs Epstein, Carroll Seron, Bonnie Oglensky & Robert Sauté, *The Part-Time Paradox: Time Norms, Professional Life, Family and Gender* (Routledge, 1999).

[12] Williams, N. 2 *supra* at p. 94.

> I did find that as I stayed [at the firm] longer, fewer and fewer of my friends were in comparable positions. I'd wonder, "How's so and so feeling about working and having kids?" I'd call and find out she had left. I'd feel a little resentful. I'd feel, "I have to work, we need the money." And then part of it was some pride that I had actually stuck it out.

For those parents who want to remain in the workforce on a full-time basis, however, or for those, male and female, who would prefer flexible schedules, there are many challenges. Although the preceding chapter established some of the systemic reasons why reduced-hour and flexible schedules haven't flourished, stereotypes about motherhood and fatherhood heap even more burdens on attempts to bring balance to the workplace.

Conflicting Roles

A Southwestern attorney, now thirty-eight and with two children, recalls the exact moment she was transformed from successful attorney to mother:

> I hid my first pregnancy for seven months, because I was afraid I would be taken off of the docket. At the very last minute I said, "Guess what, I'm having a baby next month." The head of the management committee sat me down, shaking his head with amazement, and said, "I can't believe you're pregnant. You seemed so professional." It wasn't said in a mean way—it was shock. "How you can do that?" he seemed to say. The mistake, on the one hand, was acting like a man and then, on the other, acting like a woman—wait, you were being a guy and then acting like a girl.

Upon announcing that she was an expectant mother, this woman instantly became a split personality—the nurturing mother (the "girl") competing with the aggressive, competitive lawyer (the "guy").

Many women visualize their careers as "before and after" snapshots of pre- and post-motherhood, echoing this Boston lawyer: "For me, the defining issue in my current practice is being a mother. And that is absolutely the line. Before I had kids gender was totally a non-issue." Said a D.C. female: "Within the firm they were okay with having women as colleagues. They were not okay with having a mother as a colleague." Another woman worked at a public interest agency that advocated feminist views. When she proposed a flexible arrangement after having her first child, a female colleague said disappointedly, "I was afraid you would do that."

There hasn't been much success within legal workplaces in melding the roles of mother and lawyer—the "womb/mind divide," as Kathleen Jamieson calls it.[13] This is because motherhood still carries with it overwhelming expectations. As Joan Williams points out, the assumption about mothers is that they should have "all the time and the love in the world to give."[14] Further, collected research about gender roles reveals that the trait most often associated with motherhood is nurturance, and the fact that women give birth to and nurse children is generalized to a broad and ongoing capacity for nurturance.[15]

Women in legal workplaces chafe under persistent stereotypes. Even in harmonious working relationships, lawyer/mothers detect that colleagues have different expectations for mothers than for fathers. A partner in an East Coast firm discusses her supervisor's attitude:

> He's wonderful—I love him and he's done all the right things. You see, he's thrilled that I'm still doing what I'm doing, because I'm so valuable. And some people might put me to the choice of practicing or taking care of kids. He doesn't have that view, but he doesn't assume that my husband has flexibility in his schedule. He assumes that women really should be raising kids, that women are better at it, and men can't do it, that it's not realistic for them career-wise.

A sixty-year-old man in a Southern law practice talks about the clash between understanding the demands of motherhood versus valuing the norms of full-time lawyering:

> The guys in our firm, every guy in this firm that has a wife and children, his wife doesn't work. So the guys don't need to leave to get the kid out of day care, or stay home when the kid is sick, or take the

---

[13] Kathleen Jamieson, *Beyond the Double Bind: Women and Leadership,* p. 53 (Oxford University Press, 1995).

[14] Williams, N. 2 *supra* at p. 31.

[15] Virginia Valian, *Why So Slow? The Advancement of Women,* at p. 115 (MIT Press, 1998).

kid to the doctor, or any of those things that take time away from the clients. But of course the lady lawyer has to do those things. We understand that, we say fine, you go, but that has a subtle effect: "We can't put her on this case, because it will be out of town." I think it's just the mothering instinct to say, "The baby's sick and I'm going to stay with the baby." I don't argue with that. I just say this: My partner, Don, who works like an absolute dog, who had nearly 3000 hours of time last year, you don't hear him saying, "I'm taking the day off today, I'll be at home, I'll take a few files with me." We've never had a big showdown argument about it, but there is this issue.

This lawyer's observation is a jumble of understanding and resentment. Although women logically want to spend time with their children, their absence leaves others to toil in the workplace. Indeed, the process of assigning cultural judgments can start very early. Dr. Fraeda Klein, the San Francisco consultant, says:

I watch how law firms create self-fulfilling prophecies, especially about parenting. A young woman associate becomes engaged. People notice the ring, and right away there begins speculation, especially from male partners, about when she's going to start a family. Most young women associates try to delay announcing their pregnancies as long as possible, because they are all aware that there's a sea change in their treatment. So what happens is it becomes an uphill battle. Their assignments start changing, they get left off important e-mails or memos, they don't get invited to meetings, and they fall farther and farther out of the loop. It becomes more and more difficult to keep up, and more and more frustrating. And it then does become more of a choice about whether to go back or not, because it seems so daunting to juggle everything.

Suspect Mothers

One might anticipate some ambivalence from males on this topic. At the same time, one might also expect that women within the legal profession, with or without children, would be sympathetic towards their female colleagues who are mothers. But behind closed doors the level of hostility is striking. High-powered female lawyers with kids are viewed as suspect parents, far more so than their male counterparts. For instance, a divorced single mother in her forties, of counsel to a mid-sized East Coast firm, has harsh words for women partners with children:

> Women partners, I often find that they don't approach motherhood like I do. I haven't really met female partners who are nurturing, loving mothers. Not homey-type people. You can't! The demands that are placed [on you] make it impossible.

A thirty-eight-year-old man in an East Coast firm is taken aback to hear just as much hostility from women as from men on this issue:

> I hear these comments all the time, disparaging remarks about women who are really successful: "She must be a crappy mother, her kids must be all screwed up." Why do you even have that thought? Why can't it just be, "Goddamn, she's a great attorney"? Those remarks come from men and women equally. I've heard plenty of women disparage other women for their lack of maternal instinct, all ages, too. Some of the cattiest remarks—they almost knock me off my chair, you feel like you're picking your jaw off the table—they come from women. It's like Fred Flintstone. It's really odd.

Attitudes outside the workplace can compound the disapproval within and further isolate working lawyers who are mothers. A female partner in a small Southwestern firm sidesteps the stay-at-home mothers she meets at her children's school:

> I get the sense that they think that my children don't have as much attention. I downplay my career to them. If they ask me what I do I say I work at an office. I don't say I'm a lawyer. I might say I work at a law firm. I do that to avoid getting their attitude. I'm trying to downplay anything that's going to intimidate them.

In this instance the woman maximizes her "good mother" role by "downplaying" her position, which can be perceived as conflicting with the maternal role—that of the ambitious attorney. By all outward appearances she confirms the validity of the conflict, treating her success as a guilty secret whose revelation would mark her as a bad mother. She wants to shield herself from hurtful assumptions, as does a full-time female partner in a Southern firm who has three children:

> I've had people in the community continually asking if I'm working full time. The subtext is, "You can't do that with kids." I just say, "Yeah, I still am." Sometimes you just want to say, "Do you ever ask a guy that?" You've got to pick your battles and that's certainly a tiny one.

In contrast to the women who minimize their professional responsibilities outside of the workplace, some women downplay their maternal roles within the office. Eleanor, a New Jersey in-house lawyer, believes she was "ghettoized" in her former law firm because she was very vocal about motherhood and her children, her office overflowing with photos of her children and their finger paintings. In her new position, she's trying out a new approach:

> I have made a concerted effort not to talk about my kids. I have no baby pictures or artwork in my office. I'm doing a little test—what if I don't talk about them a lot and see whether it makes a difference, whether I end up advancing the way I want to? If I present myself as the motherly type, it won't help at all. I'm sort of like undercover. It's an experiment.

A woman who lectures at a law school and has worked for not-for-profits describes being "in the closet" about her involvement with her kids, not wanting to either offend female lawyers who don't have children or unnerve her shiny-eyed female law students, who are eager to believe that the course ahead will be smooth:

> We don't tell the truth about what it's like working and having kids. One thing I've felt reluctant to do as a legal professional is to be upfront [with her students] about how much time I've taken off to be with my kids and how important they are to me. I should be upfront about that instead of massaging what I've done. I'm an important role model for students.

A woman who is now in-house but who formerly worked at a mid-sized New York City firm, recalls, "I sort of didn't tell anyone [at the law firm] until it was obvious that I was pregnant, which gave both the impression that I wasn't that excited and the impression that I was very torn about the consequences. From the work perspective I wanted them to think that this wasn't going to change anything for me."

232

This "in the closet" approach—the "experiment" of not talking about one's kids, the feigned ambivalence—recognizes a stark fact: A woman's career stock plummets as her maternal stock skyrockets. Society applauds one moment and punishes in the next, bringing the full force of tenacious stereotypes to bear on mothers in the workplace.

Youthful Disillusion

The younger generation of lawyers, both male and female, has been particularly stunned by the difficulties involved with parenthood. They come to the workplace with different assumptions and expectations than their older colleagues. The more youthful generation has charged forward, stoked by unchallenged expectations of equality and opportunity, and has crashed into the brick wall of traditional models and stereotypes.

In fact, younger women in general (and young men, as described below) are frustrated at the lack of guidance from the generation ahead. When they are asked to describe female partners in their firms, they chronicled atypical domestic arrangements: "Her husband stays at home, she has no kids, this other one didn't get married until she was forty-two and she has grown stepkids, and another woman's husband is an academic and works flexible hours." The implication is that the senior women have simply opted out of the traditional path, making a choice that most lawyers don't have or don't want.

I also heard annoyance about the attitudes of the "typical" older male partners who have wives at home. Said a young New York female associate, married with two children:

> My generation has dual income families, where both mom and dad are juggling responsibilities at home. Older male partners have no concept, they never had to do it. They never made that 5:30 phone call, "Who's getting out? Are you getting out?"—structuring [their lives] on a night-by-night basis.

Some young women leave pressure-cooker law firms precisely because they look ahead and don't see how a manageable life is possible. A thirty-year-old woman, now in-house and remembering her stint at a big firm, says:

> I wasn't married and didn't have kids. I can't imagine trying to balance those things. Like making cupcakes at 3 a.m., being up all night. I was

having a hard enough time keeping my relationship with my boyfriend going.

Another woman said firmly, "There was no way I was going to work in a big law firm and have a child. I really don't believe in leaving your kids."

And just as younger associates think more senior female lawyers who have no children are undesirable role models, they also fear the example of the female partner who has children but never sees them. Says a male partner in a large New York firm, discussing a female partner:

> The female associates that I talk to about this partner, they all have told me, "I do not want to grow up to be like her. She has made far too many sacrifices." She never sees her kids and husband, she works like a dog. This partner is not a good role model for women in the office. They hope that their future isn't like hers. But they have concerns that they will end up in that very same boat.

Making It Work

Others are more sanguine, assuming that part-time schedules will solve their problems. Many young women assured me that they had no worries about the future, because they had been advised that their firms or departments had part-time policies. A twenty-eight-year-old woman who left a firm to go in-house thinks these women are fooling themselves: "Most of my law school friends don't anticipate dropping out entirely. People have this idealized vision of part-time work. I don't really buy it."

And it isn't easy, as a Washington, D.C. female partner with children stresses:

> I have a lot of women say to me, "I couldn't possibly do what you do. What's the secret?" The answer, if there is one answer, is you have to be extremely organized but you also have to realize that there really will be nothing in your life other than your family and your job. It's not right for everybody. I used to say that one of the ways I do it is I have good health, I never get sick. I go home at 6:30, and work for a couple hours at home. You have to recognize that you won't give to your family exactly what stay-at-home moms can give, and you have to pay for all that stuff.

A female partner in a Southern firm agrees, and says that young women should be more savvy when job hunting:

> The main thing that female associates should look for is somebody who's already done it. That's hard to do. If you can avoid being the first woman partner, you ought to. Young female associates don't understand that. They say, "I'm going to some place, they recruited me," whereas I know that the firm has recruited six other females, none of whom have stayed that long or have made partner. Women coming out of law school are somewhat naïve about what it's going to be like.

But that kind of information can be hard to ferret out. A very successful woman, who has children and is a part-time partner, knows that she's used as a sort of "advertisement" for her firm and is wary of the image she projects to hopeful female job applicants:

> I'm a good thing for the firm. Undoubtedly it's misleading also. This is not perfect. I'm very cautious about how I say things to people, because I don't like to be critical of the firm. I say, "Having children and practicing law at a private law firm can be done [but] it is not easy to be taken seriously as a lawyer and work part time."

In contrast to the "in the closet" attitudes about motherhood that some women harbor, a wave of younger women are making different choices openly. A senior female partner in her fifties increasingly observes that younger female attorneys no longer want to "sacrifice rearing their children for a career." She points to a senior associate in her firm, on the verge of making partner. She got pregnant and announced she would take off a few years and come back after her child was in school. The older female reacts: "Boy, was that brave. You would not have seen that ten years ago. A woman would not feel that she could do that. This woman felt like, 'I'll be a little bit behind, but I'm smart, I'll come back when I feel like it.'"

For all their confident assumptions about their capabilities, however, young women also are often conflicted between old and new perceptions about motherhood. Younger women repeatedly complained that there were no "normal women" in their workplaces. What they meant, it turned out, was a woman who was married with children, had typical maternal instincts, and

235

was easy to get along with. So motherhood, despite how it taints a woman's perceived competence, also confers a certain social legitimacy.

If motherhood is in some sense "normal," then women who are single or without children can feel stigmatized. One woman, age forty and now a partner at a small Pennsylvania firm, talks about her previous firm:

> Being a single woman was a little more difficult because you were not part of the mainstream. You were not necessarily brought into the group. With the younger men in the firm, a lot of them came out of law school, got married, and then announced that they were having a child, and with that news the firm seemed to embrace them even more. "Oh, you're one of us." The male attorneys who have four or five kids, with wives at home who do not work—I don't know, I think that could affect the way they deal with single women in the work-force. Their impression of what they see is different from what they have at home. It's intimidating to deal with single women.

Another woman without children also feels left out:

> Sometimes—and I always feel extremely guilty for these feelings—but sometimes I feel like people with kids are the only people whose need for balance is valued. And the rest of us, it doesn't matter. Kids are the ultimate excuse. There are no options for everyone else out there. It sucks all the air out of offering options to others. And as a non-parent, I feel like I'm expected to do more work, where I don't get those built-in excuses. There are a lot of people who say they leave early because of their kids. There's this expectation that I of course wouldn't do that.

The double bind has an extra twist for childless women. Although doubts about competence abound for women with children, women without children aren't part of the mainstream club. The leeway that mothers get, however ambivalent, includes an informal acceptance that is greater than for women who don't have kids (or husbands).

A female partner with children at a high-powered firm was surprised at the reaction she got when she told the truth about what it takes to make her life work:

I tell young women, just accept the fact that you are going to have to spend a lot of money to get the help you need. I see women negotiating with illegal domestic workers to squeeze out the last dollar, and then they end up with somebody who doesn't speak English and doesn't drive. I think there are financial concessions you make for your household to run. As a result I didn't look back. I have a nanny and I give her a car, I don't do shopping, I don't get dry cleaning. I say to female associates, "Get over it and just pay the money." I don't do anything that I can delegate to others. I said this to a meeting of women associates and somebody said to me, "That really sounds bad." The young women didn't take to that well. I don't know why—I didn't go through seventeen years of school to pick up laundry, if I can pay someone to go do it. That seems to me an easy solution to a difficult problem. I was really shocked [at the negative reaction]. They said, "It sounds like you're just throwing money around."

The woman quoted above says in retrospect, "I think that perhaps what wasn't conveyed to the women was that it is not that I don't have any time left after work to do things that I enjoy. The point was that our 'free' time is so limited that I am going to make sure that I spend it on quality things, like being with my daughter, working out, entertaining, doing things that I really enjoy. What I don't have time for is any 'have to's' that I can easily have someone else take care of for me."

The associates who listened to her were put off by her "just throwing money around," which they see as callous and lacking a human touch. They are, paradoxically, offended at the notion of a woman paying someone else to do what a wife and mother traditionally does herself. Along with all the bravado and confidence they've absorbed, then, younger women also have imbibed a healthy dose of traditionalism. Perhaps prior to motherhood they don't even realize the extent to which they are exhibiting or assuming stereotypical visions of the future. They find themselves trapped between broad aspirations—wanting a rich family life and a rewarding career—and distaste over the harsh reality of what it takes to realize that vision.[16]

---

[16] Emily Nussbaum, "Great Expectations: The Prospect for a Female Lawyer, Classes of '01, '91 and '81," The New York Times Magazine, at 118 (Sept. 8, 2001). In the article, a variety

Once they become mothers, women face an enormous challenge to maintain their image in the workplace and community untainted by perceptions of failure or neglect of their maternal role. Whether they are older and with an established career, bearing children, or merely contemplating marriage and kids, they don't see a way to steer around the obstacles.

Dads in a Box

By contrast, the role of fatherhood has always meshed neatly with the image of the driven career man. If conventional wisdom says that motherhood is a minus for working women, fatherhood is a plus. It enhances men's stature without tarnishing their legitimacy in the workplace.

But this view is true only if one assumes that men only want to work as "real lawyers" (traditional full-timers) and don't want a balanced lifestyle or reduced hours at any time in their careers. Increasingly, however, many do. According to one survey of lawyers, one in five men would welcome reduced schedules, and 50% of men revealed that they chose an in-house employer due to work/life issues.[17]

However, males get far less leeway than women to parent. Although mothers who play active childcare roles have a place in the workforce, there is little opportunity for men who want to do the same. The role of father is even more rigidly defined than that of mother, still seen overwhelmingly by men and women as being the breadwinner. Even young women, as they reach the age to consider marriage, are surprised to discover, or simply take for granted, the importance they place on potential husbands as high earners.[18]

If men are transformed when they become fathers, it is because they now carry the breadwinner mantle and are assumed to be more serious and com-

---

of women lawyers are interviewed, including some who are starting out and who speculate broadly about the future, as well as others who are well into their careers and who offer insights about retaining those careers.

[17] *Women in Law: Making the Case*, at p. 35 (Catalyst, 2001).

[18] Author Peggy Orenstein shows how young women who are nourished on a diet of superior education and ambitious expectations still find themselves looking for a spouse who will be a good provider and breadwinner, and rejecting men who don't look like they're on a fast track. Peggy Orenstein, *Flux: Women on Sex, Work, Love, Kids and Life in a Half-Changed World*, at pp. 37-40 (Doubleday, 2000).

mitted to their work, rather than less. In one firm, whenever a male got married or had a child, a lead partner would exclaim, "Oh, we love to see our associates get married and become family men. It means they work harder!" A woman who worked there recalls, "Nothing like that was said when I had a child." Some workplaces confirm the male-as-breadwinner expectation most starkly in compensation scales that assume men are the heads of households and should therefore be paid more than women, which violates Title VII and a host of other federal and state laws. A male partner at a large firm in Washington, D.C. says:

> There continues to be the view that the men are the heads of the families, so if there's a variance you have to err on the side of giving [more compensation] to the men. A lot of the compensation is [determined] by men, and they look in the mirror and see that. Even when the women are the mainstay of the family, there's still a view that you have to give the money to the men. This is still going on, which is hard to believe.

And as the man quoted above points out, this bias is unfair for women who are the main breadwinners in their families. Says a female Midwestern practitioner:

> I do believe that there is an unequal pay structure for female attorneys, based on experience and just conversations. In my case I am the major income producer in my family. People make assumptions about me that my husband makes more money than I do, and [that] I don't need to worry about it.

Indeed, an article about the effect of legal employment on fathers reports that whereas women often receive paid maternity leave, men generally don't get paid paternity leave. So they are given a different status right from the onset of parenthood. "A male associate who musters the courage to approach his managing partner and ask for time off to be with his family will have to overcome a policy that is predicated on the assumption that parental leave is women's work," author Keith Cunningham writes.[19]

---

[19] Keith Cunningham, "Father Time: Flexible Work Arrangements and the Law Firm's Failure of the Family," 53 Stanford L. Rev., 907, 977 (April 2001).

And paternity leave is rarely used even now. Men usually patch together vacation time and other days off rather than take an "official" paternity leave.[20] As one man said, in a typical comment:

> Paternity leave, it's offered and nobody [takes] it. If you exercise it you're absolutely blacklisted. Any male who did that would be in a far worse position than some women [who take maternity leave]. It's almost like it's twice as bad. And I think that's horrendous.

Even more uncommon is for men to take reduced-hour schedules or other flexible arrangements. Says a male Boston lawyer (who was very sympathetic to females who work non-traditional schedules):

> Men wanting to go part time? No way. I can think of only one or two men who ever took advantage of the paternity leave policies in the firms I was associated with, let alone reduced their status to part time. To that extent, there still is the notion that it's okay for women to be part time with various forms of asterisks connected to that—maybe they're not as dedicated, won't be viewed as partner material—but at least it's sort of tolerated in a formal sense. If a female lawyer wants to take advantage of a policy, okay, good luck to her. But very few male lawyers will do it. And that is because, reflecting broader social issues, men don't feel at all comfortable equating themselves with women lawyers in that respect.

A woman in Maine says that reduced-hours schedules are only available "if you're a woman. I have a male friend who wanted part time or extended paternity leave, and he said, 'There's no way I could do that, they would take away all my clients, they would not take me seriously any more. I'd be looked at differently.'" This underlines the radically different agendas for men versus women when they become parents. Keith Cunningham concludes that men have their own double bind: if fatherhood as defined as being a good provider, and not as nurturing, men get boxed in.[21]

---

[20] One researcher found that men who take paternity leave take off an average of a mere 5.3 days. Mary Kane, "The Daddy Track: Many Men 'Go Undercover' Rather Than Take Paternity Leave," The Star-Ledger, at 27 (June 17, 2002).

[21] Cunningham, N. 19 *supra* at 997.

The contours of this cramped box are traced in the following series of quotations. A female partner who works part time and has children remarks:

> I think that is a gender issue that doesn't get that much attention; if a man was in my position, I'm not sure he would have gotten this much support. People assume the high legitimacy of what is taking me away from work, and wouldn't assume it of a man.

This is because, according to a female attorney who left work to stay with her child, "It's even more dangerous for men to do feminine things." Correct, says a thirty-two-year-old male lawyer, who left a large firm due to lifestyle issues:

> I didn't express any of this family stuff [to the firm] when I left. The way that I expressed it is that I wanted to pursue a different career. I thought that was more acceptable to say than that I wanted a better balance in life. I just don't think that men can say that. I just don't think that it rings true with people. They would just think it was stupid.

Similarly, a forty-five-year-old male who left a big firm for a smaller firm reflects:

> I went from a big firm to a small firm to take care of my kids. I also left because of practice issues. I told everyone it was the second, but it was mostly the first. I told people that out of courtesy for my last firm, I had deep respect for them. I didn't want to look like the firm was anti-family. Leaving that firm was particularly traumatic for me. I worked very hard to be a partner, no-one ever walked away from a partnership for those reasons, not there, not overtly. Certainly some people thought I was crazy.

Often men who are open about even a minor family matter can encounter resistance. Says a male partner in a medium-sized New York City firm:

> I took Friday off to spend with my daughter on her birthday and people looked at me like I was from Mars. My partners thought I was nuts. You can tell by the looks on their faces that they wondered what was wrong with me. Inside I'm thinking, "Too damn bad." I don't directly confront it. I don't really see a point to it. A woman could get

away with it. If I had had a huge crisis I would have cancelled being
with my daughter.

The language is extreme: men going part time is "illegitimate," talk of
work/life balance is considered "stupid," taking time off for children is "nuts,"
those males acting to build work/life balance are "crazy," and such talk
"doesn't ring true." A male deliberately building family concerns into his
plans is considered aberrational.

Men feel they shouldn't emote on these points, that it's indelicate even to
bring the matter up. Indeed, men are embarrassed to talk about these things.
Although males in my interviews freely talked about their wish for a healthier work/life balance, they are also "in the closet," reluctant to talk about it
much in public, in an informal conspiracy of silence. In his article about the
effect of legal employment for fathers, Keith Cunningham said that it was
hard to conduct research: "[T]he majority of men working part time at firms
that I contacted would not discuss the situation on the record or did not
return phone calls."[22] Legal recruiters told me that men go to corporate in-
house departments in large part for the same reasons that women do, but
their public reasons often emphasize the nature of the corporation's business, or a wish for a change—not lifestyle needs.

This is a problem for women who try to enlist like-minded men to help
them encourage attitude changes for work/life issues. Dr. Ron Kimball, a
Washington D.C. psychologist who counsels many lawyers, had a client
who had problems with flexibility in her work hours:

> She tries hard to develop alliances with male associates in her firm.
> It's proven fairly difficult. Her feeling is that most of the men she's
> talked to, while they do understand and kind of see the same thing
> she sees, they feel more threatened. It's almost that they have more
> to lose if they make any noise, if they are seen by partners as asso-
> ciated with any women who are making any noise.

---

[22] Cunningham, N. 19 *supra* at 995.

These fixed attitudes about fatherhood thrive even in the face of wide-spread lip service that dads should be more involved with their kids than were their own fathers. Most firms and workplaces in general seem affable toward work/life balance, whether or not they actually support the concept. It's part of the corporate white noise. A number of women described the delighted reaction men receive by acting like "super dads" in the office, performing high-profile fathering chores while not missing a step of lawyering. A female partner with children reports:

> My husband will say that, if he takes the kids in to his office, every female secretary is giving him "attaboys," volunteering to take the kids down to the break room, saying "Isn't he a good dad?" You don't see that with women. You see mildly arched eyebrows for women who bring their kids in.

Indeed, Eleanor, quoted above as conducting an "experiment" to avoid talking about her kids, says that the man in the cubicle next to her talks about his kids constantly, his office bulging with the smiling baby shots she's carefully excluded from her office. Thus the *perception* of a father's active involvement is reinforced all around, even if actual time spent on fathering versus work remains similar to or less than that of previous generations. This allows the traditional stereotype to flourish beneath the surface while minor displays of new models of fatherhood are inflated.

An added wrinkle is that men who take time off or reduce their hours for reasons other than childcare—to start a business, run for a political office, train for a triathlon, write a novel—can come back and pick up where they left off more easily than can men or women who reduce their hours because of their children. In fact, they would not routinely be referred to as "part time" during any of these episodes, as Cynthia Fuchs Epstein points out in *The Part-Time Paradox*.[23] This confirms the idea that one can remain "in the game" and be "masculine" so long as outside activities develop one's complementary ambitions. Childcare competes with a professional orientation.

---

[23] Cynthia Fuchs Epstein, Carroll Seron, Bonnie Oglensky & Robert Sauté, *The Part-Time Paradox: Time Norms, Professional Life, Family and Gender,* at p. 34 (Routledge, 1999).

Active Dads

Like the young women who find minimal guidance from the earlier generation of dual-career couples, some young men are not impressed by hard-charging males who spend little time with their families. Indeed, many of the younger men I spoke with were passionate about wanting to be more involved, rejecting the traditional uninvolved-dad paradigm.[24] A twenty-eight-year-old newly married lawyer just assumes that when he and his wife have children their working lives will change:

> My assumption is that my hours will decrease, it's going to take priority. And I'm sure it will be the same for my wife. We will not follow the traditional model—if it doesn't work out the way I want it to I would have to leave here. I reckon I would be at home hopefully by 5:30 or 6:00 every night for dinner, and also be home on weekends to do things with the kids. That would be my goal.

A thirty-year-old associate in a large Midwestern firm spoke intensely about his dedication to being a dad to his young son:

> I have a small child. I get tired of working a lot, I don't get to see him as much as I like. We don't want our kid to be a latchkey kid; we want to go home and play baseball with our kid, every day if we could. I work here so I can go home to my family. I saw my son for fifteen minutes yesterday on my way out the door and I saw him for fifteen minutes this morning on the way out the door. It doesn't make me happy. If it doesn't change, I'll be gone, I'll go in-house, and work more normal hours.

A thirty-eight-year-old Philadelphia male partner with two children wants to be different from his own father:

---

[24] According to the Radcliffe Public Policy Center, 82% of men aged twenty-one through thirty-nine name family as their top priority, as quoted in Sue Shellenbarger, "More Relaxed Boomers, Fewer Workplace Frills and Other Job Trends," The Wall Street Journal, at B1 (Dec. 27, 2000). The article also predicts that employees will start demanding flexible work arrangements that actually work, rather than forcing employees into "career suicide."

As a kid, and this is something I still struggle with, I always was resentful of the lack of my father's presence. I understood what was going on, understood that he was trying to earn a living, make things better for us, the whole old-school male way of living life. I didn't want and still don't want my sons to view me that way. I want them to think that I am available to them.

Another man left his law firm and went in-house to have more predictable hours and time with his son:

> The primary reason I left my first law firm, after my son was born, the kicker to me, I was working these insane hours and all the weekends, and I got a Saturday and Sunday off when I didn't have to work. My son was crawling, and I ran into the other room and told my wife that my son was crawling and she said, "He started that three weeks ago, you just weren't here." I started looking then.

Leonard, who practices in the Northeast, took two years out of his career to stay home with his children. He has gotten varying reactions. First he told his boss at his former job when he left to take care of his kids:

> I gave notice to an older male partner, I gave him six weeks' notice. I said, "I'm going to leave the firm." He said, "Where are you going?" I said, "I'm going home." He said, "You mean Atlanta?" I said, "No, I'm going to stay with my kids." He looked at me, completely puzzled. He knew my wife worked, but it just didn't click. But then eventually he absorbed it and it was fine.

Thereafter, when Leonard decided to go back to work (because his wife left her pressured job to stay home), he was completely open with prospective firms about what he'd done during the time at home:

> They asked about the gap, and I'd say I stayed home with my kids, and you can call the guy I used to work with, he'll give me an excellent reference. So I was very upfront about it. It was obvious I wasn't hiding anything. Then it became, "Can we accept this, it's unusual, but okay it's fine." I did note, there were inquiries about, "Is this serious? Are you really coming back to work?" So it was surprisingly not much of an issue. I would get a lot of questions about, "How did you

deal with hanging out with moms at the playground?" They were intrigued.

Leonard's co-workers' reactions since Leonard returned to work and tells them why he took time off have also been revealing. He gets respect, but with a veiled put-down from younger male colleagues:

> They look at me like, not in a critical sense, but more, "Good for you, but I could never do that, I can't imagine doing that." There's a quality of, "That's something women do and not men, chase kids around, wipe their noses, take them to dance class. I can't see myself doing that."

Surprisingly, older men have responded with sympathy:

> From older male attorneys, I have gotten responses like, "That's the most incredible thing. My kids are twenty and hate me. I didn't know my kids at all when they were growing up. You can't believe how lucky you are. My son doesn't talk to me." That's happened to me four or five times in the past year. An attorney in his mid-fifties, with two grown children and two young kids in his second marriage, said he was trying not to make the same mistakes again. These are heartfelt responses.

That Leonard has experienced reactions ranging from incomprehension to half-hearted respect to full-blown admiration indicates that many males have complicated feelings about the definition of good fathering.

Some men are starting to be more public about their concerns, rather than complaining privately. A female partner in the Midwest sees changing patterns among the young males and reactions from the old guard:

> I'm seeing many of our young men, mostly married with small children, coming in and not wanting to work the long hours, not wanting to come in and work on weekends—they say this to anyone who will listen! The reaction is often, "Tough, you should have chosen another field." I've got two men who have cut back in my department. Both have new babies and want to be home. They come in at 9 and are out the door by 5:30 or so and very seldom in here on the weekend.

In addition to wanting to change the paradigm of fathers' involvement with their kids, males also are keenly aware that their wives also want career fulfillment. One lawyer on the West Coast, whose wife recently left a high-powered investment banking job to care for their child, is torn between guilt and ambition:

> When my wife was working as hard as I was, it made it easier. We were both killing ourselves so we didn't have to feel guilty about not being at home. We've always given each other complete freedom to get our jobs done. And it's good for us—for me—to be effective in my job right now. Ostensibly there's a total green light [from his wife], "Do what you need to do, I'll make sure our son is well cared for." It's not just guilt—I have an amazing respect for my wife and the profession that she had and will have. And I want to make her life as smooth as it could be.

In contrast to the coterie of younger men wanting new options, another sector of younger men is following a very traditional path: working long hours while their wives raise the kids at home. One female lawyer with children serves on an otherwise all-male bar association committee:

> My observation is that although a lot of these guys will say that they're very up to speed and current on these [work/life] issues, and they believe that women should have equal time in the workplace, all of them have stay-at-home wives. All of them. I'm not saying one or two, almost every one has a stay-at-home wife, and nannies and so forth. They are under forty. That seems to be a badge of honor for them. My sense is that within their own firm structures that is what is expected. They wouldn't be looking as successful or doing as well if their wives were working. It seems to be a glaring factor. That to me is very shocking and bothersome.

Agrees another woman: "The single most disheartening thing that I find is that many of my male contemporaries have wives at home. How do I measure up to that? I'm not going to be able to devote as much time to work. Nor do I want to. But that's the gold standard." A female in the South says that trying to keep up is hard:

I think about how much harder the women have to work just to keep the wheels on the bus than most of our male counterparts. Most of the men here are married to non-working spouses. So they have basically everything done for them that I either have to do myself or pay someone to do.

For the time being, males who are in the closet about their evolving attitudes on fatherhood make parenting masquerade as a women's issue when in fact it's a parents' and lifestyle issue. Indeed, given the frequent career death that females experience as a result of working reduced hours, it's small wonder that men don't publicize their interest in achieving greater balance, much less pursue it actively.

Redefining Success

Lydia, a female lawyer, who is now at home full-time with her child, left work after twenty years of intense practice. The younger generation, I told her, is not always impressed with how the first generation of dual-career couples has handled work/life balance. She responded:

Our generation didn't have a generation ahead of us to act as role models. We were destined to be role models because of demography, and to try to do it in an intelligent way was important. It's interesting that the next generation would take a lesson about our personal lives and not about our career successes. A lot of us didn't work out well how to do these things simultaneously.

I then told her younger attorneys were very worried about how they were going to navigate family life. She responded:

They are right to be worried. It's hard to get it right. I think they're being smart. My worry is that my generation didn't make enough of a difference. We haven't had enough success.

If, when women first flooded the workplace, the expectation was that "everyone would work" and someone else would take care of the kids, there's little question that the reality today is far different.

In fact, the stereotype of dad at work and mom at home has re-emerged with tremendous force. We've come upon a raging river and, because we can't figure out how to wade through the waters, we've retreated back to safer ground. Part of that has been because of a failure of planning, not taking into account from the beginning that childcare would be a major obstacle in the way of the original vision, and preparing for it. That's why so many people feel almost betrayed. "We've been sold a bill of goods," frustrated women say, in a typical comment.

Parenthood is a negative for both men and women. A woman's issue is that once she becomes a mother, that role trumps all. She is primarily a mother and only secondarily holds other roles. The double bind—the stereotypical contradiction between "motherhood" and "competence"—remains in place. For a man who becomes a father, the paternal role is all but invisible in the workplace, respected but irrelevant. His contradiction is between "fatherhood," on the one hand, and "acting as a caregiver," on the other. Women are overwhelmed by their new role, men hardly dented. Both have problems if they want to play strong parenting roles and have fulfilling careers. So long as care giving is considered role-appropriate but not worthy of respect (for women), and neither appropriate nor worthy of respect (for men), that change is unlikely.

Therefore, when it comes to combining parenthood with work in a balanced way, options have not increased appreciably. Although women have some reduced-hours and other flexible options, these arrangements don't work out well. Men still are thought of as breadwinners above all and have little access to flexible work schedules. And most people still view work/life issues as almost exclusively a women's problem, rather than a parents' problem.

So there's no question the work/life balancing act hasn't turned out to be "a piece of cake," as Jane quipped early in this chapter. But because this issue has turned out to be tougher than expected, are all attempts at new models doomed? Will female lawyers continue to drop out of practice in greater numbers than men? Will it only be women who take reduced-hours schedules? Will males continue to assume leadership positions, acting as the "real lawyers" and, in the end, being no more involved with their kids than their dads were? We stand at a crossroads where it's easy to take the path of least resistance rather than working for changes.

Some indications suggest an inevitable slide back to a traditional arrangement. Workplaces have been glacial in responding to wishes for change, and not just in the legal arena. Younger men are quite likely to accept gender equity in theory, but in their personal choices many still embrace dad at work and mom at home, an option often affirmed and celebrated in the office. Younger women, too, often "give up" the career quest and stay home. They get discouraged by trying to "keep the wheels on the bus," gulping lunch at their desks while the guys shoot the breeze. Speculation about women's availability and commitment, that starts with the appearance of a diamond ring, limits women's opportunities. All these dynamics crowd out different choices and leave people feeling that the easiest way, if not the most fulfilling way, is to do things as they've been done before. Some say women may be departing the workforce without enough forward-looking perspective. Mary B. Cranston, CEO and chair of Pillsbury Winthrop in San Francisco, says, "I see all these young women cutting off their careers in mid-stream. I wonder how they are going to feel in a few years."

So maybe things will go back to the 1950s. Or is there room to push the boundaries of stereotypes about moms and dads, and to give them more freedom to work and parent as they wish without losing respect, either at home or in the workplace?

To some extent, the wave of change is cresting and about to crash, ready or not. In Chapter 7 a list of trends in the workforce revealed a movement towards more flexible schedules. Parental duties add immeasurably to those pressures. Younger dual-career couples have little choice but to trade and balance responsibilities. Says a female partner on the West Coast, "I see more and more that the younger guys have to go home and pick up the sick kid because their wives are in court. The woman says, 'I've got to go pick up the sick kid,' but the guy just says, 'I've got to go.' They're afraid of losing face." More positively, some younger males are just as vociferous in demanding family time as are females. They rebel against what they see as arbitrary restrictions against expanding flexibility.

And although the focus tends to be overwhelmingly on childcare as the chief competition for work, working people will increasingly need time to care for elderly parents.[25] In addition, in the last ten years, the number of

---

[25] The best estimate for the percentage of people in the workforce who are at present giving care to elder relatives is 15% to 20%. Given demographic patterns, it is likely that that percentage will increase in the future. Interview with Gail Gibson Hunt, executive director of the National Alliance for Caregiving, August 20, 2002.

fathers acting as primary custodians of children under eighteen rose 62%, for a total of 2.2 million men.[26] Similarly, an increasing number of males are staying at home while the moms are going to work.[27] This provides—for people like Melinda, whose husband has cared for their children—the same kind of reassurance about good parental care as was traditionally provided by mothers. Indeed, the stigma of the "mommy track" is easing in some firms.[28] As the numbers of people who work flexible schedules increase, acceptance will also increase.[29]

Employers are innovating by making their own rules. In my interviews, I heard many answers to the clarion call for flexibility. A trusts and estates lawyer runs a thriving practice working three and one-half days a week. A Florida firm employs largely reduced-hours personnel. A husband-and-wife team alternated one-year leaves to be with their children. Offices close early on Fridays. Employers permit telecommuting; a few allow job-sharing. Some give maternity and paternity leave on a "take as much time as you need" basis.

---

[26] Carey Goldberg, "Single Dads Wage Revolution One Bedtime Story at a Time," The New York Times, at A1 (June 17, 2001).

[27] U.S. Bureau of Labor statistics in 2001 reveal that, among married-couple families with children under eighteen, only the mother works in 4.5% of the families, only the father works in 29.5% of the families, and both parents work in 63.2% of the families. Sue Shellenbarger, "Please Send Chocolate: Moms Now Face Stress Moving In and Out of Workforce," The Wall Street Journal, at D1 (May 9, 2002). Earlier Bureau of Labor figures from 1993 reveal that, among the 6.3 million married-couple families with preschoolers whose mothers worked in the fall of 1993, 25% of the fathers provided care. U.S. Census Bureau, "My Daddy Takes Care of Me! Fathers as Care Givers," Press Release (Oct. 8, 1997). See Betsy Morris, "Trophy Husbands," Fortune (Sept. 27, 2002) (online article at www.fortune.com).

[28] Bruce Balestier, "'Mommy Track' Loses Stigma," New York Law Journal (June 20, 2000) (online article at www.law.com).

[29] In a June 2001 Gallup poll, 71% of employed men and 59% of employed women said that, given a choice, they would prefer to continue working outside the home rather than staying home and taking care of house and family, whereas 26% of employed men and 39% of employed women said they would prefer to be at home. These figures actually show a fair amount of convergence. There is some difference, but not a huge split, between male and female attitudes. Indeed, the 2001 Catalyst study of lawyers showed that of the married lawyers responding to their survey, 28% of the men provide all the family income, as do 5% of the women. Those figures are interesting because they represent greater numbers of women than one might expect. Increasingly, as one spouse's career takes off, decisions are made to put that spouse on the fast track regardless of gender, and have the other parent take a back seat when it comes to career. See Women in Law: Making the Case, at p. 12 (Catalyst, 2001).

Other firms aggressively market themselves as balanced on work/life issues and find that they can attract superior talent. A partner in a mid-sized Midwestern firm boasts about its results: "We were able to get top-notch people by making this a place you wanted to go to." A woman in Idaho says, "The clients I work with are pretty accommodating. They don't seem upset if I'm not in. Today I'm doing a settlement negotiation from home, because my daughter's sick, and nobody is bothered about calling me here. And I'm drawing up a motion from home, I'll e-mail it in." Bigger legal employers say they can't afford to do these things and stay competitive. It could be that competition for top lawyers will force their hand.

Lydia, quoted above, is disappointed that her generation hasn't "had enough success." Lawyers today are re-evaluating the ambitions of the first generation of female lawyers, and concluding they didn't include enough foresight about all aspects of life, rather than just acceptance in the workplace. Perhaps the right definition of success has been elusive and is slowly unfolding. A new definition of success can challenge the traditional view that the only good lawyer is an obsessed practitioner making the greatest amount of money possible at all phases of his or her career. The new definition could be a practitioner who does superb quality work, who is celebrated—not patronized—for creatively organizing his or her life to include real time for parenting, and who includes criteria for success other than earning a significant amount of money.

It's great that Judge Earle could solve her sick child problem and still mete out justice on the bench. Parents across the legal workplace spectrum are also making individual adjustments so that the "kid thing" can co-exist with work. As this chapter shows, their one-at-a-time solutions are hard to sustain in law offices that marginalize responsible parents.

CHAPTER 9

We Care: Debating a "Good" Stereotype

———————— ♓ ————————

Empathy for All
To Be Honest
To Bill or Not to Bill
"Whose Side Are You On?"
Phony Relationships
Flying Under the Radar
The Problem Solvers
What's the Meaning of This?
A Good Shoehorn?
Too Much Caring
The Best Policy
An Advocate Above All
Re-thinking Getting Business
Getting Ahead
To Play Games or Not
What's Meaningful?
Fresh Air

———————— ♓ ————————

Christopher, a male legal aid attorney, represents impoverished housing clients on the East Coast. He says:

> I prefer to appear in front of female judges. Sometimes I think stereo-typically that there's a better chance of getting a better deal for my client. I'm assuming that the female judge will have more of a caring orientation than a male judge. Stereotypes in some ways are good because it gives you something to go on. I tend to go for the female. I know I'm stereotyping but I've got to do something. It's a starting point and I'm happy to be proved wrong. There are plenty of female judges I don't respect at all. But on the whole, I have slightly more success with the females. I feel like they're a little more willing to listen to the exceptional circumstances.

Christopher is using stereotypes to his advantage: he's making a bet that the female judge will be more sympathetic to his downtrodden poor clients than a male judge, relying on the assumption that women are good, caring, and supportive.

Most of the stereotypes examined so far have worked more to men's advantage than to women's; women's performances are usually evaluated by how much they fall short of fulfilling the ideal of an effective attorney. In this chapter, however, characteristics that are more readily identified with women are explored to determine how they provide women with an advantage over men in practice. Many women perceive, and men agree with them, that they are more likely to demonstrate a caring orientation, greater honesty, more humility, less game playing and posturing, and a desire to find more meaning in their jobs.

Everyone interviewed was quick to say that these generalizations did not apply to all men or women, and that they could readily think of exceptions: a nurturing male, a take-no-prisoners female. However, most agreed there was a "tendency" for more women to act in certain ways, and for men to act otherwise. Although women aren't credited with inventing the qualities and approaches in which they excel, many believe they have exploited these possibilities more than was done previously. In this chapter, men and women first describe the ways that they believe women have changed legal practice. They then debate the advantages and disadvantages of these approaches for any lawyer who might consider using them.

Empathy for All

Women claim, and many men confirm, that females are more empathetic to colleagues and clients, as well as to juries in the courtroom. A study of lawyers' morality, which focused on gender differences, found that more women in the sampling had a caring orientation, emphasizing interdependence, avoiding harm to others, cooperation, and compromise. By contrast, the male lawyers in the study tended to have a "rights" orientation, which stresses autonomy and a faith that adherence to rules and laws will preserve the individual from harm.[1]

A caring approach meshes well with traditional assumptions of female solicitude. Obviously, there are male attorneys whose clients revere them for their moderate temperament, but women in their law practices have seized upon the notion of caring and extended it, harnessing their inclination towards intimacy and sociability.[2] There are many dimensions to the caring orientation. A man admired the nurturing style of a female arbitrator in a matter in which he was involved:

> Her womanliness probably helped to disarm people a little bit. She had a warm personal style. She made it clear that whoever was hosting the mediation was responsible for keeping coffee and food handy. She considered care of creature comforts to be a part of the mediation process. Maybe a man wouldn't be as likely to think of that.

Her ability to relate was also important:

> She really took time to let people tell their stories, to empathize with them, to make it clear that she had a great deal of sympathy for what they had gone through. There's no doubt in my mind that part of her ability to do that resulted from the various talents she had, including

---

[1] Rand Jack & Dana Crowley Jack, *Moral Vision and Professional Decisions: The Changing Values of Men and Women Lawyers,* at pp. 11, 55 (Cambridge University Press, 1989).

[2] An analysis of women's managerial style in Chapter 5 *supra* revealed that many attorneys feel that women bring a more understanding and egalitarian approach to supervision than do men.

being a woman. I'm not saying a man couldn't do it. I suppose at least initially somebody might not have expected that same kind of empathy from a male, because of the overall image that guys aren't as sensitive.

Female trusts and estates lawyers were particularly likely to say that clients love their personal approach. One woman in the Midwest gives frequent public talks about estate planning with her male colleagues. She says that new clients follow up with her, not with the men:

> I don't know if I hit the emotional side of wills and estates, but the women [in the audience] actually take the bull by the horns, identify with me, and say, "My husband is too busy. I saw you at the seminar, and I want an appointment." I have a tremendous number of clients that come in through that route. I think in estate planning that the woman is the chief emotional officer of the household. She cares about the kids and the guy's too busy to worry about things. [My role is] just to be able to sympathize. Female probate attorneys can go much further. They don't view it as "sign here and show up at the hearing." They care. [Clients] are looking for a counselor, becoming a friend to them. You gain their loyalty over a long time.

The ability to empathize is critical, agreed another female trusts and estates lawyer, and women do that well:

> We are more empathetic, and the clients I deal with, they appreciate that. They're putting a spouse in the nursing home, they're selling the house, there's a lot of loss, and they're going through a traumatic time. We're better able to handle it than men, to talk to them, to be supportive.

Understanding and compassion can help in other settings, people maintain. A female practitioner in the East praises a woman judge for her lack of pretentiousness:

> If you come in on a motion, she will come down off the bench, she'll take her robe off and fold it carefully over the bench, and she becomes [like a host] on a TV talk show. It works every time. She is totally unconscious of doing it. She comes down to the client's level;

she's no longer a person above all of us. And she just talks. She's empathetic: "I'm talking to you, and you're the most important person in the world." A man would never do that. Male judges are too much into their authority.

Caring is also reflected in better listening skills. A male partner in the Southwest says that his firm handles some large personal injury cases:

When we have PI cases, I'm not a good one for the clients to call every day. So I'll give the case to one of my female partners, or my paralegals who are women, and they do a good job of listening. And occasionally they come up with some things that I would never have listened long enough to hear.

Women capitalize on their greater warmth to build long-term relationships with clients that are intensely personal. A New Hampshire female practitioner says:

In practice, women bring a different level of commitment to the client relationship, a more personal approach to it, a better understanding of what the client's feelings are, a better awareness of what the clients are going through. This makes it a more intimate relationship with clients than typically would have been the case before women were as involved and as senior as they are today. There's a level of loyalty among clients with the women in the firm, which to some extent seems to go beyond the average with the men attorneys in the office. I think in part it's because the women care about their clients more.

Not only do women tend to be more caring and demonstrate greater empathy and more willingness to listen patiently, "female" qualities can help win cases. A male employment practitioner notes that the many women in the field lend a human approach to sensitive cases:

It emphasizes skills that people tend to attribute to women. In employment law, I think that the people who end up having real disasters in their employment cases, with big adverse verdicts, tend to be the hard chargers. Especially when you're representing management, a lighter touch does much better. When a company is being sued, the last thing they need is a pit bull as their face in that court-room, which allows the jury to demonize them. The most effective personality style tends to be somebody who has real interpersonal appeal, who seems sincere and human, and who helps to humanize the company.

A female Pennsylvania litigator agrees:

Some cases require a lighter touch if there's a lot of animosity between the parties. I'm amazed at how many cases where it's just money, but the people hate one another. In those cases women's skills are more appropriate. I usually have a good relationship with opposing counsel, not threatening, a lot of joking. Which helps when it's tense.

Women claim that they are better conciliators and peacemakers, pointing out that mediation and arbitration have blossomed at the same time that women have flooded the profession. An in-house woman in Wisconsin says:

Look at all the movement toward mediation and arbitration. You can't go to small claims without being put in the midst of mediation. That may have been influenced by a more reasoned, calmer, less com-bative approach. I think there's some truth to the idea that, rather than picking up the sword to go to battle first, women's initial ten-dency is to try to figure out a way to work it out.

And a female litigator in New Mexico concurs:

Women, of course, would rather as a gender resolve matters in a friendly way than fight. Our nature is to want resolution and not con-flict. In the domestic relations arena, we now have mandatory medi-ations. That is completely because of women lawyers and women judges.

By capitalizing on these attributes—nurturing, empathy, listening skills, more personal relationships with clients, a lighter touch in tense situations, and peacemaking skills—women have taken advantage of their tendency towards caring to achieve professional success.

To Be Honest

Along with a more caring approach, many women commented to me that they bring greater honesty and integrity to their work. Whether or not women in fact are more honest than men, this perception is widely held. "I know from our research that women are perceived as less likely to lie for their clients and therefore have a credibility advantage coming in," says Kathleen Kauffmann, a former jury consultant who is now practicing in Washington, D.C. A 1989 survey conducted by Starr & Associates found that 60% of respondents believed that women lawyers are more ethical than male lawyers.[3] A female legal aid attorney with thirty years of experience in the courtroom says:

> I've seen an awful lot of male attorneys that I believe give a bad impression because they're cocky and slick. They seem untrustworthy, they offend the jury as much as they offend me. In [women's] approach to cases, if you convey empathy to your client, if you can stress your client as a person, you make him or her seem more of a person than male attorneys do. Perhaps the jury will accept it more since you are a woman, perceiving greater empathy and honesty.

At least two states have reported that women lawyers have far fewer ethics claims filed against them, in proportion to their presence in the profession, than do men.[4] In the non-legal sphere, commentators identify high-profile female whistleblowers as evidence of women's high standards of integrity.[5]

---

[3] Jean Maclean Snyder & Andra Barmarsh Greene, *The Woman Advocate,* at p. 196 (American Bar Association, Section of Litigation, 1996).

[4] Mary P. Gallagher, "A Legal Ethics Gender Gap," New Jersey Law Journal (April 5, 2002) (online at www.law.com); Brenda Sapino Jeffreys, "Discipline Actions and the Gender Gap," Texas Lawyer (Aug. 12, 2002) (online at www.law.com).

[5] In one article a woman commented, "It's hard to say this without having it sound like stereotyping. . . . But there is a strong moral overtone in the questions the women are asking. Do women seek a higher plane?" Mary Williams Walsh, "Preparing a Corps of Women for Corporate Responsibility," The New York Times, at C2 (Aug. 13, 2002); Paul Farni, "They're Telling It Like It Is: Why Women Are Likelier to Be Whistleblowers," The Star-Ledger, at 17 (July 10, 2002). See Richard Lacayo & Amanda Ripley, "Persons of the Year 2002: Cynthia Cooper, Coleen Rowley and Sherron Watkins," 160:27 Time Magazine (Dec. 30, 2002) (spotlighting female whistleblowers in major corporations and at the Federal Bureau of Investigation).

Women don't simply claim higher moral ground. They cite specific situations where they feel their approach is more conscientious than men's, such as scrupulously accurate billing, intellectual honesty (meaning a willingness to see both sides of a matter), and an aversion to socializing for primarily networking purposes.

To Bill or Not to Bill

A number of women lawyers indicated that women are more exact about recording their hours in private practice than men. A female partner in the Midwest relates:

> One of the things that I see happening at this firm, and other firms, too, is that every lawyer worries about billable hours. But it's only the women who are honest enough to say, "I'm spending so much time with my kids that it is stressing me out to work 1800 or 2000 hours, and I'm going to go to some kind of reduced compensation package, so that I can only bill 1400 or 1500." We've got a number of women who are part time, all women. But there are lots of guys who bill no more than those women, and they don't have the nerve to stand up and say, "I'm not going to bill as many hours, and therefore I want to be part time." I do think that for whatever reason, for women it's more of an integrity issue.

Another woman, formerly a partner in a firm and now in-house on the East Coast, grew increasingly uncomfortable at her law firm when she wasn't reaching her stated goal for billable hours, and she therefore decided to cut her hours and pay:

> I was 150 hours short, and I just hated it. No one ever said anything to me. But I just felt very uncomfortable. I hated feeling like I could not say I hit the target. I felt from a psychological perspective [that arranging for reduced hours] would allow me to take the pressure off myself, to spend more time with my kids. It was an integrity decision. I was doing something that [males] were not willing to do: I was willing to forego some money.

A woman who is now in-house, but formerly worked at a firm in Wisconsin, noticed a distinct difference between female and male lawyers:

261

More women have a more difficult time being dishonest in hours than men do. Men overbill a lot more than women do. I'd hate to think it's a basic honesty thing. In private practice, there was one woman who billed like crazy, whereas for four or five or us [women], it was a constant struggle. We were in the office a third again as much as any of those guys, and it never failed that our hours would be lower than any of the guys. It just seemed that they were better at driving in the car to get somewhere and billing someone. I don't know if they felt less self-conscious about padding hours. I always described it as, I never lost my conscience. At some point you were expected to just bill the hell out of a client. You were supposed to throw a couple of hours on there with clients who won't scrutinize the bill.

A legal recruiter has noticed that women seem to write off more time than men do, and theorizes:

It's because they have a greater sense of concern about displeasing their client, and a recognition that [the amount of the bill] really is too much. They're comfortable saying, "This is too much." I think it's because they don't get as wrapped up in things personally, it's not a battle between two boys. Women tend to write off their own time before they write off an associate's time.

Some women say their attitude toward time-keeping reflects the caring orientation discussed above. A sixty-three-year-old family lawyer in the East says:

I tend to be a fairly empathetic individual. Even today I don't think that's terribly accepted. I would sit with a client and chat for an hour and then not charge them, which was frowned upon. I would have 20 minutes of chitchat and 10 minutes of legal talk, and I'd bill 10 minutes. But you're supposed to bill. The guys would be there 7 hours, chatting with each other, and they'd put down 7 hours. Time sheets were always a bête noire for me. I stopped wearing a watch for exactly that reason twenty-five years ago. I think that's a female thing.

These women perceive that men have a hard-charging commercial approach to billing, a game or calculation where men try to see how much they can get away with in charging some clients, whereas women are more scrupulous about exact recording of time, with deviations only to decrease a bill because it's "too much."

"Whose Side Are You On?"

Women identified another aspect of the "integrity" debate: a greater tendency to intellectual, substantive honesty. Many say this isn't popular, such as this New Jersey female associate:

> It gets you into trouble by saying that there are weak points. People don't like to hear the truth. You will hear from the client, "Whose side are you on?" Every day in the law you encounter the other side's client who has stars in his eyes. You know [their perceptions of a strong case are] not true, and you wonder, why has his lawyer led him on like this? At least I don't do that with my clients. I set the expectations properly.

Jackie, a female litigator in Pennsylvania, has experienced a similar dynamic:

> I tend to have a more difficult time convincing myself that things are black and white and that my side is completely correct. Men have an easier time getting into that mindset. Clients and senior partners don't think that I believe in the case enough because I quickly see the other side's point. They look at me blankly and say, "Well, you're just supposed to argue the case." There's a lack of commitment seen. I'm a very logical person so I just try to lay out why I believe it. It doesn't mean that I don't think we're going to win, but there are people who want me to say there's no chance we'll lose, and I don't believe that. There's one case I'm working on now, and I can't convince the senior partner that it doesn't look very good. He says, "It was a good case to begin with, so you do the best you can."

A male employment lawyer agrees that females tend to assess both sides of a case more fairly than males:

> In litigation in particular, that's where I've seen the gender pattern. That's one reason why employment law works really well for women. When you read about disasters that occur, it's behavior that I would associate with men. Men go in as gladiators, not having thought

263

through how the other side's position is going to play in open court, and get a disastrous verdict. You see a lot of cases tried that get bad results, and you read the facts, and you think, "What lawyer would bring this in front of a jury?" And it's usually a male. Men think it would be fun to handle an employment case, and they handle it like a commercial case. Women are less likely to do that.

A female litigator in Michigan remarks:

I agree that women are more honest about things—there are times when men are just unwilling to see the handwriting on the wall. They have to get so invested in a case in order to process it that they can't be practical. Women are more willing to see the other side.

A male litigator believes that women are more likely to share the weaknesses of their cases with juries:

I notice that most men try to hide things from the juries, they're not really honest with juries. Whereas most women are up-front. "I've got problems," they'll tell the jury. Male lawyers won't do that as much.

A man says this is because male colleagues don't like to reveal defects in their case, even with attorney colleagues, although they know they exist and have to prepare for them:

Men are less willing to admit weaknesses for their case. I've always been a little bit puzzled by it. My tendency is to talk about the strengths and the weaknesses, and to focus on the weaknesses, so we know how to address them. It's not just zealous advocacy [by the men who won't admit weakness]. It's as if they're suggesting, "If I acknowledge the weaknesses, then it suggests I'm weak, and I'm a man and I can't be weak."

In this instance, women appear detached and dispassionate, identifying less with a client or cause. This can seem counter to the caring stereotype, but instead it draws upon the role of peacemaker, a person who tries to reconcile two sides, rather than joining the battle vociferously on one side or the other.

Phony Relationships

Another feature of the honesty debate is women's distaste for "phony" socializing with potential or current clients. Many of the women I interviewed bluntly stated that they hated business development and the fraternizing that went with it. A partner in Ohio says: "I don't know how to do any of that socializing stuff. We have firm events, a big box at the Reds baseball game. I hate that stuff. I do it because I'm expected to do it." An associate in Colorado: "I suck at it. I don't like doing it. I'm not good at it." A family lawyer in Pennsylvania: "I find the whole concept of marketing slightly repulsive." A male in the Midwest observes: "I do notice that the women here don't have the outgoing personality for business getting. One says she hates these events where you've got to go and talk to people. Maybe it's just their personality, not gender."

Much of women's aversion is related to a supposed dissonance between business development and socializing. Ida Abbott, a consultant to law firms based in Oakland, California, says:

> Women have wonderful relationships, but very often they keep those in a social box, and then there's a business box. Those two boxes tend to stay separate. If you're at your kids' soccer game, talking to other moms about kids, a lot of them don't realize that the other moms are potential clients. This is not to say that you should be dropping your card everywhere, but a lot of women like to keep a very bright line between the two.

Indeed, one woman in a Colorado firm said that a social outing featuring clients she didn't genuinely care about or like was more difficult for her to tolerate than it was for her husband:

> Maybe I'm a snob. You talk to these people and you're desperately trying to find common ground. My husband can sit there and mask all his views. Me, if this person is going to tell me some view that I'm going to disagree with, my tongue will be bleeding I'd be biting it so hard. Schmoozing is hard with a person you don't genuinely like. Falseness, phoniness, that I just can't do. It's a feigned interest in somebody else's interests, like, "I love going to bars and drinking beers and hitting on women." I can't say that. My colleagues feel the

265

same way. Most attorneys are introverts. They like working on their own, they don't like to be bothered.

Thus, some women see socializing for business as a violation of roles, a pretense of liking people, which is inauthentic and uncomfortable. They feel they are being dishonest in pursuing relationships where they don't actually care about the people, but are merely using them for personal advancement.

Flying Under the Radar

Along with being more caring and honest, women point out that they are more humble and less boastful and arrogant than men. They say they prefer to just do their work well, rather than bragging about it or tooting their own horn. A woman in Maryland saw some competitive jousting among males in her firm start at the time of a merger:

> With the merger, this male machismo—"I've got to show you up and I've got to strut my peacock feathers"—became more and more evident among the male partners. Every conversation is about, "I'm better than you." It's not something I want to do. I was raised to downplay my credentials. I'm typically female, I didn't want to play that male game.

Many women assert that humility is a sound strategy for advancement. Elise, a successful practitioner with her own firm in the Midwest, deliberately cultivates the image of a humble helpmate:

> I don't know anybody else like me. Why? I don't think most people realize how successful we are. And in some ways that is intentional. I think there would be resentment if they realized that a little upstart girl was doing what I do. I tend to be very humble about what we're doing, never egotistical. We frequently act as co-counsel, and I'm always willing to do the researching and putting the case together. I'm always willing to let somebody else go out and get the glory. We're not perceived as a threat. A guy wouldn't do this. I drill this into my attorneys. There's no ego in what we're doing, we're just trying to make a lot of money. That's hard, because lawyers tend to be arrogant. This is not to say that we don't have cases where we're top chair. But it would be terrible if I acted more flamboyantly. Men could

get away with it but I can't. I think that there is a relatively deep prejudice that runs through [the local] bar and probably this society here in [the state], and a woman who does what I do is unusual. As long as I seem like a nice, friendly, hardworking, helpful type of person, then I'm not resented. But as soon as I start acting like I'm just as good as the boys, then I'm resented. Never be uppity as a woman. With clients I know really well, I will frequently refer bigger things to big firms. Clients say, "You act so humble with them," and I say, "I'm just happy to be alive, and I don't want to give them an idea of what I'm doing."

She believes that adopting a modest façade allows her to quietly achieve success.

Some observe men posturing more when they are managing others. One woman, in a typical remark, says that many of the men she works with seem to manufacture baseless "emergencies." She says:

I think a lot of the demands that we place on ourselves and on travel and "this must be done tonight" really are optional. It's muscle flexing. Men do this, and women don't.

In effect, she says, male lawyers proclaim, "It is an emergency because I am thinking about it." Junior associates have told her that a senior male commanded them to complete an assignment immediately, and she has then told them not to worry about it, because in her opinion there was no urgency.

Many women commented to me that they perceived that their hard work should speak for itself, and that pursuing business by boasting about their accomplishments made them cringe. "Blowing your own horn—I don't feel good about it," states a female partner in a big firm in the South. "Precisely. I'm innocent enough to think that all my work should stand on its merits alone." She said she felt like "a fish out of water" calling the managing partner to let him know she'd brought in a big matter. Some women say they were turned off by swaggering attitudes, such as this female partner in a Northeastern firm, whose male colleagues frequently circulate e-mails celebrating some success or another:

With e-mail, we now have incredible male back-patting going on each time a male has any success, large or small. Quite honestly, I don't have time for it. A lot of other women feel the same way. It's not in my nature to boast about my successes, or the successes of others. It's good for morale to recognize and congratulate deserving colleagues on major accomplishments, but not to excess.

For many women lawyers, humility is an antidote to overweening arrogance in the workplace, providing a stable foundation for getting work accomplished and avoiding excesses of ego.

The Problem Solvers

As a result of these characteristics, many women claimed that they were better at simply getting things done rather than playing games. For instance, they scoff at scorched-earth litigation tactics, which they consider more the province of males. Says a female litigator from Washington, D.C.:

> I do think there's a big difference with the way women approach litigation than men do. We do tend to be strangely much more direct about things. Normally the dynamic would be, there's a document request served, and men are objecting to every request. They fight about it, and there's a motion to compel. I think that women tend to say, "Let's just have a fight about what's really important." That is not the way the men do it. I've seen that as a gender difference. I say, "Just give them the things you don't care about." The men will say, "You women don't like to have a fight." They will characterize it as a gender issue too. Pick your battles, say women.

A woman who is now a federal judge recalls her days litigating:

> The scorched earth nature of litigation—I didn't like it. I was only exposed to it for a very short period of time. I didn't like the, "Oh, let's file a motion at 4:30 on a Friday." I just thought that was bullshit, I hated that. Jockeying for position—I will not let it happen in my courtroom. I have had several sessions with attorneys early on in cases where I've said, "If you guys can't behave, we're not having this."

A legal recruiter says this is a common attitude among women:

> Many women don't like the constant adversarial nature of a litigation practice. When you spend all day fighting over stupid things, women

find it far more tedious, far less productive, than men. It's more a chess game. They don't like that. Men like the combat. They don't mind fighting over incredibly stupid things. Women tend to get more disgusted with that.

Women think some men are too egotistical and stubborn to simply settle or conclude a negotiation, prolonging a process that otherwise would be resolved. A female partner in Oregon remarks:

> Most cases are settled, of course. Men must have been able to do it without [women in the profession] before. But I think generally speaking, women may do that a little better than men. When I think of people who are the most stubborn and seem to take the most lawyer-like approaches, they are usually men.

An in-house woman in California also notices that ego seems to be a roadblock:

> I watch in business negotiations, and often they fail, because the ego of someone, usually male, gets in the way. A lot of times you can point to someone who couldn't concede a valid concern of the other side, because they were just going to fight it out. I don't see too many women letting their ego get in the way of the best decision.

Jackie, the litigator from Pennsylvania, sees a similar dynamic in settlement conferences:

> Not settling, that's a man thing. I would always rather settle a case. I have a case now that could have been settled early. Attempting to carry it on has generated hundreds of thousands of dollars in bills. The [male] partner says, "Take it to trial, I'd rather lose than settle." It's a guy thing, a bravado thing. I asked what was driving this case, and another partner said, "Testosterone." The senior partner did the motion of banging on his chest like an ape, saying, "Let's go for it with all barrels," and we did even though it was not the smartest thing to do. Now it's like backing down to his friend to say it's not that good a case. He would rather go to court and lose and say that the judge was really stupid. Most of the power and money is with the guys, so as long as it's more difficult for women to get clients it's harder to control a lot of things.

Women contrast game playing and posturing with just "cutting to the chase" and reaching a goal. A woman in Texas talks about why she prefers dealing with female opposing counsel rather than male opposing counsel:

> It's always wonderful. I've had very few bad experiences. Usually there's this ability to get to the point, there's not a lot of posturing, there's not a lot of trying to show each other how smart we are. It's just, here's a problem, what's the answer? It's easier and more productive working with women. There's not as much ego involved, not as much testosterone floating around.

Another woman says females prefer to find common ground, versus men who believe that sharing information undercuts their position:

> There's always a risk of stereotyping, but if I had to say there was a gender difference in the approach, women tend to come into a negotiation setting looking for the common ground and trying to find a way to work a resolution as a problem solver. Men frequently come in with a more aggressive tone to try to intimidate or win. They don't come in with the attitude of, "Let's exchange a lot of information about our case, and maybe be creative about thinking outside the box."

Women say they are leery of the typical back and forth of negotiating. A female partner in a Minnesota firm recalls:

> We had a corporate retreat where we brought in a very high-profile speaker from a high-profile New York law firm to teach us about the art of negotiation. Most of the women afterwards said it was so revolting. He said, "We all know that negotiation is like a dance, and we all know what moves the person will play next, and it's the fun of the dance." Women said, "That's what I hate about that firm, that's what I hate about that style of negotiation, that sense from the beginning that we're going to go through this pointless dance and not just cut to the chase."

An experienced female Michigan trial lawyer sees different patterns between men and women for negotiating:

I believe that women and men negotiate differently. Men, if they're the defense lawyer in a personal injury case, they start out at like $5,000 when they're prepared to pay $250,000, and if you're the plaintiffs you start at $750,000 when you're willing to stop at $250,000. You do all this screwing around and bartering, it's very time-consuming. And for most of the women with whom I've dealt, I feel comfortable saying, this is what the case is worth. If you can come up with it, do what you need to do. They come back and say yes or no, without the nickel and diming back and forth. They are more practical, they cut to the bottom line. I believe that women just don't have time for that baloney. It's game playing and competitiveness.

A D.C. female litigator had a similar view:

If you're in a situation where you're trying to settle, there's this big dance in negotiation. They say $10 million, you say $2 million, and you're going to settle at $7.5 million, and everybody knows it. I go in and say my top number is $6 million, and that's it. When I tell the number, that's the number. They say, okay, well $8 million, and I say $6 million. If you have built up enough credibility so that they accept that number, then that's good. A lot of times that is foreign to how people negotiate. The usual way is a huge waste of time. It's so foreign to the man on the end of the phone. If you've set it up right, he does believe it and accepts it. I think that women are more direct about it. They are trying to get to the end quicker. Women posture a lot less than men.

These women believe they are doing a more efficient job and often getting a better result for their client, because they are not indulging in time-wasting games but instead are resolving the matter as quickly as possible, relying on the credibility of a firm amount in negotiating rather than a questionable result as the outcome of an endless "dance." This is an extension of the idea of women as humble workers behind the scenes, not seeking glory but rather pursuing concrete results.

What's the Meaning of This?

Another gender-related concept is that women perceive they want more "meaning" in their work, and get more impatient and frustrated than men with dry commercial or corporate work that has no obvious social dimension. Indeed, women are more likely to take public interest law and government jobs than are men, positions that reward less in dollars and more in social mission.[6] A man who was formerly managing partner at a major U.S. firm observes:

> I think it's something deeper in the difference in the psychology of men and women. What I've observed, and this is totally unscientific, is that men take a job like doing a set of papers for a tax-exempt bond. It's probably an incredibly boring, mechanical, pain-in-the-ass job, and for what? So some dinky town in New Jersey can buy a fire engine. It may be very educational as a professional matter, and men I think have their focus on the career aspects. They're willing to work day and night because it's what the job is, and it's what necessary for their careers. I think they are less likely than women to look at the thing and say, "What the hell am I am doing this for? I don't want to spend late hours in my life to write papers to buy a fire engine that no one will ever read again." These are deep values. Women are more likely to say, "What's the purpose of this?" in relation to how they want to spend their lives. Men are just as smart and just as sensitive and maybe just as disgusted with the pile of papers, but they keep on doing it. Women say the hell with it.

A New York male partner who sits on the personnel committee and evaluates associates notices that women are far more likely than men to report that they "really enjoy" doing their work, suggesting to him that interest in their work is more important to women than men.

---

[6] A recent report by the National Association of Law Placement indicated that 3.8% of women graduates from the class of 2000 took public interest jobs, but only 1.7% of the males did, and that 14.5% of the women took government jobs, as opposed to 12.9% of the men. "Employment Comparisons and Trends for Men and Women, Minorities and Non-minorities" (National Association of Law Placement, 2002) (online at www.nalp.org). Figures from the American Bar Association show that 11% of women lawyers are in government jobs, as opposed to 7% of men; 10% of women are in private industry or associations, as compared to 9% of men; and 2% of women are legal aid attorneys or public defenders, as opposed to 1% of male lawyers. *A Current Glance of Women in the Law* (American Bar Association, Commission on Women in the Profession, 2001).

Women say they have a better perspective about the importance of work versus life than men do, stating that men single-mindedly focus on practice to the exclusion of other worthwhile activities in life. A successful woman in her fifties sees fiercer dedication from her male colleagues:

> I feel as if I've devoted as much of my life to practice as my male partners have. But [among males] there's a certain absolute devotion to this being the most important thing in their lives that I frankly think is unhealthy. I don't accept that. If a client needs me I'll be in here any time of day. But I wouldn't subjugate my marriage or my kids. And I'm probably more devoted to my practice than most women. But I don't know if women have the absolute drive to be number one. I see guys who make more money than I do, but their drive is greater.

Indeed, a female lawyer in New Hampshire thinks that women are more likely to search for meaning:

> If men are busy, if they are successful, if they have a lot of clients, that's good enough. They're at the top of their game. Whether their particular issues have any meaning to them, internally or not, may not be a big factor in the equation for them. Whereas I think with women—and I stress that I don't like to say all women and all men—women may tend to say more frequently, even if they're busy and have a lot of clients, "What am I doing and why am I doing it? Am I adding value to the world? Is it making me feel good about the world?"

She speculates that this is because women are more in tune with their emotions than men.

This emphasis on meaning can include an assumption that women will have prescribed ideological viewpoints. A woman who has worked in public interest law, and now is a plaintiffs' employment lawyer, says that women who represent management often seem to go out of their way to justify their position:

> Sometimes where it's a gender case or sexual harassment case, the women [representing management] feel defensive. They overcompensate by being very tough about it. What I hate to say is, I sometimes get

273

more [combativeness] from women on the other side, women who like to think of themselves as on the right side of these issues, who do management work, and who have to convince themselves that the employee's case is without merit. They become more difficult to deal with, because it's not just another case. They get more difficult about resolving scheduling and depositions. They say, "Oh, your client is hurting all women, and that just makes me angry." Women want to convince themselves that the case is meritless. It's annoying. I think to myself, "If you feel this strongly about the issues, why are you representing management?"

Both women are vying for the crown of ideological purity in this instance, claiming that their position is the one that best advances women, rather than viewing the matter as "just another case" without political overtones.

A Good Shoehorn?

Women lawyers have carved out a distinctive niche built around positive traits: that they have utilized caring to a greater degree, challenged how integrity and intellectual honesty are interpreted, and sharpened the quest for finding meaning in one's work.

The obvious problem of linking women with even a positive set of stereotypes is that it puts women back in a box. A male practitioner in Arizona muses:

The downside to it is, any time you start stereotyping, you start shoehorning. Although in the abstract this is a good shoehorn, you don't want to have women being nudged in a certain direction, because what you do is start pushing them to certain fields. And women, with the practices they pursue, some of it is by choice and some of it is a little stereotypical, such as juvenile law, probate, domestic relations, as opposed to hardcore litigation and hardcore transactional.

Another woman maintains that when women themselves tout their womanly characteristics as qualification for practice, it "perpetuates stereotypes about certain practice areas, that women are limited to areas in which their womanly attributes help them master their craft."

It also reduces women's available strategies. If a woman is expected to be humble and without excess ego, it is more difficult for her to be known and recognized and to advance professionally. If women tout their caring sensibility as well as greater conciliation and peacekeeping abilities, this can detract from their option to duke it out if necessary. Women who take a hard line frequently are labeled "bitches," but a difficult opponent will often respond only to a combative approach.

In addition, if conciliatory qualities are strongly identified with women, it also reduces those qualities as tools available to men, who may seem too soft or malleable if they adopt nurturing approaches. Similarly, if men are routinely expected to do the traditional "game" approach in negotiating and settlement, they will be limited in offering their clients the more expeditious approach of straightforward conciliation. Men also like these approaches (many who were interviewed said, "I agree with the women on this"), but they noted that the rough and tumble of practice made it hard to put these concepts into practice.

As with any stereotype, the perception of the "caring" woman can become a straitjacket that limits women's effectiveness in many client situations. It's more helpful to debate the potential usefulness of these approaches for all practitioners, not just for women.

Too Much Caring

The caring orientation is in many ways positive. Men, too, are at pains to be considerate of clients, especially in such a competitive age where clients feel less loyalty to counsel than previously. But this orientation has downsides as well, for both men and women. For instance, it makes it harder to detach from a case or client. Christopher, the male legal aid attorney quoted earlier, says his strong identification with clients causes problems at times:

> It's harder to put work away when you go home. From the attorney's perspective, your clients are with you. I do all sorts of extra stuff for my clients, and it becomes a little more dominating in your life than perhaps is healthy. It makes it harder to let go. When I lose, it hurts more and it's harder to do the job. I've never befriended a client—I don't go to the movies with them—but I still care about them.

Too much identification can confuse one's roles with a client, veering more towards therapy than legal advice. Lydia, a Pennsylvania attorney, says:

275

> A lot of women do tend to listen more to the emotional side of it. Whereas the men try to deal more with the finances, [saying] "Don't tell me about the argument you and your husband had." Some women will sit there and listen. When I started out, I would listen to the clients cry; now I realize it's not relevant, but you let them do it to an extent, because they have to vent. Some men don't tolerate that as well, they are more gruff. Although some men are very, very good at it.

In this particular situation, many domestic practitioners refer the client who needs to vent more than most to a therapist to resolve emotional and psychological conflicts so that counsel can concentrate purely on the legal matters at hand.

Another potential pitfall is that a compassionate attorney can appear too soft, not tough enough to deal with the brutal realities of corner-cutting opponents or manipulative clients.

Although, as was noted above, women are generally more intellectually honest about their cases, a dimension of being caring is that sometimes women can be overly passionate about a case and not see its drawbacks. A woman in New Hampshire says:

> Sometimes women can get too emotionally committed to a cause or to an individual and not see the bigger picture. They lose their perspective on where the case fits in the overall proceeding. I think they can sometimes dig into positions based more on emotion than a reasonable view of the risks and benefits. It's a blessing and a curse. The passion sometimes puts them over the top, even when they don't rationally deserve to be there, because they really fight for things. It can also be a roadblock to getting things resolved. It can be a real turnoff in terms of communicating with the other side. Opposing counsel can be disgusted, because the person is so passionate and so emotionally involved that it turns them inside out and you can't communicate with them. They're just dismissed. It's great that they understand their client's perspective, but you're not really doing your client a service if you don't also see things from the other attorney's point of view.

Christopher talks about a female colleague who is blindly devoted to her clients:

> An attorney I worked with for a long time did family law. But she was completely cut-throat. She litigated everything, she was known to be scary, she was always fighting and always pissed off. She was extremely effective, because people did not want to mess with her. And she was also sympathetic and empathetic to clients. I can't judge, but to me it seemed that both things got in the way. She cared so much about her clients that she was going to fight tooth and nail to get things done for them. I took over some of her cases and I got things done that she couldn't get done. I was able to work out some stuff. Her approach is so aggressive that at times it hurt her. She might say I compromised so much that my clients didn't get as much.

A more prosaic point is that caring can take a lot of time that may be difficult to bill for. The woman who took off her watch twenty-five years ago believes it's more ethical and caring to charge her clients only for time spent in legal counsel. Others, hard-pressed to earn a living or more ambitious, may believe that aggressive billing is perfectly ethical, and in any event they may place more status on a high income.

With colleagues, an intensely personal orientation can also backfire, making it harder to bury personality clashes for the best interests of the workplace. A female partner in a Midwestern firm, Julie, contrasted her behavior with that of another female partner:

> I did some political maneuvering to get something done. It was not malicious. And because of the type of law I practice, I've had to learn that you cannot integrate your personality into business decisions. You've got to keep those all separate. I've got to deal every day with people I don't like. Or deal with people in my practice whom I like but have to say "no" to. My [female] colleague gets overly involved in likes and dislikes so she can't see the business side. She would have personality conflicts with people. She's been isolated, and her credibility is minimized on certain issues. "That's just her," people would say. "She doesn't like so and so, so she would say that." I had to learn to withdraw my own personality issues, and I watched how the guys did it. Even though the people sitting at the partners' table had an extraordinary dislike for one another, it didn't cause them to derail the law firm. They still made decisions in the best interests of the law firm. I grew to understand that when I watched it more.

277

In addition, the concept of a caring orientation is not uniform. Christopher, the legal aid attorney, initially touts a typical definition: "It makes you more accessible to clients, makes you more dedicated to people you're working with; they see that and are more willing to open up with you, work with you and maybe even trust your judgment more when it comes to settlement." But he also tries to understand the opposition. He says he has been successful because he is more conciliatory toward the landlord bar than the typical tenant's attorney:

> They know that I don't write off the landlords, that I don't think they should rot in hell. I am more sympathetic to the landlords, who are not exactly in great shape: None of the tenants are paying the rent, they're going to lose their buildings, they can't pay their mortgages, and I'm sitting there working for free [for the tenants]. Perhaps one of the reasons I settle cases is that I can see the other side's perspective better. I understand where they're coming from.

Obviously, although a caring orientation has many advantages, practitioners believe it is best deployed cautiously, with an understanding of when it helps and when it hinders.

The Best Policy

The "honesty" debate doesn't lend itself to the same pro-and-con dynamic as "caring"; obviously no-one's going to openly advocate dishonesty. However, many people identified other explanations for supposed gender differences. Some said that men tended to be less organized and therefore didn't keep as close track of their hours as women, underestimating their time as often as overestimating. Others said that people underestimate their time due to embarrassment over how much time they've worked on an assignment. Also, although men are less likely to make voluntary adjustments to their time-keeping, a majority are major breadwinners for their families, and suffer more in the workplace for being perceived as working only part time. This perception makes it far less likely that they can afford to exercise "integrity" by declaring themselves part-timers. Women have served a useful role by identifying the limitations and inflexibility of the billable hour as a business model.

In any event, even though women are generally considered more honest than men, there are plenty of exceptions. A female permanent associate who has practiced for twenty years is frustrated that women don't seem to have brought the kind of change to the profession that she would like to see:

> I don't think women have changed the profession. While they haven't turned out to be the same kind of blowhard posturing attorneys, they are obnoxious in a different way. Women attorneys in closings don't fight over knobs on the front porch, or show off for their clients. Their way of being obnoxious is that sometimes they are screechers and whiners. In my present practice, the hardest ones to deal with are the women who can talk a mile a minute. They get so many words in before the judge, and they say so many things that aren't true, that you just can't contradict them. You're always on the defensive, because there are so many quasi-facts that are in the judge's mind, and there's nothing much you can do about it. It's exasperating. I have always expected women lawyers to be better, to be more decent. I know it's naïve.

And although some women may adhere to strict moral codes, there's no indication that women have changed the profession as far as honesty is concerned. As other commentators have pointed out, honesty per se is not a good thing to encourage as a womanly trait. Cynthia Fuchs Epstein writes that an expectation of honesty from women lawyers limits options, makes women apologize or feel guilty for being ambitious and pursuing cold business interests, and tends to drive women towards low-paying public interest jobs out of a sense of duty and ideological purity.[7] Aiding and abetting this stereotype is that it is proudly touted not just "by male gatekeepers seeking to keep women out of the profession," as Epstein writes, "but also by feminists employing it out of a sense of mission to achieve social goals."[8] She observes further: "The notion that women should do good, while a worthy sentiment, inflicts a special burden on those who become lawyers, adding to their responsibilities while lessening their privileges. In the view that women are good or ought to be so, 'good' usually translates as 'too good'

---

[7] Cynthia Fuchs Epstein, *Women in Law,* 2d ed., at pp. 268-276 (University of Illinois Press, 1993).

[8] *Id.* at p. 269.

. . . too good to make deals and therefore to enter business, too good to be tough-minded and therefore to make good . . . lawyers."[9]

Similarly, Mona Harrington gives the following warning about women lawyers: "I do not think that women should accept the role sometimes thrust on them of natural carriers of a morally superior approach to professional life. . . . The belief in the moral superiority of women is just another version of the old dichotomy that requires distinct behaviors from the two sexes and inevitably connects public power to the behavior of men."[10]

An Advocate Above All

Many men and women said that intellectual honesty is indispensable to good lawyering. Some said they thought that younger lawyers with less experience were more likely to display stereotypical gender roles: the women painfully honest about a case's weaknesses, the men blustering that their case is air-tight. Experience and some hard knocks teach people that they have to heed their case's deficiencies while also retaining their clients' confidence. One lawyer explained it as a problem that plagues all lawyers at first: "A phenomenon that every litigator knows, you can get whipped up in your own advocacy, and you fail to see the other side very clearly. Good lawyers are able to see the other side, and they manage to explain well the strong sides of the other side of the case."

The "intellectually honest" claim also has pitfalls. Like too much reliance on a caring orientation, it can undercut the advocate's role. One female partner told of her reaction to an associate who was panic-stricken after reviewing a motion from an opposing party:

> She immediately jumped to, "I don't know what we can do, we're in trouble, we're going to lose" [when she read the motion]. It made me mad. I'm going to meet with her about this. It took away a lot of confidence that we all had. It doesn't need to be that the sky is falling. Being an advocate, whether or not you're a litigator, is part of being a lawyer. The "sky is falling" approach is something I see more with

---

[9] *Id.*

[10] Mona Harrington, *Women Lawyers: Rewriting the Rules,* at p. 149 (Penguin Books, 1993).

women than with men. I think that in some ways, for women, honesty is really valued. If you don't really know the answer, [women believe that] you shouldn't act like you do. You sort of get in and talk about stuff, talk it through. That drives guys crazy sometimes. You need to think through issues honestly. But I think the "sky is falling" approach doesn't have a place. You've got to think about it as, what is my role here? It's to be an advocate. It's to do an open and honest evaluation of the problem, but it is with the goal of solving the problem, not just wallowing in it. And you're not supposed to communicate everything you feel. We choose how we project, we choose how we communicate. If a female associate wants to come in and say, "I'm overwhelmed, I can't come up with a response," I'll sit and work with her. But that knee-jerk response of "we're screwed" is what I don't like.

She says she will meet with the associate and emphasize that her confidence as a partner in the associate's basic commitment and ability was shaken by the associate's response. "It makes me wonder if she's motivated, or if she will give it 100% or even knows how to do it," the partner says. "I would have liked her to say, 'Look what they've done, we're not going to win all of it, but here's what we're going to do about it. We're going to do A, B and C.'" A male attorney says he's familiar with this syndrome, sometimes feeling stricken at the first sight of bad news, but quickly recovering:

You can really lose sight of the good side of your own argument. Every lawyer goes through this sinking feeling when he gets the brief from the other side. You can feel down at first, then a few days later you're writing the reply brief and remembering the strong points of your own case. Every lawyer goes through this.

Sometimes people can identify so much with the other side that they undervalue their own case and rattle their clients. A male in the Southwest remarks:

There's a woman attorney I work with a lot, and I think she goes overboard. She's so much more convinced of the other side's case that they should hire her. She tends to be a little strong on the devil's advocate side. Sometimes she ends up undervaluing her position, paying too much to settle cases. She's afraid of what will happen. She loses sleep so much over minutiae in the case that she cannot be positive; she winds up being overly objective.

He says that on occasion he's taken over her cases, to be greeted by clients who say, "Finally, someone believes me!"

Practitioners identify a desirable approach as one that includes a healthy perspective on the strengths and weaknesses of a case, allowing one to make decisions that balance an aggressive desire to do the best for a client while also recognizing limits.

Re-thinking Getting Business

Many people can understand women's distaste for getting business. Most people don't like doing it. As a woman now in government, who formerly practiced in a Washington, D.C. firm, says:

> I hated it too. However, so did most of the men that I knew. And we all would put on a good face and do it anyway. Some people thrive on it, I guess, but most of the men didn't like it either. I hated wining and dining people and pretending all sorts of interest in every possible aspect of their lives and work that I didn't feel. It felt very phony. It's one thing to advocate someone's legal position; that's your job as a lawyer, which I've always been comfortable with. I didn't enjoy asking for business. But I liked it when I got business; that made me feel really good.

Moreover, the distaste for socializing-cum-networking can be interpreted more charitably as an effort to earn trust and respect. A female partner in the West reasons as follows with younger women:

> Women have to understand how business is done. A lot of women think if they work hard and get in their hours and give the client good products, then they'll be fine. I think I kind of ignored how important it was to get to know clients and do social things. I've talked to other women about this, and said, "Who do you like to work with? You like to work with people you respect, but you like to work with people you like. A lot of it is personality. Most clients think one law firm is as good as another. Surveys show the quality of product is surprisingly low on the list of things that matter; a lot of it is valuing personal relationship. Clients have to be able to trust you, and how do they know about

that? A lot of it is getting to know you." I try to tell this to young women.

Another way to recast the debate is to think of business development more as "part of the job" than as an unsavory add-on. A female practitioner in Texas says men adopt this approach more than women:

> I don't like [business development] either. But I do it. You don't get a million dollar case without doing it. I go into a funk about how much I have to do. Women will always feel like they have choices. That choice extends to, "I don't want to have cocktails with that guy." Men don't have that choice. A man will feel like it's his job. Since there's no choice in the job for men, they just do it without complaint. Women can say, "Let me just suck it up and get through this hour."

Getting Ahead

A reliance on humility also has negatives. At a meeting of female corporate executives, there was widespread agreement that women were ineffective at promoting themselves: "Women tend to sabotage themselves with excessive modesty."[11]

Although circulating self-congratulatory e-mails may seem over the top, this tactic also can highlight accomplishments of both males and females, make people aware of others' accomplishments, put people on the radar screen who would otherwise be ignored, and give positive reinforcement (often sorely lacking in legal workplaces). As the female partner who reported the "male back-patting" conceded, "The problem is that when women don't play this game, their successes can become invisible."

Indeed, women's tendency to modesty is a well-known obstacle. Elise's "stealth lawyer" approach—quietly achieving success without bragging about it—avoids making her a lightning rod for attention, but also prevents her from gaining the respect and attention she may deserve. She is deliberately trying to be small, almost disappear. Any indicators of visibility—being

---

[11] Mary Williams Walsh, "Preparing a Corps of Women for Corporate Responsibility," The New York Times, at C2 (Aug. 13, 2002).

"uppity," "flamboyant," or trying to "get the glory"—would be "threatening" and perceived as "egotistical" coming from an "upstart little girl," so the key to success is to appear nurturing and supportive, a "nice, friendly, hard-working, helpful type of person." Elise fulfills the image of the modest woman who doesn't toot her own horn.

And too much humility makes it hard to get business, without which, at least in the private law firm world, it's hard to progress. Phyllis Weiss Haserot, president of Practice Development Counsel, a New York-based business development and organizational culture consulting and coaching firm, says women often assume that they have more issues with business getting than do men, which is not really true:

> I feel that clearly there are some differences, but that many of the issues that are considered women's issues are true of men also. Women think that they have problems with marketing based on gender, and they perceive erroneously that men don't have issues about it. But with a lot of these things, it's more a matter of behavioral style than gender.

Business development doesn't necessarily require a distasteful approach, as Haserot observes:

> There are some people who are very successful, usually men, who are just able to be very bold. Maybe that's what women are thinking is required. They are very aggressive, assertive, out there people. Women see that and they think, "I can't do that, I don't want to do that." If a firm wants to use their rainmakers in the firm as role models and examples in training sessions, I always say, "Don't just have one person. You have to have several." There isn't a case where everybody would relate to one particular style.

Moreover, according to consultant Ida Abbott, a lawyer who thinks of herself as a potential or ongoing helper who solves clients' problems can shift away from feeling like a pest or annoyance. She says that getting over a distaste for networking and business development requires not bull-headed selling, but instead asking questions to identify the potential client's issues:

> Then they don't have to think about selling themselves. That's where the discomfort lies, and that's for lawyers across the board. They find

it demeaning. They think, "People should just come to me because I'm so smart, I don't want to have to grovel." So they should find out as much as they can about the other person, not concentrate so much on selling themselves as on finding out what the other person needs. If there's something you can do for them, you're then providing a service that meets a need.

Moreover, empathy, listening, and problem-solving—all highlighted here as female skills—are also classic selling skills. If women (or men) who are put off by networking consider it to be an opportunity for clients to build a stronger relationship with them based on trust and respect, rather than faux socializing, they can lay the groundwork for a long-term relationship and be at peace with themselves.

To Play Games or Not

Regardless of whether women may negotiate more directly than men, many people felt that using a style that is appropriate to the setting makes more sense. Many men and women agreed that a "cut to the chase" approach is preferable, but said that an aggressive opponent, pressing every advantage, forces them to respond in kind. A female former litigator, now in government, relates:

> My own approach would vary by the situation, by how good a case I had, by who's my opponent. Sometimes I play all kinds of games, sometimes I don't.

Jackie from Pennsylvania talks about negotiating:

> I do a fair amount of negotiating. I find it tough to be the firm jerk in negotiating. It's rare that it's black and white. It probably depends on context. Sometimes you are between a rock and a hard place, holding firm and threatening. That works better for men in general. Because I see both sides I don't take a hard-line position, and men have an easier time doing that. There are some situations where it's better to do that hard-core type of thing, particularly with an intransigent person. Some people need the fear of God put in them.

An in-house woman in California says:

285

Any time you say accommodation, you think, "Is that a positive or a negative?" Because maybe the strongest leader should be accommodating. I think it's a good trait in a successful lawyer, because you are then able to address the needs of your client. But I can also see other people say they're too willing to accommodate.

One male in Texas says he prefers the more straightforward approach described by women because he thinks you get a better deal for your client:

You may ultimately get more for your client [by playing games]. That wouldn't surprise me if it were true. But it's going to be only marginally more. You're going to ruin more deals than you make. You have to cut to the chase pretty quickly. If you view it as something that is going to be a long protracted battle, you're ultimately not going to do your client a service, even if you do better occasionally, because you'll lose some deals. The biggest enemy of any deal is deal fatigue. You have to do your job, but there is a clock. You have to be thoughtful about what you push for.

But many people said they felt they had to do the game playing, even if they don't really want to. A New York male practitioner says:

I feel the same way as the women. I used to think it would be great to say, "Okay, it's 50 grand and that's that." But I've realized that in most cases, once you put something out there, if you're not near the end of the negotiating, you're establishing the next floor from which you're going to go up. I've learned that the hard way. While I really wish I could sit down with my adversary and say, "This is the deal," it doesn't work that way. If I do that too early in the process it's going to come back to haunt me. I find that I've always got to play the games. When I'm dealing with men or women, there's no difference. Even when somebody tells me, "I'm not into playing games," I don't trust them.

Another male partner, based in Oregon, agrees that there are times when the "direct" approach can backfire:

I have tried saying, "Look, this is what we'll settle for, this is the number we mean." Most people have mixed results. It gets taken as part of the dance, you end up with a lower number, and you're disappointed because you find yourself negotiating further even though you gave your real number. The dance always seems so artificial, everybody knows it's not the real number when you're starting.

Many said that greater experience led to less game playing, and to more debate over pivotal provisions and less over inconsequential items.

What's Meaningful?

The assumption that women prefer more meaning in their work is problematic. First, virtually all lawyers, male and female, who are drawn to public interest or legal aid work, are mission-oriented. Christopher, the legal aid attorney quoted above, is passionate about his job and believes it has more meaning than a corporate job, partially because it's less desirable:

I feel like there are so many other people who are willing to [represent employers and management]. I partially find meaning in the fact that not many people are willing to do what I do. All the landlords' attorneys I deal with, they think they're helping landlords to get rid of the scum tenants. If they run the business well, they can provide more apartments. They think they're doing good stuff. In a way they clearly are. I just don't care, because I know that these big management companies have plenty of money, they can always get an attorney to come in. It's easy to find meaning when you're making money. I'm more micro-oriented. One woman whose apartment isn't gone just means a ton more to me than a corporation. You see the impact a lot better. I see individual families helped; I can walk away each day and say, "Did I help someone today? Yes."

But more pointedly, who decides what's meaningful? For instance, some women who work for management and corporations say they have more opportunity to effect change because they work within the system. A woman who does employment law in New Jersey for a large firm says:

People who know me well think it's odd that I represent management rather than employees. I recognize injustice, that's my counseling hat. I try to prevent problems in the workplace, I try to be a force for change. People have seen me as someone who's going to be there for the little guy, the underdog. I'm definitely more of a people person

287

than a money person. Which is why I love employment law. I also don't tolerate bullshit. A lot of the cases I get are just absolute bullshit. But when I get a case where [a company has] done something wrong, we advise that they settle. I don't want to say I'm creating a better world because I advise them to settle. Changing those types of things will go a long way to make a better workplace. I think I do have a positive effect, although I understand that's not, strictly speaking, my role. I can't push my own social agenda on my clients.

A female environmental lawyer agrees:

I work with a lot of corporations, and I am frequently defending them against EPA civil penalties. My role there is to try letting EPA do its job, while allowing the client to continue to do business as profitably as possible under the circumstances. Is that terribly meaningful to me in the day-to-day stuff? No. But when I look at it in the big picture, to allow manufacturers to make things and yet balance the environment, yeah, that's good. The counselor role, that part of it is fun for me. With my clients, it's saying, "You've got to do this."

She, like others, also finds meaning in personal relationships with clients:

One of the things that's become meaningful is having very long-lasting, close relationships with clients that I've worked with for years. I just love the fact that I have this enduring friendship as well as relationship, and I feel like that's something meaningful in and of itself. Even though some of the stuff I do may be mundane, the more important aspect is that I have these wonderful friends.

Some may think it's not meaningful to find fulfillment as a traditional breadwinner, but many people (increasingly females too) find great satisfaction in supporting a family. One man, a partner in his late thirties who works in a large firm, spoke ardently about finding satisfaction as a provider for his wife and children:

Men still see for themselves much more the burden of providing for the family, for the children. For women there is still sort of the question mark, "Do I want to devote my life to the practice of law, or do I want to be with my family and raise children and be a stay-at-home mom or some combination of the two?" So I think women are indulging in that debate more than men, who I think to some extent just feel like, "To heck with meaning, the meaning is, I'm providing for this family. If part of that is my wife gets to stay home, and my wife does something different, that's the meaning." Providing is a very big part of meaning for me. That has been a big driver for me. It's my job to make the ends meet for the family, and to do the kinds of things we want to do.

He also says that he finds meaning by being a positive agent within his firm for progressive management practices, such as being fair and encouraging and praising lawyers for good results.

Another man thinks that women go for more "mission-oriented" jobs because they have different motivations and bear fewer responsibilities:

There are things in people's lives that give you a good jerk on the collar and make you say, "Is this what I really want to be doing?" Childbirth for women tends to be one of these things. They put a different value on things. If they're going to be away from their kids, they want to get something more out of it than just money. Regardless of kids, a lot of times women are not the only breadwinner and have a husband who's making more, and they have the luxury of doing the $55,000 job as opposed to a $100,000 job. I know a lot of very unhappy men lawyers. Half the time they're bitching about their job, and how screwed up the profession is, but their kids are in college, and this is the most financially rewarding thing they can do. If it's not meaningful—oh well.

Indeed, the man quoted earlier who noted that women are more likely to report that they "really enjoy" their work than men, theorizes, "I think men look for the highest-paying job in order to make the most money and eventually put bread on the table, whereas women are not usually required to be the [primary] breadwinner, and therefore they have the luxury of just finding a job that they enjoy."

Along the same lines, a man in New York said that men are more often pushed by their families into occupations they may not want, in order to be good providers, whereas women are given more of a blanket "do what you want and be happy" message:

It happened to me and it happens to other males. We're nudged in the direction of an accountant or an engineer or a doctor. We end up being there because that's the expectation of those around us. I will tell you that it happened to me, I was nudged very hard in the direction of being a lawyer. At first I hated it. I don't know that that happens to women so much. Women can do what they want, go into public interest, that's great, or be a high-powered corporate lawyer, that's great too.

He resolved his own ambivalence about pursuing the legal career his father favored by going into the one area of law he found that he enjoyed, employment law:

I related to it. Everybody can relate to employment situations. That's how I've found meaning. I enjoy handling these situations, helping the people on the employer side work through issues and problems in this maze of federal and state laws and regulations that tell them what they can do and what they can't do.

The question of meaning is one that varies from person to person, tapping into different concepts of what's important and how to accomplish critical goals.

Fresh Air

New recruits add fresh air to organizations. They're useful because they can cause an organization to stop and take a look at itself, to reformulate what's best, what works and what doesn't, relying upon the objectivity that a new hire automatically possesses. In a broad sense, women are the new recruits for the legal profession. Because they have been in practice for a relatively short time in significant numbers, they bring a different perspective and more scrutiny to traditional practices.

Some things have changed in the legal profession by virtue of the mere presence of more women. For instance, women have caused radical change in regulating sexual harassment. They also have introduced concerns about family and lifestyle into the workplace, championing innovations such as flexible work arrangements that are now permanent features, however imperfectly they may be implemented. Greater numbers of women also have changed social patterns within legal workplaces. When the professional population was virtually all-male, offices were more united and unified; now the workplace is more fractured while men and women sort out their awkward interactions. Women practitioners have also presented new strategies for appealing to juries and clients, such as when women represent men accused of rape or sexual harassment, or when women reach out to female general counsel to bond and get business. This development has given men an array of female general counsel and female supervisors to relate with, in contrast to the all-male authority structure of the past.

Beyond that, it's harder to say what definitive changes females have brought to the law. As one man said, "I've heard and read things that [the presence of more women has] softened the profession. I'm not sure that it has. In some ways the profession is more mean-spirited, not because of women, but because the timing of women getting into the profession coincided with the decline of professionalism." Many believe, however, that females have injected their own orientation into practice, as reflected in this chapter's discussion.

Some of the same women who complain about the tyranny of negative stereotypes still revel in the advantages that "good" stereotypes confer upon women. But more useful and less divisive is a debate about how some of these "good" things work as a tool for both men and women, providing the common ground that can help promote change. Everyone can demonstrate caring in creative ways. And all lawyers can promote intellectual honesty without jeopardizing zealous advocacy. The arguments for using traditional negotiation tactics versus more straightforward approaches can result in better outcomes for clients. Finally, an exploration of meaning on the job is especially relevant, given the negative views that the general citizenry has of lawyers, and the widespread unhappiness that lawyers report about their own work lives. Women have provided some fresh air simply by injecting these topics into the ongoing dialogue about effective practice.

CHAPTER 10

Conclusion: Snapshots, Present and Future

IMMIGRANTS NO LONGER
Individual Initiatives
LONE RANGERS
COpERS
Trailblazers
ORGANIZATIONAL INITIATIVES
SYSTEMS SOLUTIONS
ENGAGING IN DIALOGUE
RE-IMAGINING THE FUTURE

Each story, thought, and viewpoint that the men and women of the bar voiced in this book added more clarity to the fine-grain photograph of the profession that has developed since women entered the profession, a snapshot filtered through the lens of gender issues.

Lawyers have debated everything from lingering bias to whether to hug or shake hands. Their topics were as weighty as the dearth of women partners and as fleeting as what to talk about while waiting for the ninety-eight-page fax. They worried about broad trends such as pay disparities, and everyday dilemmas such as dressing properly to appear before a jury. Their concerns ranged from global to local, their emotions swung from confident optimism to frustrated alienation. Their comments show that although the mightier issues that dominate the gender-bias debate are doubtless important, resolving smaller predicaments on a day-to-day basis is at least as urgent.

In this final chapter the fundamental points of this book will be outlined, surveying the findings of the research. This will be followed by an exploration of the ways that individual practitioners have met gender challenges, with approaches ranging from resolutely ignoring bias to making proactive efforts to influence debate. Next is a discussion of the methods that organizations can use to resolve these issues within their offices, including a focus on revamping systems and challenging entrenched attitudes. Finally, the conclusion will sketch a vision of the future, anticipating a new picture that is emerging based on the myriad views aired in this volume.

Immigrants No Longer

This book began by identifying an "expectations gap," starting with the assumptions that by the year 2003 there would be greater equity between the sexes and that most of the tired old stereotypes would be neatly packed away. However, those expectations have been dashed in large part due to entrenched gender roles, a hard-to-define but surprisingly steely framework of cultural expectations that hasn't collapsed overnight.

To be sure, female lawyers aren't freshly arrived immigrants any more, whose hosts isolate and reject them; rather, the host country accepts them for the most part. And many new options for men and women have emerged, including more flexible work arrangements; greater acceptance of sexual behavior and relationships in the workplace; and a baseline acknowledgment of women's capabilities. Similarly, some of the old "double binds" have unraveled: that an attractive woman couldn't be competent and that "female-ness" itself battled with professionalism. At the same time, the very inclusion of men as part of the "gender issues" rubric shifts the debate from one that isolates women to a more holistic and healthy analysis of all lawyers. Indeed, it turns out that some issues are less influenced by gender than might be thought, as evident in the discussion of "real lawyers," which established that ironclad expectations of commitment apply to all practitioners.

Despite this progress, women remain outsiders in many respects, the targets of lingering gender stereotypes that reflect positively on men but negatively on women. This is in part because the default image of a lawyer remains solidly male, dominated by men in numbers, attitudes, expectations, and assumptions. And many conventional dictates still dominate the landscape: the bossy woman continues to alienate, a "working mother" is an oxymoron, a dad who wants to work reduced hours violates the breadwinner role, workplaces hesitate to anoint women as leaders. Indeed, the simplest and most successful way many women deal with entrenched stereotypes is to embrace them in order to pursue their professional goals. That is, the attractive woman tries to attract a client, not a mate; the motherly woman supervises associates, instead of toddlers; the nurturing woman holds the hand of a paying client, rather than an ailing relative.

Although these are not objectionable approaches, as long as both men's and women's success are defined in terms of traditional stereotypes (adapted or otherwise), the gender roles remain inviolate and limit options for individuals based strictly on their sex. The most difficult course for men or women is to stray out of accepted territory. Compounding this dilemma is that it's often hard to pinpoint the causes for workplace obstacles. As respondents mused so frequently, "Is it gender or is it personality?"

This results in a peculiar dissonance. A woman is accepted, and all the surface talk and platitudes assume equity, yet very traditional ideas reign unchecked, leaving her hamstrung. Men experience less dissonance only if they adhere to traditional behaviors. Those who deviate from norms look even more suspect than women because men's "typical" behavior is the gold standard for success.

As the chapter about dress indicated, gender stereotypes can change in response to such factors as the influence of large numbers of women in the profession, confident people who openly challenge accepted "rules," and shared goals among men and women. In fact, it's evident that the mere process of deconstructing gender roles makes "solutions" easier to visualize.

For example, one explanation for the stereotype that marginalizes authoritative women is that females prefer to maintain egalitarian ties with other women, rather than hierarchical structures. Identifying this assumption makes it easier to isolate its premise, and to see how it might be susceptible to influence and change.

Another finding is that when men and women share common ground on issues, accepted behaviors for both sexes expand much more easily. A posture of males versus females leaves the sexes stuck in battle mode, rather than working together and looking to the future; there's little question that problems defined as "just about women" will attract less credibility than those that involve both men and women. Finally, "genderation gaps" suggest that the younger generation has a less combative view of many current gender issues and will, as a matter of course, resolve some of the conflicts.

Statistics and anecdotes reveal that there are more gender issues in the private practice of law than in other workplaces, including in-house departments, government agencies, and public interest organizations.[1] This is in part because of the billable-hour model that prevails in private practice, which puts tremendous focus on the sheer accumulation of hours and leads to a tendency to minimize risk. Also, the business model creates greater competition, making relations between the sexes more awkward than among men alone. And a tradition of informal management tends to perpetuate the *status quo*. (However, firms that are trying to land government contracts, as well as government units, have experienced pressure to achieve success with diversity.)

Along with revealing the components of stereotypes, the respondents talked about the many coping mechanisms they use to "manage" their gender. Those efforts suggest that there are specific steps individuals and organizations can take to nudge the workplace beyond an unthinking acceptance of prevailing stereotypes.

---

[1] Most surveys reveal greater satisfaction in settings other than private law firms, especially with respect to gender issues. See *Women in Law: Making the Case, passim* (Catalyst, 2001); "Gender Equity in the Legal Profession," passim (New York State Bar Association, Committee on Women in the Law, 2002).

Individual Initiatives

Some personal initiatives resemble a "Lone Ranger" approach, ignoring obstacles and barreling ahead. Others use a "coping" method, managing gender to bolster individual standing. Finally there's a "trailblazer" model, affirmatively reaching out a hand to others to change the *status quo*. People borrow from these approaches at different times, depending on their seniority, the varying challenges they face, and their personal styles and capabilities.

Lone Rangers

A common individual approach, particularly for the female pioneers in the profession, was simply to ignore the obstacles, redouble efforts, and triumph through sheer force of will, effort, and quality of work.[2] Indeed, many people use this approach today, and it has some appeal: the brave battler, undaunted by challenges, who fights all foes and eventually triumphs, her skills vanquishing all doubts. Moreover, as some respondents commented, reacting to all instances of suspected bias is unproductive and distracting. There are times when females have to ignore bias sideshows. This approach also sidesteps any accusations that a woman is a "whiner" or "victim" who appears to blame troubles on others.

The "lone ranger" approach, however, has only partial utility and appeal. It limits success to those few women who are willing to accept the added challenges; it makes it far more difficult for those with family responsibilities, because of the added time it requires; it excludes those who are unquestionably competent, but aren't pioneers; it keeps the *status quo* in place; and it guarantees that change will be slow. Even though it has been successful for many women, it makes the overall task of proving equity much harder because it makes success appear so difficult to attain and so unattractive due to the sacrifices required. It also appears to acquiesce to a pretense that gender bias is nonexistent. To date, the "Lone Ranger" approach has been the main vehicle for change, and the unfortunate results are persistent stereotypes and continuing low numbers of female leaders.

---

[2] See Judith Richards Hope, *Pinstripes & Pearls: The Women of the Harvard Law Class of '64 Who Forged an Old-Girl Network and Paved the Way for Future Generations* (Scribner, 2003), which makes this point repeatedly.

Copers

Rather than ignoring gender bias, those people who adopt a "coping" approach are more reactive to inequities found in the work environment. They use self-help, develop confidence, use their legal training, and hone political skills to meet challenges.

Self-Help

Many people meet gender challenges simply by observing how others act and conducting themselves accordingly—"self-help" for the individual lawyer. Examples of this approach recur throughout the book. The mild-mannered male litigator learned to take breaks when the pressure built up during litigation, to get the job done but also to mold the job to his personality. There was the female who took to heart her male mentor's words, "You have to ask for business," going on to become a superstar rainmaker. Remember the woman who wanted at first to be the "senior associate everyone liked," but who cultivated a frosty manner when no-one took her seriously? And recall the older woman who abandoned her whispery "Jackie O" voice for a more commanding tone? An aspect of self-help is to rethink basic assumptions, such as the woman who urged putting loss into perspective, comparing losing in the courtroom to losing at sports (because "no matter how hard you work, on some days you lose"), or the people who learned to think of self-promotion more as providing helpful information than as unseemly boasting. All these people took advice on board or adopted successful approaches that they observed in order to repair performance defects.

Developing Confidence

A key step seen throughout the book was building confidence. Many people feel that they are not entitled to ask for anything, as if they don't deserve advancement or more money or better assignments and are brazen to suggest a change. But confidence in one's position is critical for the stamina necessary to push for change. The woman who learned about "sisterhood" from a male partner—who said the firm wouldn't dream of cutting her compensation while she was out with a difficult pregnancy—concluded that people shouldn't feel they need to meekly request things that they deserve as a matter of course. The women who were quoted as role models in

Chapter 2 simply put on their pantsuits or purple scarves without waiting for permission. Leonard, the man described in Chapter 8 who stayed home with his children, insists on publicizing his pride: "I had nothing I was embarrassed about. I am proud of it. I raised my kids very well during two years. It's kind of like, if you have a problem with it, just get over it." And the woman who has a solid book of business doesn't apologize for working unpredictable hours: "I say, 'This is how I'm going to do things, and you can accept it or not.' The other women that tried different arrangements weren't as forthright." All these individuals were convinced that their attitude was sound, that they were not taking advantage of anyone, and that their focus balanced their personal concerns with the best interests of the workplace. Related to this confidence is a willingness to take a risk, which many successful females complain that other women avoid.

Legal Skills

Many people rely on their lawyering skills to improve their lot, such as the in-house woman who marshaled facts and figures and "pleaded her case" with the CEO to ask for a raise, and the female associate who wrote a long memo justifying her "air-tight" proposal to become a partner. Dealing with facts is much easier than dealing with emotions and generalizations. As a result, finding a factual basis for discussing loaded issues can be effective.

Political Skills

Some gender bias situations are resolved only by developing political awareness. Sometimes people can be tone deaf, such as the associate in Chapter 6 who failed to see that her mentor/partner and another associate, Joe, had a closer relationship than she had with the partner, despite the fact that the partner was "sarcastic" and was "dissing Joe." Others learn to be more savvy, such as the women who aligned with unexpected partners, and split with expected allies (especially other women) to increase their credibility. Julie, for instance, a partner in the Midwest, learned to put aside her personal feelings about colleagues and vote in the best interests of the firm. Her female colleague, by contrast, allowed personal grudges to dictate her actions, prompting other colleagues to dismiss her viewpoints: "That's just her," and, "She would say that." Others learn they can't just let their good work speak for itself, and that they must publicize their triumphs, like the female associate in New York who went on her own "personal PR campaign" to inform her colleagues of her activities, paving the way to becoming a partner. These political skills increase the likelihood of winning important battles. A prevailing rule of thumb is always to look to the business case for support, and thereby cast an issue in terms of fulfilling the goals of the workplace.

Trailblazers

In addition to the Lone Ranger and coping approaches, the third category of individual initiatives is the trailblazer approach, characterized by help and understanding for others as well as efforts to change the *status quo*. These include reactive skills such as subtle interventions and confrontation. These initiatives are also proactive: reemphasizing common ground; using leadership, mentoring, and preventive skills; and reformulating rhetoric.

Subtle Interventions

Those who push back in the face of gender bias often use indirect methods, such as the in-house woman who listened quietly to a biased commentary about female candidates for hire, and waited until the group considered a male candidate to repeat the comments ("Did you hear his laugh?" "Didn't you think he was heavyset?"). Other people picked their opportunities for identifying gender issues, doing it sparingly to avoid being tuned out. Many relied on humor to get their point across while preserving a relationship, like the woman who parroted men's words back to them: "Hi, honey!" One in-house man challenged people who made biased generalizations, gently questioning how they came to their conclusions, trying to unearth the factual bases of their opinions rather than simply telling them they were wrong or being judgmental. These subtle approaches are important, given the prevailing ethos that everyone "already knows" about avoiding sexism and presumably doesn't need direct tutoring. Those people who adopt indirect approaches make their points adroitly so their objects don't feel attacked and can adjust their behavior without feeling humiliated or singled out.

Confrontation

Rather than using more roundabout approaches, some people rely on direct confrontation. One woman pointed out a disparity in pay between two quirky lawyers, one male and one female, to prove bias against the woman. Others bluntly rebuked colleagues who made off-color jokes or who were involved in questionable relationships. Direct confrontation as a tool to effect change is especially effective when it is wielded by those with enough seniority and credibility to avoid suffering politically.

Seeking Common Ground

There's little question, on issues from dress to flexible work arrangements, that the more men and women formulate issues based on common concerns, rather than on points that divide them, the easier it is to find solutions. Common ground provides a way to talk about sensitive issues that avoids divisiveness and limits defensiveness. The easiest way to find commonalities is to align the objective with the interests of the workplace, such as the woman who intervened when an incident appeared to present a sexual harassment risk for the firm. Similarly, recall the in-house counsel who expressed her reservations about a new advertising campaign because of the effect it might have on the company. Another approach is for males and females to "borrow" from one another's profiles. For instance, a general counsel in California suggested that men mimic the female tendency to take criticism seriously and seek to improve performance, while women learn that a façade of confidence, even if it covers up fear, can be effective. These measures broaden the dialogue from one that pits the sexes against one another to one where they sit on the same side of the table.

Leadership Skills

Promoting leadership skills entails spearheading change, by people such as Jane, who pushed for the election of a woman to the executive committee, actively lobbying the candidate to agree to the post, and urging others to back her. Her example and others prove that it doesn't require a whole workplace to take a risk or drive new ideas. Even one determined individual can make a difference. For instance, a Midwestern firm had divided into two camps over flexible work arrangements. "It was almost at the point of being two political parties," recalls a partner in the firm. "The younger partners wanted to push the move towards flexibility, whereas the older, more traditional partners were in the opposing camp. It was not a totally peaceful transition. The firm could have broken apart five years ago over these issues, because of this philosophical split." The head of the recruiting committee, who was deeply committed to alternative work arrangements, won over the doubters by using innovative work/life policies as a lure to attract higher-caliber lawyers than those hired in the past. "She really sold the place as a kinder, friendlier, gentler firm," the partner related.

Mentoring Skills

A mentoring skills approach assumes that people can learn and develop. One key to successful mentoring is a willingness to take a risk, such as with a female leader or with an "outsider" whose potential isn't immediately evident. Many respondents helped out seemingly hopeless young practitioners who were halfway out the door, and watched them transform into superstars. Others made their mentees "rehearse" important skills, such as the senior female partner in Florida who coached younger women to practice three-minute speeches about themselves to hone their networking skills. A mentor can also give a mentee the confidence to take a risk, such as the senior associate in Boston who gave a junior associate "permission" to take on more challenging tasks. Another aspect of mentoring is to bring outsiders within the insiders' circle, much like Maria, who gave work to a woman who was being sidelined, liked the results, and then actively praised her to others ("building a buzz"), so that colleagues began funneling work to her. Another example was the male litigator in Washington, D.C., who deliberately mentored women, reasoning that they were otherwise more likely to be left out. Others identified the support they valued as they progressed in their careers and passed it on to others, such as the African-American woman in California who had been mentored by African-American female judges and lawyers. She in turn now advises other minority women, deconstructing minutiae ("Why didn't you object?") to reduce their anxieties.

Preventive Skills

Rather than sitting back and waiting for problems to occur, many try to prevent them in the first place. One man observed sexual banter between a male lawyer and a female staff member. He asked the woman in private whether it made her uncomfortable. She said no, but this question signaled to her that he was aware and concerned, making it easier for her to approach him in the future if a problem develops. And recall the women who vetoed hiring the "blustery young men" who seemed like they might have trouble working with female colleagues and clients. Another woman, in New York, "front loaded" assignments for men, giving them a thorough background on the cases so that they understood why the detail-oriented work might not be "sexy" but was still vital. (A similar approach could be used with work/life issues. Managers can talk with new hires from the beginning about planning their working lives, molding their careers with family in mind if they intend to become parents, so that their careers don't resemble "before and after" snapshots once children are in the picture. Similarly, meeting with people before launching flexible work arrangements allows participants to talk through foreseeable problems, and to model a two-way communication approach for solving unanticipated problems in the future.)

All these success stories come from people within legal workplaces who have painstakingly cobbled together ways to advance, protect themselves, or adapt their behaviors for better workplace success, managing their gender so that it doesn't hinder their progress.

Reformulating Rhetoric

I would add another approach that respondents didn't identify, but that would be effective. Change agents can use rhetoric to alter the terms of the debate, because the very words people use can make others think differently and accelerate change. For instance, in the past, it was thought unnecessarily precise to say "he or she" when one referred to both men and women because the pronoun "he" covered both genders and was sufficient. It is now common to hear the phrase "he or she" uttered automatically. Previously in this book we have highlighted words that people use to describe their situations, such as the rhetoric that surrounds the work/life debate: part-timers who are "slackers" and not "real lawyers," who "lack commitment," and whose flexible arrangements are described as "accommodations" and "special deals." These familiar phrases, so common that they're rarely challenged, set the terms of the debate. Accordingly, a manager who is determined to make flexible work arrangements a success won't let putdowns about "slackers" and "special deals" slide by, but instead will emphasize the business arrangement that the relationship rests on, point out the needs of "working parents" (instead of "working mothers"), and identify the value of retaining good lawyers rather than contributing to high turnover and associated costs when people leave.

There are many other examples where adroit word choice can subtly alter the terms of debate. One would be to resist linking a "good" stereotype with one sex or another, in order to avoid the backlash that accompanies so many of the stereotypes, already analyzed in this book, that shed a negative light on women. This means avoiding statements such as, "Women are much more empathetic," and instead advising that, "Empathy is effective in certain instances." In this way, one can be aware of how words can define and limit a debate, and use that awareness to shape a different environment.

Organizational Initiatives

The above are all effective steps that individuals have taken. But they are all one-person-at-a-time baby steps. What about organization-wide giant steps to institute and revamp existing systems and to identify and challenge underlying attitudes? There's little doubt that well-designed organizational initiatives can have a far more powerful impact than the accumulation of scattered individual efforts. Legal workplaces can borrow ideas from other organizations to combat some of the concerns highlighted in this book. Indeed, in-house departments have been the beneficiaries of corporation-wide programs that drive change and influence attitudes.

Some people may ask why organizations should care about these issues on a global basis. Some organizations lead the way because their leaders believe that increasing diversity is the right thing to do. Champions within those workplaces push the causes of increasing female participation, confronting stereotypes, devising work/life balance initiatives that work, and communicating a broader view about the issues that men face. For example, the Bar Association of San Francisco launched the "No Glass Ceiling Task Force" in 2001, challenging legal workplaces to take specific steps to promote women into leadership positions and proposing criteria for organizations that publicly committed to the challenge, such as achieving a 25% representation of women at the partnership level in law firms by the end of 2004.[3]

Other organizations won't be motivated by a social justice dimension, but may be spurred by a business case argument. For instance, the workplace may consistently lose high-performing lawyers due to family issues and lifestyle concerns such as long, unpredictable hours; Chapter 7 outlined the business case for flexibility. An emerging issue, one that will only increase in the future, is the increasing presence of women in the ranks of general

---

[3] Letter from Angela Bradstreet and Mary Cranston, of the No Glass Ceiling Task Force of The Bar Association of San Francisco to area law firms (April 12, 2002).

counsel—in other words, as clients. That fact, more than any other, is likely to cause change within law firms, as corporate legal departments seek to do business with law firms whose values are aligned with theirs.

Each of these views can inform the other. Workplaces that are driven by a "socially just" mission must integrate the business case so that good intentions aren't swamped by the realities of trying to make ends meet (and so that expectations aren't raised unduly only to be dashed when the economics won't support ambitious changes). And those firms that are driven by business concerns will find greater dedication to their initiatives if they develop a consensus to eradicate gender bias within their offices.

Systems Solutions

Assuming that a workplace wanted to make some change, what might its leaders do? Many respondents complained that systems within organizations often were nonexistent, or poorly designed to prevent inadequacies. The value of a good system is inestimable; a host of gender issues occur because of a lack of openness or a lack of alignment between a professed policy and actual practice. The temptation, particularly in smaller workplaces, is to eschew processes and systems as overly formal and bureaucratic. Even some larger offices celebrate informality to reduce red tape. But informality is the enemy of diversity, whether in hiring, work arrangements, the personalities and skills that different people bring to the table, or work assignments and promotions. Fair, well-designed, streamlined systems (not cumbersome, make-work procedures) are the key to building trust among employees and convincing them that equity and fairness rule, not informal "who you know" ties or inconsistent approaches from department to department. Carefully crafted systems for performance reviews, mentoring, work assignments, and flexible work arrangements yield countless benefits.

Performance Reviews

Performance reviews that feature rigorous, detailed criteria, and that are regularly scheduled, taken seriously, and conspicuously tied to compensation and advancement, are a critically important factor for easing gender bias. For instance, successful evaluation programs will alleviate many of the concerns about competence, because there will be greater trust that advancement is based on merit, rather than politics. In addition, performance reviews reduce speculation that arises about people who are involved in romantic relationships within the workplace, providing a performance context to counter the suspicion of favors granted or denied due to an alliance. Comprehensive reviews also help with the "real lawyer" issue. It's harder to denigrate people with flexible schedules who have attained top billing on performance reviews. This is also true for issues involving confidence; performance criteria that are gender-biased can be revamped for greater fairness. The more formal a workplace performance framework may be, the more likely that judgments about the true worth of individual lawyers will be deemed credible.[4]

Mentoring Systems

Formal mentoring systems can help prevent some of the sidelining that occurs when people informally pick out favorites, choices that are often based as much on personal comfort as on ability. Mentoring systems are especially important in view of widespread informal socializing and its quasi-mentoring effect. Remember the male department head who took a new male hire out to lunch, ignoring the women he had worked with for a decade, or the guys who invited a male summer associate to lunch but not a female, thinking she wouldn't be interested in their sports talk? The women who were left out felt aggrieved and resentful. Many employers in other industries don't socialize with underlings at all, believing it is a conflict of interest. Or if they do, they go out with all their staff, not just a select few.[5]

Work Assignments

Since people demonstrate their worth based in part on the quality of their assignments, determining how assignments are made is also vital for an equitable workplace. Distribution of work assignments is most successful if it's very transparent, in terms of criteria, i.e., who gets assignments and why, emphasizing giving people a variety of assignments of varying skill levels. If work assignments are meticulously tracked, the workplace can work with

---

[4] Excellent guidelines on bias-free performance reviews are found in Jeanne Q. Svikhart & Abbie Willard, *Fair Measure: Toward Effective Attorney Evaluations* (American Bar Association, Commission on Women in the Profession, 1997).

[5] A guide to a mentoring system is found in Ida O. Abbott, *The Lawyer's Guide to Mentoring* (National Association for Law Placement, 2000).

facts to accurately determine if there's a concern about equity. Better assignments systems also can demystify the procedures relating to inheriting files and criteria for promotion. In addition, when work assignments are integrated with performance reviews, they can be helpful components of a development plan.

Flexible Work Arrangements

Flexible work arrangements often founder due to concerns about equity on both sides. Carefully constructed policies on hours, salary, bonuses, promotion, benefits, "overtime" if appropriate, adjustment of hours in the event of an emergency, as well as guidelines governing issues like communication can alleviate these concerns.[6] If the factors governing flexible work arrangements are well publicized and understood, the workplace can alleviate the misunderstandings and misconceptions that so typically deepen into disregard and alienation on both sides.

Measurements for Success

Critical to the success of all these systems is that whenever possible, measurements for success be included, providing accountability for the success or failure of the efforts. Linking results to compensation is the fail/safe method for encouraging compliance. People often complain that intangibles such as professional abilities are difficult to break down into categories and measure. But corporate America has had great success in measuring even abstruse qualities, by thinking deeply about what skills, traits, and attitudes

---

[6] Guidelines for policies are outlined in Joan Williams & Cynthia Thomas Calvert, "Balanced Hours: Effective Part-Time Policies for Washington Law Firms," at pp. 20-41, *The Project for Attorney Retention, Final Report*, 2d ed. (Aug. 2001), and in Deborah L. Rhode, "Balanced Lives: Changing the Culture of Legal Practice," at 31-41 (American Bar Association, Commission on Women in the Profession, 2001). In addition, an article in Harvard Business Review identified the components of successful reduced-hour schedules in corporations. Most of the tips included in the article are highly proactive and some are defensive in nature, such as: making the schedule clear to everyone; broadcasting the business case and emphasizing the positive results for the workplace; establishing routines to protect time at work and at home; cultivating champions in the workforce who will protect part-time work but also advocate for the arrangements; and actively reminding colleagues that one is still "in the game." Vivien Corwin, Thomas B. Lawrence & Peter J. Frost, "Five Strategies of Successful Part-Time Work," Harvard Bus. Rev., at 123-126 (July/Aug. 2001).

contribute to a top-flight environment. And as with any innovative program, there must be follow-up, fine-tuning, and periodic assessments; once a program is up and running, it can't just be forgotten or ignored.

Risk-Taking

Another requirement of a successful system is a willingness to take a risk as an organization, not just for individual efforts. One man comments on risk in the context of building a more flexible law firm: "Lawyers aren't risk takers. They're afraid to take risks. They think, 'We're going to be taken advantage of, she's not really going to work, we're going to be angry at her, we're not going to be able to handle it, we're not going to trust that she's doing the job.' It's about trust and risk. If you're trained to believe that you can't work from home, or that you have to be in the office, sacrificing to show you are truly committed, it will never work for you." Similarly, there aren't many women leaders, often because of fear or a lack of familiarity. One argument is that people are still simply unaccustomed to women as leaders, and that over time female leaders will gradually be legitimized. Others say that it's necessary to take a risk with women who have proven themselves, pushing change before people are absolutely "ready," having faith (just as one would with a similar male) that a female will grow into the job.

And beyond established systems within the workplace, there's a natural role for formal training programs, to make the workplace comfortable for all employees while also maximizing performance. For instance, communication training can help with competence and confidence issues, because well-delivered feedback helps immeasurably with performance review issues by focusing on delivering hard messages, rather than ignoring or soft-selling them. This is key to getting beyond snap judgments, refuting the Darwinian model that "only the strong survive," and promoting lawyers' abilities to develop and change. Another area of training would focus on effective styles of leadership. Such training can help some people to gain the courage to stop being consistently "nice" when urgency is necessary, and to identify pitfalls of abusive or bullying leadership styles, as well as suggest alternative behaviors.

Engaging in Dialogue

However, systems alone can't solve the dilemmas explained within this book. A lack of dedication to making a system work will doom it to failure:

evaluations will be perfunctory and slap-dash if they are completed at all, and formal mentoring systems will fizzle. Organizations that seek to reconcile clashing views often employ open group debate and dialogue techniques to reach a consensus and find common ground. More specifically, dialogue focused on diversity has sought to sensitize people about how they might inadvertently discriminate or harbor assumptions that are invalid or hurtful. Exchanging views can help people understand differing perspectives, reveal underlying assumptions, examine those assumptions for their validity, and above all, work towards identifying common ground. Legal workplaces haven't widely utilized formal dialogue as an approach for organizational change. But in situations where underlying attitudes and a lack of consensus are major roadblocks to change, dialogue is a vital step towards greater equity.

Such an approach was used to great effect by then-Deloitte & Touche (now Deloitte Touche Tohmatsu), a professional services firm, which was losing women in droves. To stem the tide, the organization initiated workshops for all employees in which they debated scenarios involving gender issues. People with different viewpoints confronted one another head on, resulting in greater enlightenment and understanding. Significantly, the debates revealed that many of the retention problems stemmed from inaccurate assumptions made about women: that they didn't like to travel; that they were satisfied with low-profile assignments; that they would prefer not to work with "tough clients." As a result of these initiatives, the retention of women and the percentage of women partners both improved significantly.[7]

The issues raised in this book suggest two categories of topics that could be debated profitably in organizations: workplace responsibilities and underlying attitudes.

Workplace Responsibilities

One effort would clarify the responsibilities that a workplace actually has, versus those issues for which it shouldn't logically be held responsible. Perceived responsibilities within the workplace have shifted over the years,

---

[7] Douglas McCracken, "Winning the Talent War for Women: Sometimes It Takes a Revolution," Harvard Bus. Rev., at 162-165 (Nov./Dec. 2000).

but rarely with any real perspective or analysis about defining them. For example, before the 1960s and 1970s, household concerns and private issues such as child care impinged little on the workplace, and some people would argue that that remains the proper model. They would maintain that individuals should work out household arrangements for themselves and not expect the workplace to do that because work is only for work. Other people would say that failing to recognize recurring, anticipated private concerns means that each individual has to solve his or her own problems individually rather than as part of a more efficient collective effort.

Another issue involves clients and the effect their attitudes have on the workplace, such as the supervisor who told a young woman who complained of a client who was harassing her, "Would it really kill you to have a drink with the guy?" and women who require male backup for a balky client. What obligation does a workplace have to educate clients about gender issues? Is "the customer always right," or is there an obligation to try to influence a client's attitudes? Some people maintain that business reality requires giving the client more leeway, and that the lawyer's role does not include fostering greater social consciousness. Others argue that in the past, some workplaces took the lead in insisting that clients accept a woman on a case, when there were objections. If those actions seem unquestionably correct in retrospect, following the same logic, might a workplace not insist that a client behave appropriately, such as not engaging in sexual harassment?

Yet another issue is, what obligation does a workplace have to educate all its participants about how to get ahead and succeed, even if some are "outsiders" who do not immediately adapt to the workplace? After all, resources for developing people who don't "get it" right away are limited, and it would benefit the employer if such people found a workplace with a better fit. One could respond that the employer has a responsibility after hiring people to do the utmost to help them, especially if they are from an "outsider" group such as women or minorities who might be expected to encounter obstacles. And the business case once again must be considered: hiring is expensive and high turnover is disruptive and enervating.

Still another controversy concerns informal networks, which impact negatively on women's advancement. What responsibility does the workplace have to replace informal systems with more formal systems to distribute work, cases, and referrals in a more equitable way? Some will say that these are issues of personal chemistry, that trying to influence them with formal systems is doomed to failure, and that it is best to let things develop naturally. Others will argue that a laissez-faire attitude inevitably preserves the *status quo*, and that even artificial manipulation of human relations will help derail informal systems that benefit those who most resemble the people in power.

Organizations must debate where workplace responsibility ends and that of society or an individual begins, so that the workplace doesn't embark on a misguided initiative. More positively, if members of a workplace talk through their responsibilities and agree on them, they will share a publicly voiced commitment to realizing that goal, making it easier in the future to refer to and focus on their shared commitment.

Underlying Attitudes

This book shows that many gender issues have conflicting fundamental attitudes at their root. I would suggest that honest discussion about persistent sex stereotypes can help clarify existing attitudes, and help participants work toward a consensus about how to solve workplace-wide problems. It's harder to dismiss the views of colleagues when you know with certainty what they believe, and when they deliver insights that are unavailable when one speculates alone or only with like-minded colleagues. Discussing these hidden views can include speculation about worst-case scenarios, tapping fears about what might occur should existing assumptions be upended, as well as evaluating the "pros and cons" of preserving the *status quo*. We can speculate about what such exchanges might reveal.

For instance, there are differing views of aggressive men and women. Some reject all "alpha male" behavior, whether it is exhibited by males or females, and argue that allowing strident behavior by women only encourages behavior that should be eliminated. In response, others might point out that, realistically, many larger-than-life practitioners often have some negative personal characteristics, but their success usually assures them a place at the table; therefore, some allowance for excesses from both sexes is preferable.

Another debate could focus on the pros and cons of sticking with the "real lawyer" model versus allowing more flexible systems. One viewpoint is that the real-lawyer model has stood the test of time, that clients get the best service from people who are deeply engaged, and that it's unfair to value lawyers who only spend part of their time working just as highly as those who are always on duty. Another perspective is that a consequence of including parents in the workplace is that children need care; that childcare duties don't last forever; and that treating part-timers as second-class citizens alienates them and jeopardizes any possibility of a long-term relationship.

Similarly, attitudes about parenthood can be explored. What are the consequences of speculating about a woman's future as a wife and mother? Some people insist on speculating in order to protect the workplace and plan for the future, and not be caught flatfooted when people leave. However, the mere act of speculating leads to a mindset that subtly edits people out of a vision for the future.

There are many other scenarios for debate. Suppose women had just as much latitude in their sexual behavior as men have. What are the pros and cons of preserving a stricter moral standard for women than for men? In another vein, what are the fears about a woman as leader? What qualities does a man have that women are thought to lack? What are the pros and cons of preserving the notion of sisterhood among women, versus more hierarchical behavior for women? What's won, what's lost?

I suggest that such discussions would clarify a vision of the future that minimizes sexist attitudes. Dialogues on attitudes would help recognize the benefits of evaluating people more on their individual traits and less on how they conform—or don't—to expected gender roles. The purpose of healthy debate, as in the above examples, is to expose hidden attitudes that may underpin many policies or decisions, but that rarely are invoked overtly. Other benefits of frank discussions are that they build self-insight and cultivate greater responsibility about how individuals' own attitudes contribute to persistent problems, and build greater empathy for viewpoints that were previously considered baffling. Most important is that talking through thorny issues is more likely to result in an organization-wide consensus. The ambivalence that often sabotages well-intentioned systems is less likely to occur when hidden demons are recognized and exposed. Discussing challenging and conflicting ideas results in more common ground than people initially expect. As a result, they can put conflicts behind them, having hashed out the differences, or at least having become better equipped to tolerate remaining divergent opinions. This allows firm leaders to utilize revamped or new systems that actually work because the workplace is philosophically committed to the systems.

Re-imagining the Future

At the outset, I proposed three aims for this book: to provide a new starting point for debate and dialogue; to expand the gender-issues focus from solely about women to all lawyers, men and women alike; and finally, to articulate a vision for the future.

The new starting point for debate is one without any "expectations gap." This book helps to narrow that gap by offering a realistic assessment about the status of gender issues in the profession, tempering disappointment of any perceived lack of progress with the realization that stereotypes don't disappear overnight, and that one generation is a short time for major social change. On this basis, expectations can be adjusted, injecting a little patience into the formula while women still anticipate equity. Women continue to be a minority in the profession, and therefore the dynamics that govern minority/majority scenarios continue to prevail; that women still perceive they must work harder than men to succeed is the starkest proof. The new starting point for dialogue acknowledges a mismatch in expectations, and adjusts them accordingly.

But this re-calibrated understanding shouldn't be an argument for abandoning efforts to influence change. The question is, how can change be pursued profitably and without rancor? Right now it's often difficult to even bring up these issues. Therefore the assumption of a "no problem" problem needs to be confronted. The many voices in this book, and a survey of the data, signal that significant issues remain and that the "no problem" assumption is not valid. Similarly, the idea of aligning public and private voices, which came up in the chapter on sexuality, is critical. Clearly, there is too big a gap between what some people think and what they say. The two must align more closely so that public statements will be more honest.

It is difficult to talk about these issues without impugning people's integrity, without casting some as victims, others as bad guys, and a few as relentless ideologues. We need a common set of principles to bracket discussions. Searching for common ground between men and women is less threatening and more productive than a relentless focus on women's issues alone. So we have our new starting point, and a suggested organizing principle for dialogue—a tight focus on common ground between males and females.

A final technique to spur the debate is to articulate a vision of the future. Chapter 1 highlighted scenarios that were expanded later in the book, some showing great progress, others the continued effect of long-held rigid stereo-types. Now I'd like to include some thoughts about an imagined future.

Usually these visions concentrate on numbers—more women in leader-ship, more women partners, more women general counsel. That goal may spur women, but may not be of much interest to men. In fact, because that goal focuses strictly on women, men may be alienated. They're not going to see a lot of benefit from their standpoint. Why should men be dedicated to a goal that seems to read them out of the picture? What benefits accrue for males from a simple accumulation of women at the top? Although many men might have a benign, even supportive view, of increasing female visi-bility, they may not feel much urgency to do the hard work to help make it happen. (Nor do numerical goals provide an obvious roadmap to get from here to there.) We need a vision that motivates both men and women to spend time and energy making the future look different from the present.

I would therefore suggest a different view of the future, one that empha-sizes everyone's concerns and deals with concepts rather than stark num-bers, favoring personality and skills over gender. We can't get to the numer-ical goals without embracing new, broad ideas. One way to do that is to go back to first principles about how best to deliver legal services, who makes a good lawyer, the best way to manage a workplace, and the most effective way to deal with the intersection between personal and professional lives.

First, there can be fresh thinking about how legal services are delivered in the most effective way possible. Clients want to have the most capable peo-ple working on their cases. This goal isn't furthered when men and women are pushed apart as a result of informal networks, fear of lawsuits, and ram-pant rumor and speculation, which result in less collaboration and trust between male and female lawyers. Rather, lawyers can provide superb client services if the awkwardness between men and women working together on a daily basis is relieved. A workplace that features healthy relationships between men and women will be one in which they don't avoid one anoth-er, but instead find topics and issues in common so that they can enjoy good working relationships. In such a workplace, lawyers will recognize when sit-uations might be awkward and employ creative solutions to ease the ten-sion, pursuing socializing and entertaining that allows bonding without threatening social norms. In short, they can make an art and science of mix-ing the sexes to work together effectively, not hindered by any discomfort because of interaction between the sexes and uncertainty about how to avoid speculation and rumor. The benefits include a higher-performing workplace with employees who deliver a better work product for clients and gain a higher profile and more success.

Another new vision would adjust views regarding the traits that make a good lawyer. Although this analysis could draw upon the perceived strengths and weaknesses of males and females, its purpose is to formulate a new consolidated model with room for a wide variety of personality types, and less reliance on the masculine model of brash confidence. For instance, having the confidence to give a client assurance is good, but empty bluster, especially when covering up ignorance, is not. Carefully phrased honesty to set appropriate expectations is helpful; panicky, unvarnished "truth telling," disregarding business and political realities, is not. Sometimes a game-playing approach to negotiation will be required; other times it is more effective to get straight to the point. By re-thinking the qualities of a good lawyer, there would be an opportunity for each practitioner to add new tools and approaches to his or her everyday practice. The benefit would be a more thoughtful understanding of what traits contribute to good lawyering, which, again, leads to better, more professional performances.

Still another concept is to re-think ideas of authority and leadership. A new model would borrow from what both men and women have typically brought to the table and draw the best from each, depending on the workplace situation and other factors. For instance, some men already have benefited from integrating inclusivity, collegiality, understanding, and patience into their leadership styles, traits that have been considered more the province of women. In turn, women can borrow from the male model, including having the backbone to make hard decisions, wearing a face of confidence at times to cover inward doubts, and unapologetically requiring superior performance from underlings. Women can recognize that exercising authority at times, whether done by a man or woman, is necessary to spur a workplace onward, thus easing advancement of authoritative women. The benefits would be better management skills for both men and women; a more congenial environment for all lawyers and staff; more room for authoritative women; and less tolerance for abusive personalities of either sex.

There also can be a different, more flexible view of "commitment" to work during a person's life span. Rather than viewing every new lawyer as a potential lifer, working day in and day out, this vision assumes from the start that there may be times in people's lives that they need to expand and contract their work schedules. A workplace can commit to help people cope with changing priorities, if possible, given business realities. This goal could be realized with dedication to a lifetime perspective on lawyers and their careers, transparency about policies, and a shared agreement that the policies are fair. The benefits would be that flexible arrangements would thrive; people's careers would expand and contract according to family pressures and other personal needs, and proceed with whole-hearted endorsement; the turf war between full-timers and part-timers would wane; and perennially unhappy lawyers would find greater job and life satisfaction.

There also can be a different conception of parenthood vis-à-vis professionalism. Rather than view men and women differently when they become parents, the workplace would embrace a more balanced notion: that both may want time at work and time with their families. A man who wants reduced hours would be considered a good father, not a bad lawyer/breadwinner, nor "stupid" or "crazy" for publicly making lifestyle decisions about jobs. Similarly, women who work after they become mothers would continue to be lauded for their legal work, not denigrated as bad mothers. The result would be that work patterns among parents of both genders would even out, with less reliance on the traditional model of fathers as breadwinners and mothers as nurturers at home. Again, the chief benefits would be greater job and life satisfaction.

More broadly, the future could include more support of people who step outside stereotypical norms. There would be a recognition of how hard it is to violate the borders guarding stereotypes, a recognition of the benefits when people have more opportunities to express their personalities and individual qualities, garnering support rather than jeers from onlookers. The workplace would then reap more positive input from people rather than suppressing some of their skills and personalities due to arbitrary conclusions about sex.

One of the most striking stories I heard was from the in-house woman who had to "smooth the ruffled feathers" of a male peer who bristled when the woman questioned him closely. She said: "It's a pain in the neck. I really shouldn't have to do that. There's a lot of extra stuff that has to get done as a woman, just in order to maintain a position." The ways that women manage their gender are well-documented, in this book and elsewhere; what this book also highlights is that men have to do the same, albeit not to such an extent. An overarching goal is to work towards the day when men and women spend less time doing "extra stuff" managing their gender and more time just doing their work.

Much of the hard work on gender bias has already been done. There remain some frustrating, hard-to-budge last obstacles that need to be removed. Often the last tasks prove the hardest; people get tired of a particular "cause," they assume it's resolved, and they don't want to devote resources to persistent problems. Let's move forward with a cult of personality and push aside the cult of gender. We can look forward to a day when we hold a snapshot in our hands that is sharper, clearer, and more inspiring than the one we now possess.

BiblioqrapHy

Abbott, Ida O., *The Lawyer's Guide to Mentoring* (National Association for Law Placement, 2000).

Abelson, Reed, "Men, Increasingly, Are the Ones Claiming Sex Harassment by Men," The New York Times, A-1 (June 10, 2001).

A Current Glance of Women in the Law (American Bar Association, Commission on Women in the Profession, 2001).

Auletta, Ken, "In the Company of Women," The New Yorker, 76 (April 20, 1998).

Baker, Debra, "Plague in the Profession," ABA Law J., 40 (Sept. 2000).

Balestier, Bruce, "'Mommy Track' Loses Stigma," New York Law Journal (June 20, 2000), www.law.com.

Banerjee, Neela, "Some 'Bullies' Seek Ways to Soften Up," The New York Times, C1 (Aug. 10, 2001).

Batchelor, Jennifer, "The Perfect Fit: Dissatisfied Female Attorneys Start Own Firms," The Legal Intelligencer (Sept. 16, 2002), www.law.com.

Benali, Rosemarie Clancy, & Sara Yoon, "Breaking Through: Women Hold the Top Legal Job at 60 Fortune 500 Companies," Corporate Counsel (May 20, 2002), chart at www.law.com.

Braverman, Paul, "Manhandled," The American Lawyer (Aug. 2, 2002), www.americanlawyer.com.

"Breaking Through: Women Hold the Top Legal Job at 60 Fortune 500 Companies," Corporate Counsel (May 20, 2002), chart at www.law.com.

Buchanan, Paul, "Love, or Harassment? How Employers Should Deal with a Touchy Issue," 11:1 Business Law Today (Sept. 2001), www.abanet.org.

The Burdens of Both, The Privileges of Neither (American Bar Association, Multicultural Women Attorneys' Network, 1994).

Carson, Clara N., *The Lawyer Statistical Report: The U.S. Legal Profession in 1995* (The American Bar Foundation, 1999).

Carter, Terry, "Paths Need Paving: Women and the Law," ABA J., 35 (Sept. 2000).

Case, Mary Ann C., "Disaggregating Gender from Sex and Sexual Orientation: The Effeminate Man in the Law and Feminist Jurisprudence," 105 Yale L. J., 1 (1995).

Corwin, Vivien, Thomas B. Lawrence & Peter J. Frost, "Five Strategies of Successful Part-Time Work," Harvard Bus. Rev., 123 (July/Aug. 2001).

Coscarelli, Kate, "Legal Bills Are Even Upsetting to Lawyers," The Star-Ledger, 1 (Aug. 9, 2002).

Cunningham, Keith, "Father Time: Flexible Work Arrangements and the Law Firm's Failure of the Family," 53 Stanford L. Rev., 907 (April 2001).

Dobrich, Wanda, Steven Dranoff & Gerald L. Maatman, Jr., *The Manager's Guide to Preventing a Hostile Work Environment: How to Avoid Legal and Financial Risks by Protecting Your Workplace from Harassment Based on Sex, Race, Disability, Religion, or Age* (McGraw-Hill, 2002).

Dusky, Lorraine, *Still Unequal: The Shameful Truth About Women and Justice in America* (Crown Publishers, 1996).

"Employment Comparisons and Trends for Men and Women, Minorities and Non-Minorities" (National Association of Law Placement, 2002), www.nalp.org.

Epstein, Cynthia Fuchs, *Women in Law,* 2d ed. (University of Illinois Press, 1993).

Epstein, Cynthia Fuchs, Robert Sauté, Bonnie Oglensky & Martha Gever, "Glass Ceilings and Open Doors: Women's Advancement in the Legal Profession," 64 Fordham L. Rev. 200 (1995).

Epstein, Cynthia Fuchs, Carroll Seron, Bonnie Oglensky & Robert Sauté, The *Part-Time Paradox: Time Norms, Professional Life, Family and Gender* (Routledge, 1999).

Farni, Paul, "They're Telling It Like It Is: Why Women Are Likelier to Be Whistleblowers," The Star-Ledger, 17 (July 10, 2002).

"Flirting the Key to a Pleasant Working Day," The Times (Nov. 7, 2001).

Gallagher, Mary P., "A Legal Ethics Gender Gap," New Jersey Law Journal (Apr. 5, 2002), www.law.com.

"Gender Equity in the Legal Profession" (New York State Bar Association, Committee on Women in the Law, 2002).

Glater, Jonathan, "Software Trains Employees and Limits Liability," The New York Times, C-1 (Aug. 8, 2001).

Goldberg, Carey, "Single Dads Wage Revolution One Bedtime Story at a Time," The New York Times, A1 (June 17, 2001).

Harrington, Mona, *Women Lawyers: Rewriting the Rules* (Penguin Books, 1993).

Hope, Judith Richards, *Pinstripes & Pearls: The Women of the Harvard Law Class of '64 Who Forged an Old-Girl Network and Paved the Way for Future Generations* (Scribner, 2003).

Jack, Rand, & Dana Crowley Jack, *Moral Vision and Professional Decisions: The Changing Values of Men and Women Lawyers* (Cambridge University Press, 1989).

Jamieson, Kathleen Hall, *Beyond the Double Bind: Women and Leadership* (Oxford University Press, 1995).

Jeffreys, Brenda Sapino, "Discipline Actions and the Gender Gap," Texas Lawyer (Aug. 12, 2002), www.law.com.

Jenkins, Alan, "Losing the Race," The American Lawyer, 1 (Oct. 4, 2001).

Kane, Mary, "The Daddy Track: Many Men 'Go Undercover' Rather Than Take Paternity Leave," The Star-Ledger, 27 (June 17, 2002).

Kaufman, Leslie, "Return of the Suit, Tentatively; Some Men Are Dressing Up Again, but Casual Still Lives," The New York Times, C1 (April 2, 2002).

"Keeping the Keepers" (National Association for Law Placement, 1997).

Lacayo, Richard, & Amanda Ripley, "Persons of the Year 2002: Cynthia Cooper, Coleen Rowley and Sherron Watkins," 160:27 Time Magazine (Dec. 30, 2002).

Lawyer's Handbook (American Bar Association, 1962).

Longman, Jere, "Debating the Male Coach's Role," The New York Times, D1 (Mar. 29, 2002).

Mackenzie, Donald, "Workplace Flirting Has Negative Impact on Life at the Office: Poll," The Canadian Press (July 21, 2002), www.cp.org.

Massachusetts Bar Association, "Part-Time Schedules for Attorneys Available, But Used Infrequently in Law Firms," Lawyers J., 13 (Sept. 1999).

McCracken, Douglas M., "Winning the Talent War for Women: Sometimes It Takes a Revolution," Harvard Bus. Rev., 159 (Nov./Dec. 2000).

Meyerson, Debra E., *Tempered Radicals: How People Use Difference to Inspire Change at Work* (Harvard Business School Press, 2001).

Meyerson, Debra E., & Joyce K. Fletcher, "A Modest Manifesto for Shattering the Glass Ceiling," Harvard Bus. Rev., 127 (Jan./Feb. 2000).

Mitchell, Mary Stewart, "When Actions Speak Louder Than Words Between the Sexes," Law Practice Management (July/Aug. 2000).

"More Than Part-Time: The Effect of Reduced-Hours Arrangements on the Retention, Recruitment and Success of Women Attorneys in Law Firms" (Employment Issues Committee, Women's Bar Association of Massachusetts, 2000).

Morris, Betsy, "Trophy Husbands," Fortune (Sept. 27, 2002), www.fortune.com.

National Association for Law Placement ("NALP"), *2000-2001 National Directory of Legal Employers* (2000).

Newport, Frank, "Americans See Women as Emotional and Affectionate, Men as More Aggressive," Gallup News Services (Feb. 21, 2001).

Nussbaum, Emily, "Great Expectations: The Prospect for a Female Lawyer, Classes of '01, '91 and '81," The New York Times Magazine, 118 (Sept. 8, 2001).

Oakley, Judith G., "Gender-Based Barriers to Senior Management Positions: Understanding the Scarcity of Female CEOs," J. Bus. Ethics, 321 (Oct. 2000).

Orenstein, Peggy, *Flux: Women on Sex, Work, Love, Kids and Life in a Half-Changed World* (Doubleday, 2000).

Pearlman, Laura, "Whistle a Happy Tune," American Lawyer (Sept. 28, 2001).

"Perceptions of Partnership: The Allure and Accessibility of the Brass Ring" (National Association for Law Placement, 1999).

Pierce, Charles A., Herman Aguinis &. Susan K. R. Adams, "Effects of a Dissolved Workplace Romance and Rater Characteristics on Responses to a Later Sexual Harassment Accusation," 43:5 Academy of Management J., 869 (Oct. 2000).

Poirier, Marc R., "Gender Stereotypes at Work," 99 Brooklyn L. Rev. 1073 (1999).

"Reflections on a Glass Ceiling: How Women Are Faring in the Profession, Part 2," The Recorder (Mar. 18, 2002), roundtable discussion at www.law.com.

Rhode, Deborah L., "Balanced Lives: Changing the Culture of Legal Practice" (American Bar Association, Commission on Women in the Profession, 2001).

Rhode, Deborah L., "The Unfinished Agenda: Women and the Legal Profession" (American Bar Association Commission on Women in the Profession, 2001).

Rhode Deborah L., & Jennifer A. Drobac, *Sex-Based Harassment: Workplace Policies for the Legal Profession* (American Bar Association, 2002).

Saad, Lydia, "Women See Room for Improvement in Job Equity," Gallup News Services (June 29, 2001).

Samborn, Hope Viner, "Higher Hurdles for Women," ABA J., 31 (Sept. 2000).

Schaefer, Cindy M., & Thomas R. Tudor, "Managing Workplace Romances," 66:3 S.A.M. Advanced Management J., 4 (Summer 2001).

Shannon, Marcia Pennington, "Charting a Course for Satisfaction and Success in the Legal Profession," Law Practice Management (Mar. 2000).

Shellenbarger, Sue, "More Relaxed Boomers, Fewer Workplace Frills and Other Job Trends," The Wall Street Journal, B1 (Dec. 27, 2000).

Shellenbarger, Sue, "Please Send Chocolate: Moms Now Face Stress Moving In and Out of Workforce," The Wall Street Journal, D1 (May 9, 2002).

"SHRM Survey Finds That the Number of Sexual Harassment Complaints Is on the Rise," Society for Human Resource Management (March 15, 1999), www.shrm.org.

Snyder, Jean MacLean, & Andra Barmash Greene, eds., *The Woman Advocate* (American Bar Association, Section of Litigation, 1996).

Svikhart, Jeanne Q., & Abbie Willard, *Fair Measure: Toward Effective Attorney Evaluations* (American Bar Association, Commission on Women in the Profession, 1997).

Tannen, Deborah, *Talking from 9 to 5: Women and Men in the Workplace: Language, Sex and Power* (Morrow/Avon Books, 1994).

Thomas, David A., "The Truth About Mentoring Minorities: Race Matters," Harvard Bus. Rev., 98 (April 2001).

"21% of Women Surveyed in the Latest National Poll Report Having Been Sexually Harassed at Work," U.S. Newswire (Feb. 5, 2002), www.usnewswire.com.

U.S. Census Bureau, "My Daddy Takes Care of Me! Fathers as Care Givers," Press Release (Oct. 8, 1997).

Valian, Virginia, *Why So Slow? The Advancement of Women* (MIT Press 1998).

Van Engen, Marloes L., Rien van der Leeden & Tineke M Willemsen, "Gender, Context and Leadership Styles: A Field Study," 74:5 J. Occupational & Organizational Psych., 581 (2001).

Walsh, Mary Williams, "Preparing a Corps of Women for Corporate Responsibility," The New York Times, C2 (Aug. 13, 2002).

Weitz, Rose, "Women and Their Hair," 15:5 Gender & Society, 667 (Oct. 2001).

Wells, Susan J., "A Female Executive Is Hard to Find," 46:6 HR Magazine, 40 (June 2001).

Wilkins, David B., *The Black Bar: The Legacy of Brown v. Board of Education and the Future of Race and the American Legal Profession* (Oxford University Press, forthcoming).

Wilkins, David B., & Elizabeth Chambliss, "Harvard Law School Report on the State of Black Alumni 1869-2000" (Harvard Law School Program on the Legal Profession, 2002).

Williams, Joan, *Unbending Gender: Why Work and Family Conflict, and What to Do About It* (Oxford University Press, 2000).

Williams, Joan, & Cynthia Thomas Calvert, "Balanced Hours: Effective Part-Time Policies for Washington Law Firms," *The Project for Attorney Retention, Final Report,* 2d ed. (Aug. 2001).

Williams, Joan, & Cynthia Thomas Calvert, "The Project for Attorney Retention, Interim Report" (Mar. 2001).

Women in Law: Making the Case (Catalyst, 2001).

Ziewacz, Elizabeth K., "Can the Glass Ceiling Be Shattered? The Decline of Women Partners in Large Law Firms," 57 Ohio State L. J. 971 (1996).

ALSO FROM ALM PUBLISHING:

The Essential Guide to the Best (and Worst) Legal Sites on the Web
by Robert J. Ambrogi, Esq.

Full Disclosure: The New Lawyer's Must-Read Career Guide
by Christen Civiletto Carey, Esq.

On Trial: Lessons from a Lifetime in the Courtroom
by Henry G. Miller, Esq.

Going Public in Good Times and Bad: A Legal and Business Guide
by Robert G. Heim

Inside/Outside: How Businesses Buy Legal Services
by Larry Smith

Arbitration: Essential Concepts
by Steven C. Bennett, Esq.

Courtroom Psychology and Trial Advocacy
by Richard C. Waites, J.D., Ph.D

Negotiating and Drafting Contract Boilerplate
by Tina L. Stark

The Practice of Law School
by Christen Civiletto Carey, Esq.
and
Professor Kristen David Adams

Other publications available from AMERICAN LAWYER MEDIA:

LAW JOURNAL PRESS professional legal treatises—over 100 titles available

Legal newspapers and magazines—over 20 national and regional titles available, including:

The American Lawyer
The National Law Journal
New York Law Journal

Visit us at our websites:
www.lawcatalog.com
and
www.americanlawyermedia.com